Sandpiper

CELIA THAXTER AT EIGHTEEN WITH HER SON KARL

Sandpiper

THE LIFE & LETTERS OF
CELIA THAXTER

and her home on
THE ISLES OF SHOALS

her family, friends & favorite poems

Written & Compiled by
Rosamond Thaxter

PETER E. RANDALL
Publisher

Fifth printing, February 1999
Printed in the United States of America

Peter E. Randall, Publisher
Box 4726, Portsmouth, NH 03802

Distributed by University Press of New England
Hanover and London

The assistance of the following is gratefully acknowledged for help-ing to produce this fifth edition: Celia Thaxter Hubbard, Celia Thaxter's great-granddaughter; Stephanie Nugent of Artists Collaborative Theatre of New England (ACT ONE); Miller Library at Colby College for permission to use the front cover photograph; and Mary Jo Brown of Brown & Company, Portsmouth, New Hampshire, for the cover design.

Library of Congress Cataloging-in-Publication Data

Thaxter, Rosamond.
  Sandpiper: the life & letters of Celia Thaxter, and her home on the Isles of Shoals, her family, friends & favorite poems.
  Reprint. Originally published: Rev. ed. Francestown, N.H. : M. Jones, c1963.
  Includes bibliographical references and index.
  ISBN 0-914339-01-X
  1. Thaxter, Celia Laighton, 1835-1894. 2 Authors, American–19th century–Biography. 3. Isles of Shoals (Me. and N.H.) -Description.
  1. Thaxter, Celia Laighton, 1835-1894.
  11. Title. Ill. Title: Sandpiper
                              [PS3113T45 1982] 811.'4 [B]
                                                   82-16531

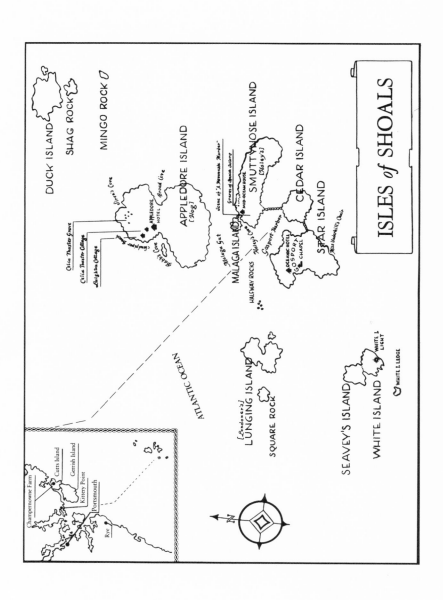

ISLES *of* SHOALS

DUCK ISLAND

SHAG ROCK

MINGO ROCK

APPLEDORE ISLAND
[Hog]

Sirens' Cove
Broad Cove
Celia Thaxter Grave
Celia Thaxter Cottage
APPLEDORE HOTEL
Leighton Cottage
Babb's Cove
Caswell Point

Malaga Gut

Scene of "A Memorable Murder"
Graves of Spanish Sailors
MID-OCEAN HOUSE

SMUTTYNOSE ISLAND
[Haley's]

MALAGA ISLAND

HALFWAY ROCKS
Haley's Cove
Gosport Harbor
OCEANIC HOTEL
GOSPORT
CHAPEL

CEDAR ISLAND

STAR ISLAND

Miss Underhill's Oven

ATLANTIC OCEAN

LUNGING ISLAND
[Londoner's]

SQUARE ROCK

SEAVEY'S ISLAND

WHITE ISLAND
WHITE I. LIGHT
WHITE I. LEDGE

Champernowne Farm
Cutts Island
Gerrish Island
Kittery Point
Portsmouth
Rye

N

PREFACE

Over the years, I have gathered together everything I could find concerning the life of the gifted woman who, as poet and author, was an important literary figure of her time. To family letters I have added reminiscences of those who knew my father's mother and done my best to piece together the story of Celia Thaxter's unusual life, from the day of her first trip to the Isles of Shoals at the age of four, through the joys and sorrows and accomplishments of her fifty-nine short years.

Her own way of telling a story was always so vivid that I have quoted freely from her letters, as well as from her books — *Poems, Stories for Children, Among the Isles of Shoals* and *An Island Garden*. Quoted also are excerpts from *Collected Letters of Celia Thaxter* and other letters written to Celia by her many friends in the artistic and literary world, for the reflection they give of the esteem in which she was held by such people as John Greenleaf Whittier, James T. Fields, editor of the Atlantic Monthly, and others. I have drawn also from her brother's book, *Ninety Years at the Isles of Shoals* by Oscar Laighton, from the diary of Levi Thaxter, her husband, and a scrapbook of clippings kept for me by my mother. To these I added all my father, her second son, had told me. Also my cousins Barbara Durant and Margaret Forbes have lent me their father Cedric's letters: they were Celia's own nieces and remembered her well. Also included are a few brief memories of Katharine Thaxter, daughter of the third son Roland, the granddaughter whom Celia was able to enjoy. The first grandchild, little Eliot, who was so passionately loved by his Granna, only outlived her by twelve years. Another grandson, Edmund Lincoln Thaxter, was born even later and is the last male Thaxter to bear the name and although named for both grandfathers, is affectionately called by his friends Ted. I have written this simple story with the deep regret that I opened my own eyes just one year too late to know the grandmother of whom others have told me so much.

Mr. Lyman Rutledge has been of the greatest assistance — his untiring historical research has brought to light several hitherto unknown facts about the Laighton and Thaxter families, which he has most generously shared with me, as have many personal friends who have lent or given me letters written in Celia's clear unmistakable hand.

The Huntington Library of Pasadena, California, the Houghton Library of Rare Books at Harvard, the Boston Public Library of Rare Books, the J. P. Morgan Library of New York and the Public Libraries of New York and Providence and the Essex Institute of Salem and the Boston Athenaeum have also most graciously allowed me to have photostatic copies made of material in their possession. I have quoted freely from the hundreds of letters written by Celia thus preserved. May I also express my deep gratitude to my dear friends, the late Rosamond Dana Wild and Elizabeth Hoxie, Helen Laighton Delano, John P. Marquand and Ellnora Richter Rice, also Miss Evelyn Benedict of Newport, R. I., and others, who like Mrs. Sidney Lanier and Loulie Albee Mathews, Margaret Hale Thomas, Hugh Payne Greeley and Mrs. Roland H. Woodwell, have told me what they can still remember of the beautiful white haired Celia Thaxter, busy among her flowers, or reading her poems in her famous parlor.

The reception of the First Edition of *Sandpiper* has been a continuing source of unexpected pleasure and interest. I have received countless delightful letters from old friends and from total strangers into whose hands the book has fallen. They have all been most appreciative that these family and personal memories of Celia Thaxter and the Isles of Shoals have been recalled to them. It has made me very proud and happy and more than repaid my amateur effort of writing.

Other sources of material were: *New England Summer* by Van Wyck Brooks; *Authors and Friends* by Annie Fields;

Memories of a Hostess by M. A. DeWolfe Howe; *The Un-discovered Country* by William Dean Howells; *Life and Letters of J. G. Whittier, Vol. II* by Samuel T. Pickard; *Talks in a Library With Lawrence Hutton* by Isabel Moore; *Acres of Flint* by Perry Westbrook; *Literary Friends and Acquaintances* by Louis C. Cornish; *The Isles of Shoals* by John S. Jennis; *A Hearsay History of Curzon's Mill* by John P. Marquand; *History of Watertown* and *A Little Book of Friends* by Harriet Prescott Spofford; *So Early in the Morning* by Loulie Albee Mathews; *Chapters from a Life* by Elizabeth S. Phelps; *Sketches of Concord and Appledore* by Frank Preston Stearns; *Thomas Wentworth Higginson* by Mary T. Higginson; *The Bostonians* by Henry James; *Reminiscences of a Flower Painter* by Ellen Robbins.

CONTENTS

POEMS

LIST OF ILLUSTRATIONS

Sandpiper

1

PORTSMOUTH AND AN AUCTION
1831 - 1839

ON A BRISK September day in the year 1831 all men and women who walked down the poplar lined streets of Portsmouth were stopped by a little boy who handed each in turn a flyer with the printed word AUCTION, in big letters. Most gave only a glance, and passed on. But one young man, Thomas B. Laighton, read the handbill carefully and brought it home to show his wife, Eliza, whom he had married only three months before, in the Old Parsonage in the nearby town of Greenland, New Hampshire. That evening, while Eliza prepared the meal, Thomas read the handbill to her.

Thomas Laighton was a promising youth of good, if not college, education. One of a large family of brothers, he was handicapped by a slight limp caused by an early fall. He was eager to make a good living, either with an active political career, or through a share in his brothers' ships which carried lumber and freight along the coast to family owned wharves in Portsmouth. At that time he was employed as clerk in the local U.S. Customs House, where all imported goods to the area passed through his hands. There was a store of valuable articles which had been brought into port by Portsmouth sea captains who had sailed to the Orient, to Europe, and returned with various cargoes in their merchant vessels. The possibilities of the auction fascinated him.

1

Weeks later he re-read the now weathered copy tacked to the door of the handsome red brick government building in which he was employed. He realized that this was not an auction of goods, but of three islands lying some ten miles off shore from Portsmouth, the city of his birth, where his brothers already owned property.

Laighton remembered that a century before the first William Pepperrell, stopping on his way from England, had so developed the fishing trade on those islands, that he had made a large fortune there before moving to the mainland where he later lived in great prosperity. Thomas' mind raced over all the potentialities which ownership of the islands presented. He could arrange with the fishermen to buy their catch and then re-sell to the captains of the Spanish and British trading vessels which made the islands their last stop before the Atlantic crossing. These ships left home heavily loaded with merchandise of all sorts, — yard-goods, furniture, china, silver and all household needs for America, but they needed to carry back some salable cargo, if for no other reason than ballast.

On the appointed day of the sale, Laighton betook himself by rowboat to the village of Kittery Point, Maine, across the Piscataqua River from Portsmouth, and tied up at the wharf of Gerrish Warehouse. The auction was held as scheduled and Laighton made his bid, but before the young man of twenty-seven fully realized it, the hammer had fallen and John Smiley became the owner of the three islands in the Atlantic Ocean — Hog, Smutty-nose (or Haley's) and Malaga. These three islands comprised the largest part of that rocky group known as the Isles of Shoals, all belonging to the State of Maine. Wistfully Laighton watched the lawyer arrange to have transfer papers drawn.

The sale had happened all too quickly for him but before he returned to Eliza, Thomas sat down on a gravestone in the old church yard of the nearby white meetinghouse to think things over. At the time he could not produce the money, but the price was not high. Although he might have

AUCTION.

To be sold at Public Auction at **J. L. Lawrence, Esqr's** dwelling-house, at Kittery Point, in the County of York,

On *WEDNESDAY* the
12th of October next, at 11 o'clock A. M.

By virtue of a license from the Hon. Wm. A. Hayes, Esq. Judge of Probate within and for the County of York and State of Maine,

All the right, title, interest, and demands that Benjamin Haley, late of Portsmouth, in the County of Rockingham, State of New-Hampshire, mariner, deceased, had, at the time of his decease, in and unto the island, commonly called Hog Island, one of the Isle of Shoals, in said County of York.

Also, all the right, title, and demands that said Haley had at the time of his decease, in and unto the islands commonly called Smutty Nose and Malaga Islands; together with all the said Haley's right he had at the time of his decease, to a large two story **DWELLING HOUSE**, lately built by said Haley, and his right to a number of other Buildings, all of which are on said Smutty Nose Island, with the Dock and Water Privilege; to be sold to raise twenty-two hundred and twenty-five dollars to pay the claims and demands against the said Haley's estate, with incidental charges.

Conditions of sale will be made known at the time and place of sale.

Sept. 6, 1831.
ELIZA H. HALEY,
Administratrix.

to borrow a little, Thomas felt sure that he could soon buy Smiley out, and then make a profit on the fish business.

Before him ran the peaceful Piscataqua River, with New Castle and its old Walbach Tower on the opposite shore, and where the stream broadened to the lower harbor, beyond the Whalesback Lighthouse, lay the open sea and the Isles of Shoals. Looking inland from where he sat, he could see the long avenue of elm trees leading from the beautiful Colonial home of Lady Pepperrell to that of her daughter, who had married young Sparhawk, who later took his wife's name. Sir William Pepperrell had been able to build both of these stately mansions with the fortune partly amassed by his father in the fishing trade on these very Isles of Shoals. Thomas wondered if he might not have an equal success? The problem was how he could oversee and expand the declining fish business on the islands, which were far away and hard to reach. Soberly he arose and returned to Portsmouth.

For the next few years Thomas Laighton spent many hours discussing what might have been had he made his impetuous purchase. In their small house near Market Square, Eliza loved to listen to his stories of the early history of the Isles of Shoals, from their discovery by John Smith to the present time.

He told her that in 1614 settlers from southern England had stopped to fish at the largest island in the group, Hog Island. There they had built shanties in which to live during the fishing season and named their little settlement for the English town of Appledore. Fish caught — cod, haddock, mackerel and the rest — were cleaned, split, salted for preservation and spread out to dry on long racks. The dried fish were then packed and sent to Spain and England aboard trading ships returning to those countries. It had been a rough life at Appledore, with only men living on the island, there having been an old law forbidding women to live on the Shoals. In 1650, however, the Reverend John Brock went to live among the Islanders, and marriages and other rites of the Established Church could then be administered, so the old law was abandoned.

This latter story especially interested the pious Eliza. She had been born Eliza Rymes, in Newington, New Hampshire. The small town had no Established Church and, whenever possible, the Rymes family had attended Queen's Chapel, in nearby Portsmouth, to which an ancestor had given a beautiful Communion chalice. Now Eliza had only to walk up the hill to sit in the Chapel's successor, the newly erected red brick St. John's Church.

From the house on Daniel Street, the young Laightons could see Market Square, only a block away, where wide spaces of the Parade were full of horse or ox drawn carts loaded with hay and farm produce. This was an age of barter and exchange — hay for potatoes, eggs for flour and apples for dress material — goods brought in for sale on market day. Down Daniel Street in the other direction, beyond the stately Macpheadris-Warner House, lay the wharves owned jointly by Thomas' brother Joseph and himself, where fish was a good item of trade. He could also see schooners owned by two other brothers, Mark and John, which sailed from further down east along the Maine coast to the more southern ports.

Portsmouth, New Hampshire's only seaport, was a city with an interesting past. In 1603 an English navigator, Martin Pring, seeking water and a harbor, first landed on Odiorne's Point and then, sailing on up the Piscataqua River, found rest and refreshment from the strawberries on a sloping bank by the river's edge. These berries gave the town its first name, Strawberry Banke.

Like Boston, Salem and Newburyport, Portsmouth had grown and prospered from the time of its early settlement. The wealth which had been acquired by the Langdons, the Wentworths, the Sherburnes, leading families in the East India trade, was used to build and furnish stately homes, Colonial and Georgian, mostly square and three-storied, with the inevitable balcony or Widow's Walk on the highest part of the roof. From these lookouts returning ships could be sighted far down the river, and sometimes lonely widows or heartbroken sweethearts watched from them and waited in vain for mariners who never returned.

After the War of 1812, the period of the privateers and the subsequent embargo on imported goods, ships owned by rich sea captains no longer returned from East and West laden with rare, sweet smelling treasures, and cargoes of rum, molasses, Canton china, mahogany and teakwood furniture for their gentry. The Langdons, the Wentworths, their neighbors the Pepperrells and other wealthy Tory families, because of steadfast allegiance to the King had lost estates and fortune. Many of them returned to England. Coastal trade in the early eighteen hundreds was fast supplanting foreign trade and cargoes then consisted principally of prosaic lumber and fish. Still every well-to-do family in the area had as a matter of course, a full set of Canton china — enough for a large family Thanksgiving dinner — gray ginger jars, rose medallion punch bowls, Lowestoft tea sets and teakwood sewing boxes.

Politics were of great interest to Thomas and he gave a dollar to fire a salute before the brilliantly illuminated Jackson Hall, in Portsmouth, when President Jackson vetoed the Bank Bill. The excitement of the event, the undue exertion of walking to New Castle and to the Navy Yard, all in one day, so greatly overtaxed the strength of Thomas' father that he died within the week! His son recorded the event in his diary, also that he spent $4.00 for mourning articles for his mother and sister and that the postage on two letters was forty cents and fifty cents respectively. Political excitement flared high and Thomas showed how very strongly he felt when he made a bet with Ebenezer Wentworth that General Jackson would be reelected to the Presidency. Each man placed the huge sum of $50.00 with Sam Larkin and eagerly awaited the election. News traveled slowly, but on January 8, 1833 a salute was fired in honor of Jackson's victory and the full sum of $100.00 was handed

to Thomas. It was indeed a fortune at a time when a good
house could be rented for $40.00 a year and twenty-two
bushels of potatoes brought only $7.33.

Thomas took an active part in the political life of Portsmouth. He served as Postmaster and was representative to
the New Hampshire Legislature, traveling to Concord by
stage coach to attend the summer sessions.

He took pains to be at home though, June 29, 1835. The
air was sweet with flowers that day, mingled with the
pungency of the sea, when a daughter, to be named Celia,
was born to Eliza and Thomas Laighton. The blue-eyed
baby was doubly welcome because an older sister, Helen,
had lived but eleven months, merely long enough to have
the dates of her birth and death entered in the family Bible.

While Thomas continued to be active in Portsmouth
political affairs, he also, for one year, tried his hand as
editor of the New Hampshire Gazette, now the Portsmouth
Herald, which prides itself on being the oldest newspaper
in continuous publication in the country. For a time, too,
he was librarian for a small seaman's library, which offered
the working man a knowledge of building and sailing ships.
This library was quite different from the beautiful Athenaeum on the square where such humble readers might
not have been made welcome by the shareholders who
were proud of the building and its contents.

In March 1839, Laighton was a candidate for the office
of Selectman of Portsmouth. He was defeated by a vote
which he always considered unfair. Disillusioned, he decided to embark upon a new venture.

On April 26, 1839, Thomas and his brother, Joseph,
jointly bought Hog, Smutty-nose and Malaga Islands. To
their scant available equipment, they added what they could
afford to purchase. After a summer spent in working out
plans, they were ready to begin business. Meanwhile, on
June 30, 1839, Eliza gave birth to a son, Oscar.

Fortunately for the Laightons, the post of lighthouse
keeper for White Island, most westerly of the Isles of

Shoals, became vacant. Thomas' excellent reputation, and his willingness to assume the responsibility, were helpful in obtaining for him the government appointment as keeper. The lighthouse had at its base a small, well-built, white-washed cottage for the keeper and his family. Once established therein Thomas could live in solitude with his family, far away from the jealousies and intrigues of small-town political life. There he could oversee his own islands and conduct the fishing trade.

The fact that Eliza had never ventured beyond the mouth of Portsmouth harbor was no deterrent.

From the moment of her father's decision to take his family to the Isles of Shoals the story of Celia Laighton becomes an unique one. At the age of four, she was transported from the security of a little wooden house on a quiet street in a small New England city to a group of barren islands· where the inhabitants were often completely cut off from reach of human aid, and were isolated even from the nearby fishermen by the dangerous landings. Ten miles of ocean, often lashed to insurmountable fury, lay between the islands and the mainland. But the wildness and beauty of sea, wind and sky were so impressed upon the mind of the child that they became forever part of the very life of Celia Laighton.

2

WHITE ISLAND LIGHT
1839 - 1841

THE MOMENTOUS move was made to the Isles of Shoals when the baby Oscar was just three months old. On that fateful day a small pilot boat bore Eliza and her children, with their personal possessions, from the foot of Daniel Street to their lighthouse home to begin a new life.

Little Celia sat perched among household provisions with which the boat was loaded. Oscar, in his mother's arms, received his baptism of salt sea spray. They sailed through the narrows of the Piscataqua River at Pull-and-be-damned Point and on to the lower harbor at Kittery Point, past Fort Constitution on the New Castle shore. At Whalesback Light they left Portsmouth Harbor and all land behind and fixed eager eyes on the ever-growing line of the islands which were to be their only world. Theirs would be the only household on White Island, though Star Island, two miles distant, had the small fishing village of Gosport.

Celia felt the pleasant and unaccustomed ripple of the waves against the boat's sides. She enjoyed the sight of wide water, limitless sky, and the warmth of the late afternoon sun, which made her blink like a young sandpiper.

Some years later she described her arrival at White Island:

> It was at sunset in autumn that we were set ashore on that loneliest, lovely rock, where the lighthouse looked

8

down on us like some tall, black-capped giant, and filled me with awe and wonder. At its base a few goats were grouped on the rock, standing out dark against the red sky as I looked up at them. The stars were beginning to twinkle; the sound of many waters half bewildered me. Someone began to light the lamps in the tower. Rich red and golden, they swung round in mid-air; everything was strange and fascinating and new.

On this lonely rock they were met by Thomas Laighton, who had preceded his family by three days, to see to the simple furnishings of the small cottage, which consisted of kitchen, bedrooms, cupboards and clothes presses. He had been helped by Ben Whaling who had agreed to leave the mainland and share the lot of the Laightons on White Island.

Celia's description continued:

We entered the quaint little stone cottage that was for six years our home. How curious it seemed, with its low, whitewashed ceiling and deep windowseats, showing the great thickness of the walls made to withstand the breakers, with whose force we soon grew acquainted! A blissful home the little house became to the children who entered it that quiet evening and slept for the first time lulled by the murmur of the encircling sea.

From that first evening Celia was enchanted by all she saw in the little kingdom. Sure-footed, she was to climb up and down over the rocks with ease and grace in spite of her long skirts, morning-glories ran wild, knotting and twisting among rocks and loose boulders.

Celia played alone until her brother Oscar grew old enough to accompany her. Then they would play in and out of the caves and crevices, looking for shells and picking the flaming blueberry leaves and rose hips to make necklaces. Each season was to bring its own special charm. Even in the coldest winter days, when they must stay inside, they could amuse themselves for hours on the high window ledge, warming pennies — "for which they had no other use" — to melt the frost on the window pane into peep holes through which they could see the roaring waves around them.

Winters were to come quickly and terrible storms to shake the high tower and little cottage, bringing tragedy to their very door. During that first winter one storm, more fearful than the rest, washed off the rowboats and carried away the long covered walk over the chasm leading up to the light. Hens and henhouses were blown seaward by the furious northeast wind, and floated away on the high waves. The only way Thomas Laighton and the hired man could save the one cow was to bring her into the kitchen. Fortunately most of the family supplies were securely stored at the base of the lighthouse tower and were unharmed.

The unforgettable experience of that first storm impressed itself sharply on the memory of the four year old girl. Twenty years later she described every detail of the terror in *Wreck of the Pocahontas.* (See page 247)

This and later tempests gave Celia an early knowledge of how cruel the sea could be, but when the storms of winter were past, spring and summer brought wonderful days to children who were never lonely in the years spent at the lighthouse. Long afterward, when ninety years had not dimmed his memory, Oscar Laighton wrote: "Many people have said, 'You must have been very lonely at the light.' They did not know that where our mother dwelt there was happiness also. I am sure no family was ever more united and contented than the Laightons on White Island."

All through the life of Celia and the Laighton family, Eliza Laighton stands out as the dominant figure, the matriarch, to whom everyone turned for comfort, understanding and cheerful common sense. Her fortitude never wavered, her loyalty never flagged and she was adored by her husband and sons and almost worshiped by her daughter. All turned to her in need and she never failed anyone.

Each year the family waited for spring with eager longing. During long winters, with the exception of Ben

Whaling, they saw hardly a human face besides their own. But each year the first soft warm southern breeze returned life to their lonely rock. Celia describes watching the migrating birds which flew against the light and were killed:

> Many a May morning have I wandered about the rock at the foot of the tower, mourning over a little apron brim full of sparrows, swallows, thrushes, robins, fire winged blackbirds, many colored warblers, and flycatchers, beautifully clothed yellow-birds, nuthatches, cat birds, even the purple finch and scarlet tanager and golden oriole, and many more beside — enough to break the heart of a small child to think of!

At last, with smoother seas, the pilot boat would come from Portsmouth laden with supplies of food and news. Thomas Laighton arranged with pilots to bring his mail to the light every ten days in summer but often only once a month in winter. There were three of these pilot boats to guide the shipping bound in and out of Portsmouth, second only to Salem in importance as a port. Four shipyards were busy building the fine vessels that passed the Light.

The parents talked of war in Mexico and famine in Ireland, news of the world, but the children took little heed. Their big news was the finding of a tiny blade of grass pricking through the shallow soil. They listened to insects humming in soft sunshine, and wondered over the everlasting beauty of a thousand tender tints of seashell and mosses reflected in the pools. "Better than a shopful of toys," the treasures of nature seemed to Celia and little Oscar. One of their greatest delights was to watch and wonder over the scarlet pimpernel, the flower so much wiser than they. Poor man's weather-glass, it was called, for even before human eyes could detect a coming storm, "the pimpernel clasped its small red petals together, folding its golden heart in safety from the shower that was sure to come." Because there were few flowers, each and every one was precious. Bluets, morning-glories, wild roses, elder-bloom and goldenrod all delighted the wondering children.

Often Celia dressed herself warmly and crept out of the house before anyone was awake. With scarlet cape closely wrapped around her to keep out the chill wind of dawn, she would climb the highest cliff, called the "Head," to watch the sun rise. Spellbound she stood as the flame of the lighthouse paled before the dawning day. East and south the wide Atlantic stretched before her and deepening rose color flushed the delicate cloud flakes that dappled the sky. She watched her dearest friends, the gulls, take on a rosy hue as they soared over the blushing sea below.

One of Celia's early tasks was milking the little cow, Betsy. Later, if the tide were low, she would guide her four-footed friend over the stones to tiny Seavey's Island where Betsy found just enough grass to nibble before returning water would leave the animal marooned, which meant a swim home. The cow soon learned to plod back unaided ahead of the tide and chew her cud near the cottage.

A year after their arrival on White Island the family grew larger with the birth of a second son, Cedric, on September 4, 1840. There is no record but Eliza probably returned to the mainland for the event. She now had more than enough to occupy every minute of her days, with Celia, five, Oscar, a year and a half, and the new baby. Nancy Newton, a girl from Star Island, came to help. The two brothers so near of an age yet so different in temperament, were, in the future, inseparable companions always. Oscar, full of romance, open-hearted and improvident, Cedric with a keen business sense, frugal and cautious, were alike in their devotion to their family and the sea.

When weather was calm, a black oil schooner would come lumbering to the Island with several months' supply of whale oil. The oil was stored below the lighthouse tower where a roomy cellar contained also a large cistern for rain water. Daily the oil lamps in the light must be filled, wicks trimmed and the huge globes of glass made spotless. Also the many-paned windows must be washed and cleaned of

spray so that the warning light could be seen for miles. The
rocks of the Shoals were very dangerous to schooners sailing down the coast or heading into Portsmouth Harbor, and
to incoming foreign shipping. All night long every night
someone must keep watch in the tower.

Thomas Laighton and Ben Whaling stood four hour
watches to insure that the light still burned. "The lantern
was kept revolving by a weight running down a pocket
in the tower, similar to the workings of a tall clock. This
had to be wound up by hand. Red and white flashes
were exactly timed enabling a vessel's captain to identify
the light and thus determine his position, 42 58" North,
70 37" West." Celia's most valued duty as she grew older
was to help her father at the lighthouse.

Several times each year the government inspector paid
a visit to White Island. He brought with him all that was
required for the light, also "a barrel of pork, and wood and
coal enough" to last until the next visit.

Every lighthouse keeper was provided by the government with an eighteen-foot sailboat and a dory. The only
landing on White Island was and is to this day very dangerous. Boats must be hauled over the long slip and into
the boathouse by a windlass. Great care has always been
required to bring a boat in safely between the timbers of
the slip and one must steer for an exact spot. The bright
light from the tower shining over the dark sea makes rocks
at the base seem even darker. Thomas Laighton often
rowed or sailed to Smutty-nose or Hog Island to oversee
the fishermen who had long lived there and were now in
his employ, catching the fish which he re-sold at wholesale.
The distance between the islands was about two miles, and
when he sailed alone he would sometimes not return until
after sunset. Celia loved to stand at the spot for which her
father must steer, holding her guiding lantern, facing seaward, and well sheltered from the wind. She often waited
hours alone in the darkness, unafraid, until at last, over the
black waves would come a welcome shout telling her that

her small light had been seen. She tells the story in her poem *Watching*. (See page 255)

After the lamps in the lighthouse tower were lit, the family would often gather in the cozy kitchen, where Ben kept the woodbox filled. The driftwood fire was cheerful but it required much fuel which was hard to find and Thomas Laighton soon imported one of the first cookstoves, of black iron, to replace the fireplace and brick oven. To make the fire, flint and steel were kept in a box on the mantel. It was here in the kitchen that Thomas read aloud to Eliza. The children, when they were old enough, listened eagerly, while outside the sea was thundering, and in these surroundings they learned their letters.

During the summer months many visitors came out to see Thomas Laighton. Among these was Richard H. Dana who, when asked about his Two Years Before the Mast, said, "There was no danger on a ship with Mark Laighton (Thomas' brother) at the helm!" Another visitor was Judge Charles Levi Woodbury, just returned from a voyage around the world.

Once a year Eliza went to Portsmouth to buy cloth to make the children's clothes and sometimes Celia went with her. The child took in all she saw and would regale her wondering brothers with stories of trees, and rows of houses, and horses, none of which they had ever seen. These vivid word pictures gave promise of her future writing.

3

JOURNAL AND SMUTTY-NOSE
1841 - 1847

THE JOURNAL of Thomas B. Laighton telling of his arrival on White Island gives a daily picture of life there. Reports of the wind's direction and the amount of oil burned in the lighthouse were noted in so clear a hand that it is easy reading more than a century later.

It must be remembered that on these islands, everything used — from fishhooks to frying pans — had to be transported from the mainland by boat. So, Thomas records that when "Mr. Rymes" (referring probably to Eliza's father) brought a supply of sugar and a pig for Christmas, he brought also some much needed nails! The diary continues its daily entries, telling of visitors, the number of fish caught, trips to Smutty-nose and Hog Islands; then adds a recommendation and detailed plan for reconstruction of the covered walk which had been carried away during the winter.

The Journal skips over the next two years to when Thomas Laighton, although far removed from his former political life, was unexpectedly elected by the voters as representative to the New Hampshire Legislature. This unsought recognition necessitated his return to the mainland for a short time both spring and fall to attend the sessions held in Concord. There he was closely associated with H. A. Pierce, brother of the future President Franklin Pierce, both of whom became close friends of the Laighton family and later often visited the islands. During these years, there was a substitute keeper at the lighthouse on White Island, while

15

the Laighton family moved to the house built and long occupied by Samuel Haley, on nearby Smutty-nose Island.

Haley also erected salt-works and manufactured excellent salt for curing fish, he stretched a ropewalk over uneven ground 270 feet, he set up windmills to grind wheat and corn grown on Smutty-nose Island, and planted an orchard. Most helpful of all, he built a sea-wall connecting his island with Malaga and thus forming a safe harbor. The funds to construct this wall he acquired when he discovered four bars of solid silver under a large flat stone on the Island, left there by one of the many pirates who often buried their treasure on or around the Isles of Shoals.

Life on Smutty-nose was pleasant and uneventful for Eliza and her children. The neighboring fishermen and their families were friendly and days passed happily. Celia loved the story of how the island's former owner, Samuel Haley, always left a light burning in his window at night, a fire laid on the hearth, should some shipwrecked mariner need shelter. Her young heart was moved by the story of the Spanish ship which had been wrecked on the island in January 1813. Not far from the house were the graves of the fifteen unknown sailors who had perished. The little girl used to climb to the lookout on the house top and fancy she could see the sails which had set out from Spain with a gay crew. She pictured the sailors kissing their sweethearts goodbye in their far off homes and promising to return. Years later she wove the story into her poem *The Spaniards' Graves*. (See page 253)

Haley's house was large and roomy, and had been built with timbers from the wreckage. During his lifetime, the house had been known as The Mid-Ocean House of Entertainment. Eliza, rehanging the old sign, conducted the house as an inn during the summer months. Many gay parties sailed from the mainland to enjoy the fresh sea breeze, good fishing and old Jamaica rum, of which a plentiful supply was kept on hand. These years of hospitality gave the Laightons their first experience of innkeeping.

Among earliest visitors were several whose names are noted for more than exploits with a codfish line. One of them, Thomas W. Higginson, made a pet of Celia, sending her a book which she treasured through life, *The Sea Side Beach.* The donor's brother, Henry Higginson, later was to give happiness to thousands by organizing the symphony concerts in Boston. Another who came to visit the newly opened inn was Richard H. Dana, young sailor and author.

Most important to the lives of the Laighton family were two Harvard students, John Weiss, a German Jew who was planning to become a Unitarian minister, and his friend Levi Lincoln Thaxter.

Levi Thaxter was born in Watertown, Massachusetts on February 2, 1824. His mother, Lucy White, married the Honorable Levi Thaxter, descendant of Thomas Thaxter who had come from England to settle in Hingham, Massachusetts in 1638. Thomas Thaxter's descendants were nearly all prominent in the annals of the state and were traditionally graduates of Harvard College. The Thaxters married into the Lincoln family, also of Hingham. General Benjamin Lincoln, an ancestor of Levi, was George Washington's aide-de-camp and received Cornwallis surrender at Yorktown. Governor Levi Lincoln of Massachusetts was also a forebear.

At nineteen young Levi was graduated with honors from Harvard and took up the study of law at his father's suggestion. His increasing interest in literature and the drama made it difficult for him to settle on a profession and he was full of uncertainties about his future, an indecision which was unfortunately to follow the student-dreamer through life.

These two young men, Thaxter and Weiss, early drawn by the fascination of the islands, were to find themselves irrevocably affected by this spot and by the Laighton family, for the remainder of their lives.

During Eliza's management of this simple "House of Entertainment," a young party of friends came over from

Newburyport — Nathaniel Hale and his sister Susan, with John Greenleaf Whittier's younger sister Lizzie and her friend Margie Curzon. The young people fished and explored Smutty-nose Island for several days. But, when they were regretfully waiting for the sailboat which was to take them home, Lizzie Whittier attempted a last climb over the slippery rocks crossing to Malaga Island. On the treacherous seaweed she lost her footing, fell and hurt her back, an injury from which she was never to recover entirely. She was carried at once to a bedroom and laid on the bed. Celia was in the room, tidying up, but she left her task quickly to help comfort the suffering girl. She brought in a big bowl of blueberries, just picked, which had left a telltale stain on her white dress. Despite the fact that Celia was so much younger than the other two, the friendship begun that day lasted throughout the lives of Margie Curzon, Lizzie Whittier and Celia Laighton.

The pleasant life on Smutty-nose continued tranquilly during the two years that Thomas Laighton served in the state legislature. At the conclusion he again assumed the position of lighthouse keeper on White Island, and the little family moved back to their first island home.

Thomas' interests now became completely centered on the rocky islands. One day a letter from his brother in Portsmouth seemed to demand his presence on the mainland, possibly in connection with the piers and vessels which the four Laighton brothers owned together. Thomas grudgingly set sail but to the surprise of the watching family, they saw him, when half-way to the mainland, tack sail and return. He tersely explained that he had thought out a plan which would not require his presence on shore. Whatever plan he had worked out was evidently put into effect, for from that day on he apparently realized his wish never again to leave the islands.

The peaceful existence on White Island continued for the next few years. The family went on living happily in the cottage at the foot of the tower, moving to the Haley house only for the reopening of the inn in the summer. Weather permitting, Thomas Laighton made almost daily trips to Smutty-nose from White Island. He painted and papered his house and planted a vegetable garden. When Sunday was fair, he took his wife and children with him. Sometimes they attended service at the little stone church on Star Island nearby. Always the idea was in his head that, although a good sum could be raised from fishing and from accommodating guests in the old inn, if a new and modern hotel were built on Hog, the largest island, the fortune of the owner could be made.

Each night, in spite of his troublesome leg, he dragged himself up the winding iron stairs of the lighthouse to tend the lamps. Through his spy-glass, he surveyed the coast from Cape Ann in Massachusetts to Cape Elizabeth in Maine, and on clear nights he could see the lights of each over a distance of about eighty miles. In the crisp days of early autumn the White Mountains of New Hampshire, and Mount Washington with a cap of new fallen snow on its summit, were clearly visible. All the while he continued to ponder the possibility of the new hotel.

During this time, Celia's childhood was carefree and full of joy, from the rising of each new sun out of the sea to its setting behind the distant hills of New Hampshire. The tower, the cottage, her father trimming the lights or mending his nets, her mother — the sun around which their little world revolved — constituted her universe. Daily play with her brothers on the rocks and in the pools, the teachings of her father, sharing the tasks of their helpers, Ben Whaling and Nancy Newton, were all she knew of occupation and companionship. (See page 255)

The children's studies were conducted by their father. He wrote a "copybook" hand and there still exists (in the possession of Cedric's daughter, Barbara) a yellow paper on which well over a hundred years ago Thomas Laighton wrote a script for Cedric, aged six, to copy: "George Washington is come. What praise is due?" The little boy shaped the letters painstakingly and correctly, smaller and smaller each time until after the seventeenth line it was so small that he could not read what he had written. His father rewrote the copy. On the last page Cedric wrote free-hand: "This is my Father's birthday, February 2, 1847, today he is 42 years old. God bless my Father. He is so kind."

One evening was much like another during those years. Chores done, the family would gather near the black coal-burning stove and, by the light of the oil lamps, Eliza knitted and Thomas read or made fishnets. The boys studied and Celia, just introduced to the world of poetry, would sometimes interrupt to read aloud from the poems of her favorite, Tennyson.

Due to their isolation, a close family relationship of mutual dependence bound them together with gentle ties that had the strength of steel cables. In later years they never were broken. The devotion between father and mother strengthened the bonds of children to parents, sister to brothers. These affections were always to prove even stronger for Celia than her later love for husband and sons. Through the fifty-nine years of her life, whenever family loyalty was divided, fealty to her parents was the more important.

Opportunity came to Thomas Laighton in the spring of 1847 to sell his share of the family holdings at the north end of Portsmouth where the incoming railroad company desired land. Here at last was some of the capital needed for the erection of a first-class summer hotel on Hog Island. A sailboat could connect with trains and carry guests to the Isles of Shoals. During the summer Thomas supervised the building of a small dwelling on Hog, which he renamed Appledore Island.

From the time Levi Thaxter first visited the Isles of Shoals, he had not only been charmed by the atmosphere, but he had come greatly to admire Thomas Laighton. In May 1847, after a month's visit at White Island he had written Laighton: "I often think of the Lighthouse Islands

CELIA'S BIRTHPLACE, DANIEL STREET, PORTSMOUTH
(*Second house left*)

CURZON'S MILL HOUSE
BIRTHPLACE OF CELIA'S SECOND SON JOHN, 1854

WHITE ISLAND LIGHTHOUSE AND LAIGHTON COTTAGE

WHITE ISLAND LIGHT AND SEVEY'S ISLAND
VIEWED FROM APPLEDORE

as I arrange my collection of mosses. I will continue to grow the beard which was started there, and I surely will return!" He regretted that his hasty departure had forced him to forego the steaming plum pudding which Mrs. Laighton was about to put on the table. He sent his love to all the household and jokingly expressed his intention "to carry away young Cedric to have as my little boy" but no mention was made of Celia, who was only eleven while Levi was an elderly man of twenty-three years.

Thomas Laighton's diary states: "Mr. Thaxter brought his parents." Levi Thaxter, in his enthusiasm for the Shoals and his friends the Laightons, had evidently enlisted the interest of his banker father in the proposed hotel — a business in which he himself was, at the time, ready to take part. Mr. and Mrs. Thaxter senior must also have approved of Thomas Laighton's plan, for after three days spent at the inn on Smutty-nose, they returned to their Massachusetts home and signified their willingness to advance a loan for the venture.

On September 10th an agreement was entered into by Thomas Laighton and Levi L. Thaxter that the Appledore Hotel should be built. After the two friends had signed their business contract and drawn their plans, a load of lumber and other building materials was ordered from Bangor, Maine, about two hundred miles north along the coast. These were loaded on one of the Laighton brothers' sailing ships and delivered at Appledore. Workmen were hired from the mainland "at 3/ per day, and found" and the stupendous venture was ready to begin.

4

APPLEDORE
1847 - 1851

A NEW PAGE was turned in Thomas Laighton's Journal with this notation:

> Thursday, Sept. 15, 1847 — Wind W. light, moved from White Island to Hog Island. Mr. Baker took charge of the Light House for me, and John Randall moved to Smutty-nose to care for the fishing business.

The Journal goes on to record that after he resigned his position as lighthouse keeper, the family made the move to Appledore the day after the papers of agreement were drawn. Celia was then twelve years old — the boys six and seven. As the Laighton family had once bidden farewell to Portsmouth and the mainland, now the lighthouse with its shelter from storms, the sunrise seen from rocky cliffs, the leading of the little cow to her scant feeding spot were left behind, as were the grassy meadows and the lonely graves of the Spaniards on Smutty-nose. These pictures indelibly impressed on the minds of the three children were treasured memories, but to explore the vastness of Appledore was to be their new adventure. White Island had possibly two acres, of which half was steep rocky cliffs, while Appledore stretched one mile from end to end. There was much vegetation there and many caves and beaches.

At first Celia, Oscar and Cedric hardly dared stray from the doorstep, but soon they began to roam over what seemed limitless hills and valleys to their short legs, accus-

22

tomed only to the bare rocks of the smaller islands. Here the huckleberry bushes with delicious fruit, the wild roses with their red but unedible haws, and the sweet smelling bayberry bushes seemed like a forest. They found "a hundred cellar holes" — all that was left of homes where inhabitants of the early Town of Appledore had lived out the drama of their lives. Celia's quick and vivid imagination wove stories about the "Fairy Dell," a certain grassy spot near the northeastern end of the island. She told her brothers this was where little people danced in the moonlight and played leapfrog over the toadstools and peeped at each other through lace curtains of cobwebs. She found everywhere on the island new beauties of nature that filled her with unbounded happiness.

In the new little house on Appledore, Eliza Laighton's kitchen window was full of sun and blooming plants. Celia had inherited her mother's green thumb and took pride in planting a small garden. There she grew marigolds and planted flax, as she later told Mr. Longfellow, to see the color of the eyes of the Captain's daughter in *The Wreck of the Hesperus* which she had begun to memorize. The same loving care that tended those earliest seeds produced in later years the riot of flowers loved by artists and poets in Celia Laighton Thaxter's island garden.

Celia had learned to swim and row a boat during the stay on Smutty-nose, but Oscar and Cedric had been too young to master the high waves and dangerous slip at White Island. However, once on Appledore, they were tempted by the sight of a dory close in shore and stole quietly away from watchful eyes. They untied the painter and each seized an oar, thinking himself a great adventurer. After the boys and boat had turned around several times, their father caught sight of the pair and called them back. Wisely they were not punished, but only told to return to the house for dry clothing.

The construction of the new building was getting under way but there was no pier or floating stage, and everything used in the hotel's construction had to be floated ashore from sailing vessels, or brought in by small rowboats. Sufficient food must be supplied to feed workmen, as well as the Laighton family. Nothing forgotten could be obtained without crossing those ten miles of choppy sea, and if a storm should blow or heavy fog roll in, the purchaser must then wait on the mainland until the weather cleared.

The problem of transporting materials and supplies necessary for building a hotel in that desolate spot would have seemed almost insurmountable to a later generation, but not to the far-seeing, determined Thomas. He had not shrunk from the difficulty of life with a young family in a lighthouse on two acres of rock any more than he had allowed his lame leg to deter him from climbing the steep stairs to the tower, or landing his rowboat on the White Island slip.

By the end of October 1847 the outside of the new hotel was completed, chimneys built and plastering finished. It was four stories high, with two chimneys, and a tower on top. A piazza across the front commanded a fine view of shore and mainland. One could look across blue water to the White Island lighthouse, and also toward Londoner's Island, but the other islands were concealed by headlands.

The winter months passed, busy for the Laightons and all the workmen, with hammering, sawing and painting. Office, dining room and kitchens were completed on the first floor, and bedrooms on the floors above.

To establish the hotel's independence, a small blacksmith shop and forge were set up on the island. There were also vegetables from the garden, milk from the cow, a flock of sheep, and a sea full of fish to satisfy an increasing number of appetites.

Levi Thaxter offered to relieve Thomas Laighton of a task for which he was better suited than for actual work on the hotel. He became tutor, or schoolmaster, to the Laighton children. To the boys he must have seemed almost as old as their father, for the beard, which he had begun to grow when he first visited the island and declaimed to the elements against the roar of the waves, was now of impressive proportion. His dramatic aspirations had been abandoned although not forgotten. Now he found a spellbound audience in the young girl just blossoming into womanhood. All the enthusiasm of romantic youth moved Celia to look upon Levi with awe and admiration.

On June 15, 1848, less than one year after the project had been started, the doors of Appledore House were opened to the public. Excitement was wild in the hearts of the little family, so long isolated from contact with their fellow-men. Breathlessly the children watched the horizon for sails.

The Springbird, a little schooner chartered to bring passengers from Newburyport, sun on her sails, moored in Babb's Cove in front of the hotel and landed her six passengers — a man, his wife and two children; also two other gentlemen, one of whom was Judge Whittle of Manchester.

Judge Whittle became annoyed at having to wait his turn and demanded immediate service. Thomas Laighton, well known for his short temper, was independent even when business was at stake, and not to be blustered at by any guest. When Judge Whittle threatened to go elsewhere, Thomas announced briefly that he could go to Hell! Only the ministrations of little Oscar, acting as bellboy, calmed His Honor's agitation. All was happy again, however, by the time the guests were seated in the dining room and had tasted Eliza Laighton's wonderful fish chowder. Later in the afternoon more people came from Portsmouth.

Word of the new hotel spread and day by day guests arrived in steadily increasing numbers, some to stay a week, a month or the remainder of the summer.

Levi Thaxter's family moved from Watertown to spend a season at the island. His parents, his sisters, Lucy and Mary, his brother, Jonas, all continued interest in the growth and progress of the new hotel. At their first meeting, Celia and Lucy began what was to be a lifelong friendship.

The Laighton boys, now able to handle a boat successfully, started a little lobster business of their own, selling a three-pounder for the sum of six cents.

As the summer progressed, many curious visitors, in addition to the weekly guests, came for the day only, lured by the desire to see the place Laighton had built and by the fame of Eliza's chowder. Business increased surprisingly for the new hotel, and for the lobster business as well. The season did not close until the end of September. Thomas Laighton, who had spent more on the building than first estimated, was filled with encouragement.

Under date September 2, 1848, the New Hampshire Journal has a column describing a visit made to Appledore which runs in part:

> Sailed out on the Fanny Elsler with obliging Capt. Tuckerman . . . rough seas, squally time . . . eager to plant our feet on Hog Island and to salute our friends Messers Laighton and Thaxter of Appledore House. To us it was a real treat . . . in spite of sea breaking over in wild fury . . . Many a countenance before joyous, on the voyage looked the picture of despondency, ashy paleness deepened as we "luffed" . . . but the little boat danced on . . . we were satisfied with our Captain, who had been upon the sea 37 years. When the ladies were sick, he promised they would soon make the Shoals.
>
> We soon sighted Appledore Island with the newly built Appledore House. It has become the resort of the "Fashionables" from every quarter, who are strangely flocking there . . . The house is four stories high with a large Cupola and wings on each side, and a piazza nearly all around the building, capable of accommodating 130 visitors. Our vessel moored in the cove and a flat bottomed boat was sent to set us on shore. Waiting to receive us stood our hospitable friend Mr. Thaxter the genuine specimen of a gentleman. We wonder why a gentleman of his accomplishments, a graduate of Harvard, should be content to settle on this barren remote Island? He told us that during the summer one day there were 98 guests from all parts of the N. E. states! They come hungry and go with satisfied

appetite, come feeble and go away strong, come pale and sick and return florid and healthy, come full of cash and return with scarcely a "Picoyune." (sic)

Then we discovered our old friend T. B. L. Esq. snugly seated in his counting room with huge piles. of bank notes laying carelessly about him, happy as a king, revelling in his magnificent wealth . . . We rambled about the Island among ancient ruins and modern improvements and found only a few sheep, but we decided this is an "Oasis in the ocean" with plenty to eat, turkey, turtle, salmon, sea bass, partridge, pigeon and little pigs and vegetables. Then we went over to Smutty-nose. There we found the old hotel, pleasanter than Appledore, with visitors from Boston and Salem . . . an old man showed us the graves of the Spanish sailors and said he had helped dig them, lining them with planks from the ship's timber. It was 36 years before, but he said he should never forget the day when the frozen bodies of the poor fellows were laid out to thaw.

In the fall after the visit thus described, the little boat Springboard was tied up for the winter at the Laighton wharf in Portsmouth. The family settled down to solitude on Appledore with time to review the success of their venture. Each one had played his part helping Thomas in his tremendous undertaking — Eliza's cooking, Celia's industry in all directions, the boy's eager interest — had added to the pleasure and satisfaction of the guests.

The next summer Judge Woodbury came again out from Portsmouth, for a stay, bringing with him fireworks for the Fourth of July, which added gaiety to Appledore. When the guests went fishing in one of the two whaleboats, which had been added to a growing fleet, the catch of fish on a good morning would average forty pounds or more. They then had the satisfaction of eating the delicious cod, haddock, flounder or mackerel for their dinner, supplemented by fresh vegetables from the double-sized garden Thomas Laighton had planted. Board and room were ten dollars a week or one dollar and fifty cents per day, and for those who came only for noon dinner, fifty cents was charged. Although Laighton relied largely on curiosity and word of mouth publicity the following advertisement did appear in his former newspaper, the New Hampshire Gazette, for 1850, the third season after the opening of the hotel:

> Appledore House, Isles of Shoals is now open for the reception of summer visitors. Dressing rooms and other improvements have been made to this establishment, securing to invalids the luxuries of sea bathing in the open ocean, without the annoyances of sand and dirt. A packet boat will run daily from Portsmouth, immediately after the arrival of the morning train from Boston, from wharf, 107 Market St.

Until the opening of the hotel, the young Laightons had known few people besides the rough fishermen and their families. Celia had had her brothers, for playmates, but as she entered her teens the four and five years difference in their ages made them less companionable. She had become a strikingly pretty girl, well developed and appealing. She was beginning to coil her long braid around her head, held in place on special occasions with a silver comb, the gift of Lucy Thaxter. No wonder the young fishermen from Gosport turned to look at her. True, they could not understand her love of flowers, or why she sat by herself out on the rocks reading from a book. One bronzed, handsome youth, more gentle than his companions, was especially attracted and shyly invited her to come along in his boat for a brisk sail or a day's fishing. Celia, pleased and responsive, welcomed his attentions, and for a time the two young islanders were gay and happy comrades.

Then, little by little, Celia came to feel shy about the companionship, as her exacting school-teacher wakened her mind to new horizons.

After the first two seasons, Thomas Laighton found it hard to agree with Levi Thaxter as to various financial details. Therefore, to their mutual satisfaction, they decided that the partnership should be dissolved. Levi was far too much of an intellectual dreamer to be very businesslike, and Thomas' quick and stubborn temper may have flared up once too often.

In November, 1849, a notary went to the Island and a formal division of all property was made, even to the heifer, for which they cast lots. Mr. Thaxter retained "all south of an E. W. line through the centre of the Stone Monument, also the right of way to the well and landing place." All other buildings, the new hotel with its many improvements, the farming utensils and livestock, were retained by Laighton, who gave a note of hand, secured by a mortgage to Levi Thaxter, Sr., for seventeen hundred dollars, payable in five years.

Levi's growing interest in Celia as more than a pupil began to be apparent. Thomas Laighton, already on the defensive, seems to have felt it time to make a change. During the year 1849-50 Celia appears to have accompanied Lucy Thaxter to the mainland and to have attended the Mt. Washington Female Seminary, operated by Mrs. Burrill in South Boston. Probably this was for one term only.

Levi's friend, Samuel Longfellow, wrote:

> Dear Fannie — August 20, 1850 — Thaxter who lives in a house a stone's throw from the hotel, with a hedge of sweet peas and mignonette of marvelous fragrance before the door, is engaged to the daughter of him who once kept the lighthouse and now keeps the hotel — a simple, frank and pleasing girl of fifteen, who has grown up on the islands, the flower of the rock; for the last year planted in the Boarding School garden or greenhouse of Mrs. Burrill of S. Boston.

Levi's friend Thomas Higginson mentions the romance developing between the two young people several times in his diary. He speaks of Celia as having visited the Thaxter family in Watertown, where they grew very fond of her. He also says "her school mistress thought her most mature with an uncommon mind, for a girl not yet 15, and Mrs. Thaxter senior was charmed with her sagacity. Mr. Thaxter senior overcame his first displeasure, pleased with his own sagacity, because he had long predicted what would happen!" Higginson continues, he "sees no decided advantage in the match, but defers judgment" and later wrote his mother that he "grew more attached to the sea maiden" and that Levi was happy.

This was the year when Celia was of an age to be eagerly storing away in her mind all she could find from books wherever she was. She felt much older than her years and her thoughts at this time must have been long, long thoughts, all too soon to be changed to those of realities and responsibilities, so heavy that she was cheated of a leisurely and carefree youth!

5

CELIA'S ROMANCE
1851 - 1852

IN MARCH of 1851 Celia wrote a long wistful letter to Jennie Usher of Maine, her first recorded correspondent. The letter is the only writing previous to her marriage which has been found to date.

Appledore
March 2, 1851

My dear Jennie,

Your letter was received last week, and I meant to have answered it immediately but I have to plead the same excuse "lack of time" which you did, I study nearly all the time. One would scarcely think in the quiet, dreamy life we lead here, there would be so much to take the time. There is no excitement of any kind except when a boat comes from the mainland bringing letters and papers, or a tremendous storm stirs us up a little. We are cut off as it were from the world, There being twelve miles of salt water between us and mankind. Our island is the largest of a group of nine only four of which are inhabited. Star Island is the largest next to ours, and has the most inhabitants. The next is "Smutty-nose" an exquisite name, isn't it? That has eleven people on it, ours has seventeen, and White Island, has two, the lighthouse keeper and his wife, no more. Two years ago now nearly three father kept the lighthouse there and five years of my life were passed on that little spot of earth only one acre in extent. I left Portsmouth at the age of five, lived two years on Smutty-nose, five at White

Island, and three here at Appledore. This Appledore was, nearly a hundred years ago, very populous, containing six hundred and fifty inhabitants. There are still the ruins of some of the houses to be seen and several sunken graveyards. No trees grow on the islands, save a few stunted Balm of Gileads. What soil there is is very rich and yields an incredible amount.

April 10th — Well, Jennie, some time has elapsed since I began this letter, don't you think so! But I have been sick, and many things have prevented my resuming this. But at last I have a little time and I will finish so I can send it by the first opportunity so you shall not think I have entirely forgotten you. I had a friend named Jennie who was very dear to me. She was a roommate of mine at school. She never would write to me though I begged her to and now I believe she has left school for I can get no trace of her. I hope our friendship will not end so my dear second friend Jennie.

. . . .

The weather here now is surpassingly lovely. Everything is expanding beneath the reawakening breath of spring. Tonight's sunset was very beautiful. There were piles of massive gigantic clouds about the sun. Those in the East were deep and dark and dewey and the slightest possible flush or rose was mirrored in the sea. We can see no land in the East. There is only the infinity of ocean stretching far far beyond the reach of human vision. I used to listen when a child to my father's words with wonder that if you should take a boat and sail as far east in a straight line from these islands the first land you would meet would be Ireland. In the West and North the far blue hills are clearly defined against the sky. Sometimes they seem very far indeed, very pale like clouds. This is owing to a peculiar state of the atmosphere. And sometimes they seem very near and stand boldly out on the horizon, dark purple and blue. Sometimes the mirage plays with them, turns them into great gigantic temples and towers and churches and strange unwieldy figures of every description. The same mirage plays with the vessels too and in the place of one vessel one can see three, one in the clouds, the real vessel, and one in the water.

April 15th — Another beginning! Indeed I am afraid you will think I have forgotten you for this letter seems fated never to go. At present there certainly is no prospect of it for the sea is lashed into a fury by a tremendous northeaster. I am longing for fair weather so we shall be able to have some communication with the mainland.

The letter goes on to mention a story written by Celia and ends with a somewhat unenthusiastic statement crisscrossed over the top of the page:

You asked me how father liked "Allen Percy." I am sorry to say he did not like it as well as I expected but it found quite an impassioned admirer in Mr. Thaxter, which more than compensated me for the disappointment in regard to father. Perhaps you do not know who Mr. Thaxter is. He is the gentleman whose wife I shall probably be next fall. I hope you will answer this soon as I shall be very anxious to hear from you and to know whether this reached you in safety.

With my love

I am yours affectionately

CELIA

This is the direction:
Miss Celia Laighton
Care of Hon. Thomas B. Laighton
Appledore   Isles of Shoals
via Portsmouth, N. H.

Until this winter there had been many lonely hours for Levi, the gifted student of drama turned schoolmaster. Now the responsive girl who loved beauty in all forms of nature was discovering that it could be found in literature and the human voice. Levi, instead of declaiming to the waves, now solaced himself through the long evenings by reading poetry aloud with vividness and fire to an appreciative girl eleven years his junior. Celia's keen mind, eager to absorb all that lay beyond her limited experience, had doubtless first drawn the scholarly student to his promising young pupil. But as winter moved toward spring the hearts of these two began to be stirred by a more human attraction than poetry.

On an evening when the delicate colors of sunset tinted clouds and sea, the school teacher came to sit on the high lookout with his pupil. He realized how beautiful the daughter of his old friend had become. Later, in an attempt at an autobiography begged for by John Greenleaf Whittier, begun but not completed, Celia described herself:

> A young girl sat there clad in a gown of cocoa brown gingham, innocent of any attempt at ornament, save for a little bunch of purple hepaticas at her waist. Her heavy braid was tied with a worn ribbon of dull purple.

It was spring and the first song sparrow sang to them of the nest he would build in the wild rose bush. Levi declared his love then, and asked her to be his wife.

As the attraction between Celia and Levi had blossomed into love, Levi perhaps thought of himself in the guise of a Pygmalion who could mould an untrained, unspoiled child into any form he might choose. He did not dream that the name of his unworldly water-sprite would later become known in literary circles beyond the ocean.

For years Levi had been like a member of the Laighton family, but Celia's father, when informed of the romance foreseen by all but himself, insisted that she was too young to be married. He all but ordered Levi off the island when he first asked for her hand. It was Celia's understanding mother who finally persuaded her husband to relent and agree to an engagement. After all, Levi was an old friend and came from a suitable family. Also Celia, though young, had been carefully trained by her mother in all necessary household arts and was blessed with wisdom and intelligence far beyond her years. However, Thomas insisted that she wait for a few months at least and help as usual in the hotel during the coming season.

The summer months passed rapidly for the young couple, with more dreams than plans. The beautiful days of September led hotel guests to remain longer than usual but at last they were almost all gone. Only a few old friends remained, which included John Weiss, his wife and baby.

Tuesday, September 30, 1851, dawned radiant. With characteristic lack of convention, Levi, suddenly and on the spur of the moment, decided he would wait no longer to be married. The license had been for some time in his pocket and he had thought that his friend John Weiss could perform the ceremony at any minute. John, however, had been ordained in Massachusetts. He had to explain, when approached by Levi, that he could do no more than assist at their marriage, since the laws of Maine required that the knot be tied by a resident of that state. Consequently Levi's brother, Jonas, was dispatched early by sailboat to secure the services of a minister from Kittery Point, to which township Appledore Island belonged.

Meanwhile Celia, in the bright September sunshine, gathered armsful of scarlet huckleberry leaves, bright rosehaws, wild asters and beach goldenrod to fill the room where she would be married. For her bouquet, she stripped the garden of its last, fragrant sweetpeas. Her mother had lately finished making a warm, red merino dress for Celia, and this she wore for her wedding gown.

The wedding, a simple one but beautiful, took place in the gaily decorated front parlor of Appledore House. The bride, slender and touchingly young, her brown hair smoothly parted in the middle and drawn back by her silver comb, held her head as always proudly high, as if to catch the sea breeze; Levi, with his full auburn beard and deep-set, piercing eyes, was a distinguished looking bridegroom. John Weiss read the greater part of the marriage service but the pronouncement that the two were man and wife was made by the visiting minister.

All the Appledore Islanders, including one Captain Fabius Becker, the Weiss family with the baby in its cradle,

Cousin Christopher Rhymes, Jonas and Lucy Thaxter, were present at the wedding. Thomas, stiffly upright, Eliza, her eyes brimming, and the two boys Oscar and Cedric looking "like seals with hair cut straight across each forehead," stood nearest the girl bride. The warm sun of Indian summer shone brightly, and all around stretched the limitless ocean, always part of the very fibre of Celia's life.

Never on the islands had there been baked a more wonderful and delicious wedding cake. Good wishes to the happy couple were drunk by the guests in champagne and home brewed elderberry wine.

"We had a merry time," wrote Levi to Thomas Higginson. "And then I took my dear wife home in the beautiful night, bright and clear with the stars and a growing moon, and prayed God to strengthen me to make the hearth happy. I shall hope and try."

Shortly after the wedding, sixteen year old Celia stood on the platform of Portsmouth's new railroad station. She held her husband's hand as she watched eagerly for the arrival of the train which was to take her out into the world. They were on their way to visit Levi's family in Watertown. What lay beyond those shining rails?

Any bride has much to learn. New sensations, sights and experiences crowded upon one another in a bewildering fashion for Celia, and Lucy Thaxter was to prove a great help to her.

Levi's parents were much older than Celia's and their house was one of elegance compared to those she had known. Good mahogany and black walnut furniture was far more handsome than the sturdy pieces with which her island homes had been equipped. There were servants to do the work. Nearby the Thaxter house was the brick dwelling of Levi's mother's brother, Abijah White, who had no less than six daughters, all agog with curiosity to see their new cousin. In every way the families lived a more sophisticated life than had been the lot of the Laightons on their small bits of rock. They all gave a warm welcome,

CELIA LAIGHTON AT FIFTEEN

CELIA THAXTER AFTER HER MARRIAGE

however, to the "Mermaid" Levi had found on the headland of her island and transplanted to the city.

The Thaxter house was not large enough for the young couple to remain permanently, for besides Lucy, there was sister Mary (soon to marry Judge Samuel Jennison) and brother Jonas. During the first winter of their marriage the newly-wed Thaxters probably occupied one of the many houses which were owned by Levi's father in Watertown. Celia enjoyed a series of new impressions, not least of which was attending the church services. She did not mind the two and a half mile walk to reach the church, especially since kind friends sometimes drove her back. Once home, before she could forget the text, she would sit down and write her parents of the stirring sermons preached by their friend John Weiss. In these letters she told her family all that happened, day by day, and of her husband's affectionate tenderness towards her. Her father at once replied, hoping that she would not become spoiled. When she announced her desire to cut off her hair because she had seen some city girls who had short hair, her mother advised her to ask her husband's opinion in the matter. Levi had plenty of time to consult with his young wife on this and other matters since he seemed unable to find any business or profession which suited his tastes. His opinion was always valuable to Celia, however, and in this instance she did not cut off her beautiful long braids.

Celia had great fun packing a Christmas box to be sent to the cold, ice-bound island – a comfortable cushion for her mother, who was always of generous proportions; a thermometer for her father, who daily recorded the temperature; and games for Oscar and Cedric. Christine, the new housemaid on Appledore, was not forgotten, and the material sent her must have been quickly converted into a dress, since Cedric wrote: "it is a pretty gown and fits very well indeed."

In January the Laighton family begged for a winter visit from the young couple, and a time was set for their arrival.

On the appointed day Celia's mother could not sit still for excitement, but only a letter was brought from the mainland. Her father's reply to the letter described its effect upon the family:

Feb. 2, 1852

Dear Celia:

. . . Mother - - unable to do anything, so great was her excitement expecting your return - - laughed and cried by turn. She rushed to Broad Cove to welcome you — but only letters. Glad you are well dear child — long to see you both . . . Oh dear Celia, imagine yourself in the little Parlor, your good kind Mother at the South window hearing Father at the East one reading your very interesting letter — Father laughing most heartily as he read the particulars of certain matters aloud, and dear Mother sobbing as if it really were a matter for tears! Dear child, you know how very anxious I am that matters should be thus. I shall rejoice if it shall be a boy — but will thank God sincerely be it male or female. Be very careful of yourself and don't leave off the bag of camomile for an instant. The sooner you can conveniently return here the better it will be for you, for in the ocean air there is strength.

This invitation was written while an extremely severe winter raged around the islands. Newspapers were full of accounts of the exceptional amount of ice and snow. There was grave fear that if the spring thaw were to come too quickly, the swift current in the Merrimac River might force ice against the bridge at Newburyport and carry the whole structure seaward. It was no time to attempt a passage to the islands. While the anxious parents were rejoicing in her pregnancy, Celia longed more than ever for the deferred visit with her mother.

6

STAR ISLAND AND CURZON'S MILLS
1852 - 1855

As SOON AS weather permitted, Celia and Levi returned to his house on Appledore Island and it was there during the summer of 1852 that baby Karl opened his eyes. He was the first child to be born on Appledore in many years. A mid-wife was summoned from the little town of Gosport on Star Island but, though she did her best, the baby must have suffered some injury at birth. Throughout his life Karl walked with a slight limp, his health was never very good and, although of a mild and gentle disposition, as he grew older attacks of violent temper were followed by great mental depression. From his birth Karl was the object of his mother's special care and tenderness, and she did her best to shield him from a world "full of people who do not understand."

For this first summer Celia was as gay as her beloved song sparrow. With her husband and her baby in her own small house, near her parents and her brothers, Celia had all those whom she best loved close at hand as at no other time. Lucy Thaxter and her brother, Jonas, were visitors often, and with friends from the hotel the young people had many a merry evening.

Among the guests at Appledore House that summer was Nathaniel Hawthorne who gives in his American Notebook an interesting picture of the young Thaxters and their islands.

39

Aug. 30, 1852

Leaving Portsmouth at 10:30 A. M. we sailed out with other passengers to the Isles of Shoals. The wind not being favorable, we had to make several tacks before reaching the islands, where we arrived about two o'clock. We landed at Appledore, on which is Laighton's Hotel — a large building with a piazza or promenade before it, about an hundred and twenty feet in length, or more, yes, it must be more. It is an edifice with a centre and two wings, the central part upwards of seventy feet. At one end of the promenade is a covered verandah, thirty or forty feet square, so situated that the breeze draws across it from the sea on one side of the island to the sea on the other, and it is the breeziest and comfortablest place in the world on a hot day. There are two swings beneath it, and here one may sit or walk, and enjoy life, while all other mortals are suffering.

As I entered the door of the hotel, there met me a short, corpulent, round and full-faced man, rather elderly, if not old. He was a little lame. He addressed me in a hearty, hospitable tone and judging that it must be my landlord, I delivered a letter of introduction from Pierce. Of course it was fully efficient in obtaining the best accommodations that were to be had. I found that we were expected, a man having brought the news of our intention the day before. Here ensued great inquiries after the General, and wherefore he had not come. I was looked at with considerable curiosity on my account, especially by the ladies, of whom there were several, agreeable and pretty enough. There were four or five gentlemen, most of whom had not much that was noteworthy.

After dinner, which was good and abundant, though somewhat rude in its style, I was introduced by Mr. Laighton to Mr. Thaxter, his son-in-law, and Mr. Weiss, a clergyman of New Bedford, who is staying here for his health. They showed me some of the remarkable features of the island, such as a deep chasm in the cliffs of the shore, towards the southwest; also a monument of rude stones, on the highest point of the island, said to have been erected by Captain John Smith before the settlement of Plymouth. The tradition is just as good as truth. Also, some ancient cellars,

with thistles and other weeds growing in them and old frag-
mentary bricks scattered about. The date of these habita-
tions is not known, but they may well be the remains of the
settlement that Cotton Mather speaks about; or perhaps one
of them was the house where William Pepperell had lived
and where he went when he and somebody else set up a
stick, and travelled to seek their fortunes in the direction
in which it fell.

. . . .

In the afternoon I walked round a portion of the island
that I had not previously visited, and in the evening went
with Mr. Titcomb to Mr. Thaxter's to drink apple-toddy.
We found Mrs. Thaxter sitting in a neat little parlor, very
simply furnished, but in good taste. She is not now, I
believe, more than eighteen years old, very pretty, and with
the manners of a lady, — not prim and precise, but with
enough of freedom and ease. The books on the table were
Pre-Raphaelitism, a tract on spiritual mediums, etc. There
were several shelves of books on one side of the room, and
engravings on the walls. Mr. Weiss was there. By and by
came in Mr. Thaxter's brother, with a young lady. Anon,
too, came in the apple-toddy, a very rich and spicy com-
pound; after which we had some glees and negro melodies,
in which Mr. Thaxter sang a noble bass, and Mrs. Thaxter
sang like a bird, and Mr. Weiss sang, I suppose, tenor, and
the brother took some other part, and all were very mirthful
and jolly. At about ten o'clock Mr. Titcomb and myself
took leave and emerging into the open air, out of that room
of song, and pretty youthfulness of woman, and gay young
men, there was the sky, and the three-quarters waning
moon, and the old sea moaning all around about the island.

. . . .

This island (Appledore) is said to be haunted by a
specter called "Old Babb." He was one of Captain Kidd's
men, and was slain for the protection of the treasure, Mr.
Laighton said that, before he built his house, nothing would
have induced the inhabitants of another island to come to
this after nightfall. The ghost especially haunts the space
between the hotel and the cove in front. There was, in
times past, great search for the treasure, which continues.

Mr. Thaxter had once a man living with him who had seen "Old Babb," the ghost. He met him between the hotel and the sea, and describes him as dressd in a sort of frock, and with a very dreadful countenance, who always carried a butcher knife.

.   .   .   .

Last evening we (Mr., Mrs., and Miss Thaxter) sat and talked of ghosts and kindred subjects; and they told me of the appearance of a little old woman in a striped gown, that had come into that house a few months ago. She was seen by nobody but an Irish nurse, who spoke to her, but received no answer. The little woman drew her chair up toward the fire, and stretched out her feet to warm them. By and by the nurse, who suspected nothing of her ghostly character, went to get a pail of water; and, when she came back, the little woman was not there. It being known precisely how many and what people were on the island, and that no such little woman was among them, the fact of her being a ghost is incontestable. I taught them how to discover the hidden sentiments of letters by suspending a gold ring over them.

Mr. Thaxter tells me that the women on the island are very timid as to venturing on the sea — more so than the women of the mainland, — and that they are easily frightened about their husbands. Very few accidents happen to the boats or men, — none, I think since Mr. Thaxter has been here. They are not an enterprising set of people, never liking to make long voyages. Sometimes one of them will ship on a voyage to the West Indies, but generally only on coastwise trips, or fishing or mackerel voyages. They have a very strong local attachment, and return to die. They are now generally temperate, formerly very much the contrary.

.   .   .   .

September 13th. — I spent last evening, as well as part of the evening before, at Mr. Thaxter's. It is certainly a romantic incident to find such a young man on this lonely island; his marriage with the very pretty Miranda is true romance. In our talk we have glanced over many matters, and among the rest, that of the stage, to prepare himself for which was his first motive for coming hither. He appears quite to have given up any dreams of that kind now.

What he will do on returning to the world, as his purpose is, I cannot imagine; but, no doubt through all their remaining life, both he and she will look back to this rocky ledge, with its handful of soil, as to a Paradise.

. . . .

Since dinner, the Spy has arrived from Portsmouth, with a party . . . from the interior of New Hampshire. I am rather sorry to receive these strangers into the quiet life that we are leading here; for we had grown quite to feel ourselves at home . . . Mr. Thaxter, his wife and sister, and myself, met at meal-times like one family. The young ladies gathered shells, arranged them, laughing gently, sang, and did other pretty things in a young-lady-like way. These newcomers are people of uncouth voices and loud laughter, and behave themselves as if they were trying to turn their expedition to as much account as possible in the way of enjoyment.

. . . .

As to newcomers, I feel rather a distaste to them; and so I find, does Mr. Laighton, — a rather singular sentiment for a hotel-keeper to entertain toward his guests. However, he treats them very hospitably when once within his doors.

. . . .

Ordinarily, since I have been here, we have spent the evening under the piazza, where Mr. Laighton sits to take the air. He seems to avoid the within-doors whenever he can. So there he sits in the sea-breezes, when inland people are probably drawing their chairs to the fireside; and there I sit with him, — not keeping up a continual flow of talk, but each speaking as any wisdom happens to come to mind.

It has been raining more or less all the forenoon, and now, at twelve o'clock, blows, as Mr. Laighton says, "half a gale" from the southeast. . . . All around the horizon, landward as well as seaward, the view is shut in by mist. Sometimes I have a dim sense of the continent beyond, but no more distinct than the thought of the other world to the unenlightened soul. The sheep bleat in their desolate pasture. A wind shakes the house. A loon, seeking, I suppose, some quieter resting-place than on the troubled waves, was seen swimming just now in the cove not more than a hundred yards from the hotel. Judging by the pother which this "half gale" makes with the sea, it must have been a terrific time, indeed, when that great wave rushed and roared across the islands.

. . . .

As we sat under the piazza in the evening, we saw the light from on board some vessel move slowly through the distant obscurity — so slowly that we were only sensible of its progress by forgetting it and looking again. The splash and murmur of the waves around the island were soothingly audible. It was not unpleasantly cold, and Mr. Laighton, Mr. Thaxter, and myself sat under the piazza until long after dark; the former at a distance, occasionally smoking his pipe, and Mr. Thaxter and I talking about poets and the stage. The latter is an odd subject to be discussed in this stern and wild scene, which has precisely the same characteristics now as two hundred years ago. . . .

. . . .

September 9th. — Mr. Thaxter rowed me this morning, in his dory, to White Island, on which is the light-house. There was scarcely a breath of air, and a perfectly calm sea; an intensely hot sunshine, with a little haze, so that the horizon was indistinct. Here and there sail-boats sleeping on the water, or moving almost imperceptibly over it. The light house island would be difficult of access in a rough sea, the shore being so rocky. On landing we found the keeper peeling his harvest of onions, which he had gathered prematurely, because the insects were eating them. His little patch of garden seemed to be a strange kind of soil, as like marine mud as anything; but he had a fair crop of marrow squashes, though injured, as he said, by the last storm; and there were cabbages and a few turnips. I recollect no other garden vegetables. The grass grows luxuriantly, and looked very green where there was any soil; but he kept no cow, nor even a pig or hen. His house stands close by the garden, — a small stone building, with peaked roof, and whitewashed. The light house stands on a ledge of rock, with a gully between, and there is a long covered way, triangular in shape, connecting his residence with it.

We ascended into the lantern, which is eighty-seven feet high. It is a revolving light, with several great illuminators of copper silvered, and colored lamp-glasses. Looking downward, we had the island displayed as on a chart, with its little bays, its isthmus of shingly beach connecting two parts of the island, and overflowing at high tide; its sunken rocks about it, indicated by the swell, or slightly breaking surf. The keeper of the light-house was formerly a writing-master. He has a sneaking kind of look, and does not bear a very high character among his neighbors. Since he kept the light, he has lost two wives, — the first a young creature whom he used to leave alone upon this desolate rock, and the gloom and terror of the situation were probably the cause of her death. The second wife, experiencing the same kind of treatment ran away from him, and returned to her friends. He pretends to be religious, but drinks. About a year ago, he attempted to row out alone from Portsmouth. There was a head wind and head tide, and he would have inevitably drifted out to sea, if Mr. Thaxter had not saved him.

. . . .

On our way back we landed at another island called Londoner's Rock, or some such name. It has but little soil. As we approached it, a large bird flew away. Mr. Thaxter took it to be a gannet; and, while walking over the island, an owl started up from among the rocks near us, and flew away, apparently uncertain of its course. It was a brown owl, but Mr. Thaxter says that there are beautiful white owls which spend the winter here, and feed upon rats.

At the base of the light-house yesterday, we saw the wings and feathers of a decayed little bird, and Mr. Thaxter said they often flew against the lantern with such force as to kill themselves, and that large quantities of them might be picked up. How came these little birds out of their nests at night? Why should they meet destruction from the radiance that proves the salvation of other beings?

Mr. Laighton says that the artist who adorned Trinity Church, New York, with sculpture wanted some real wings with which to imitate the wings of cherubim. Mr. Thaxter carried him the wings of the white owl that winters here at the Shoals, together with some other birds, and the artist gave his cherubim the wings of an owl.

Mrs. Thaxter tells me that there are several burial-places on this island; but nobody has been buried here since the Revolution. Her own marriage was the first one since that epoch, and her little Karl, now three months old, the first-born child in all those eighty years.

Mr. Hawthorne ends his Notebook with paragraphs singularly appropriate to the lives of those left behind him on the Isles of Shoals — where love was to pass all too soon, and the hotel to end in fire:

> I burned great heaps of old letters. . . . preparatory to going to England. . . . the world has no more such, and now they are all dust and ashes. What a trustful guardian of secret matter is fire! What should we do without fire and death?

Hawthorne gone and the hotel closed, winter found the young couple househunting again on the mainland, unhappily from temporary quarters. In spite of their uncertainties and disappointments, Celia's letters home were full of the baby Karl and his doings. Her father wrote her to be very careful during the critical period of teething: "Do not wean him until the worst is over. Next to God, should anything ail him, put your trust in Lobelia." (A patent medicine of that day.) Then he inquires about Levi's "new business," and if Celia thinks "he will succeed?"

This inquiry referred probably to a plan for Levi to assume the temporarily vacant position of preacher in the stone chapel on Star Island, his duties to include the teaching of the fishermen's children in the little town of Gosport. Homesick Celia had been begging Levi to try the experiment. Gradually attracted by the idea, Levi finally agreed.

Throughout the following year they occupied the old parsonage while Levi took up his new duties. Celia was very happy on Star Island and often in later years looked back wistfully to those months wishing that they might have continued. But by the fall of 1854 an ordained minister was sent to Gosport and Levi surrendered his post.

After leaving Star Island, Celia, Levi and two-year-old Karl accepted the hospitality of the Curzon family of Newburyport, Massachusetts, who had urged the Thaxters to occupy their Mill House on the bank of the Artichoke River. Margie Curzon was living with her parents next door in the Mansion House. Naturally, it was a great help to the young Thaxters to be established near friends.

Celia enjoyed quietly sitting and watching the tidal stream turn the mill wheels, grinding meal for the farmers who drove in bringing fat bags of corn. And here at the Mill House on November 29, 1854, the Thaxters' second son was born. Celia was tenderly cared for by Mrs. Curzon, Margie's mother, who was most kind to the young mother of nineteen and her two babies. She took the place Eliza Laighton would have filled so gladly had loyalty to Thomas and their sons not kept her on Appledore.

Christmas arrived before the parents settled upon a name for the new baby. "Rupert" and "Victor" had been discussed, but sounded too fancy to their ears, so they finally decided on the name of John, used for generations in the Thaxter family.

The Thaxters had a happy Christmas that year at Newburyport. Little Karl, only two-and-a-half years, enjoyed his stocking and his Noah's Ark. His mother wrote home describing how he loved the new baby, and sang to him:

> *Dance little baby, dance up high.*
> *Never mind baby, Karly is nigh.*

Celia told proudly how clever the little tot was to repeat her song, putting "Karly" in place of "Mamma," as she sang it. He made a baby of his kitten, she reported, and often talked about "Dominy Laty" and her kitchen. These sayings warmed Eliza Laighton's heart.

Eliza, herself, had done all she could at a distance for her daughter's Christmas and had packed a wonderful box for

Newburyport. There were buns, spare-ribs, sausage-balls, hog's head cheese and bread which, when received, was "as fresh as the day it was baked." Little Karl sat on the floor peeping under the lid while his father opened this, and another box from the family in Watertown, "red apples, sweet cookies for Karly, a great ham, a large lump of butter and a bushel of rye and wheat."

Celia sat by the fire warming her feet on the fender, and little Karl who had placed his father's slippers to warm on the hearth, was running to get them for Levi to put on, when the expressman made his third visit.

Celia stopped writing the letter in her lap, describing the day to her brothers, and looked up in surprise. This time a large bandbox was handed in to be opened by the delighted young woman. It contained a "wonderful dark winter bonnet, all trimmed and fixed, but with no note, no explanation."

This small mystery, like many greater and more serious ones which came to Celia as the years rolled on, was never solved. But Celia spinning around for her husband and babies to admire the bonnet on her head, enjoyed one of the few frivolous moments of a youth which was flying by too quickly.

Another frivolous moment of those days was when she went coasting on the frozen river. She wrote Oscar on February 12th, 1856:

> . . . The Merrimac is a great deal better than the land, it is like a great flat marble floor and the amount of sleighing down on it is remarkable. I tried to skate the other day but kept falling down and my king Levi laughed, so I gave it up in great disgust. I kept faithful to coasting and yesterday coasted away from the top of a high hill, plump down on the frozen Artichoke all across to the other side, a long coast, I can tell you. . .

7

LEVI'S SHIPWRECK — NEWTONVILLE
1855 - 1861

AFTER THE winter in Newburport, Levi, Celia, Karl and baby John returned for another long summer on Appledore. Levi enjoyed the companionship and conversation with the summer guests at the Appledore hotel, and went sailing and fishing in the same waters which had first attracted him ten years earlier.

In the fall of 1855, however, an event occurred which, though less tragic than it might have been, had a permanently disturbing effect upon the lives of Levi and Celia.

One afternoon at the end of their happy summer, Levi and Oscar Laighton sailed home from Portsmouth, where they had gone in the little skiff to bring back household supplies. Celia was giving baby John an airing on the rocks when she suddenly became aware of darkening clouds. Her senses were long trained to changes of wind over the water and she realized that a squall was blowing up. Running back to the cottage, she placed the baby in her mother's arms and rushed to look for her father.

She found Thomas stationed at the highest window of the tower, spyglass to his eye, watching the black water and approaching storm. In the far distance was a tiny speck of sail. As the storm was about to break, he shouted: "Down with your sail!" as if his voice could be heard over the howling of the wind and the roaring of the waves.

Celia took one desperate look, then leaving him, ran downstairs and out into a torrent of rain so fierce that she could hardly stand, as the wind split the shingles off the roof, whipped her skirts about her and lashed her face and hair. She strained her eyes over the boiling water, where all the coastline was completely blotted out. In the darkness of the storm and as the waves rose and fell, she lost sight of the sail, then regained it again. Nearer and nearer it came — then suddenly it was lost from sight once more! Had the two men been able to lower their sail? Would the fierce storm blow them past the island and out to the open seas? Or would they be smashed against the sharp ledges of Duck Island? These were the thoughts that rushed through Celia's mind as she stood scanning the sea, knowing that the little skiff was just a pawn, little more than a cockle shell, in the midst of the angry, churning sea.

All at once, on the farthest rocks of the island, her eye caught sight of moving objects. Wild with hope, she rushed forward. There, creeping on hands and knees over the slippery water-beàten rocks,,crawled her brother and husband, rescued by a miracle. One wave, higher than the others, had tossed the tiny boat with its occupants up on the rocks, beyond the clutches of the boiling breakers.

As suddenly as it began, the storm cleared, and the setting sun shone out. The little family was re-united by God's mercy. Levi's experience, however, had been so terrifying to him that he became dominated by fear of that trip, and for the remainder of his life made all possible excuses not to revisit the Isles of Shoals. (See note page 265)

He was so shaken that his one idea was to leave Appledore Island and never return. He conferred with his father-in-law and agreed to sell him, for six hundred dollars, his fifty acres on the south side of the island and the little house where he had taken his bride on the moonlight night of their marriage.

This was the first rift, the opening wedge which tended as the years passed, to separate Celia's and Levi's lives, sending them along paths leading in different directions. Celia's ideal of marriage had been founded on the devotion and understanding between her parents, as shown in a letter written by her father to her mother at the time of one of their rare and brief separations.

My cherished and beloved wife,

A week has elapsed since you left our peaceful home and brief though it be, appears an eternity. You cannot imagine my dear wife, how necessary your presence is to the happiness and comfort of my life. Your absence and Oscar's at the same time is tearing away the best part of our home — he is the music and you the sunshine of our solitary life. But the time wears away, and then to meet you again, safe, contented and happy, what a glorious moment that will be for all of us.

Give yourself no uneasiness about our well-doing. We are getting along famously as can be possible to do without you. Though I must confess, I regard everything as unsettled with us, until I again hear the merry music of your sweet voice in our home.

I had a letter from Celia yesterday dated Monday saying she had arrived safely at Curzon's and Levi with Karl had gone to Watertown. She desired you to call and see her as you came back. You will probably see Levi if you go to Watertown. Tell Oscar to be very careful and keep out of danger. I have seven letters to write in two hours, which must excuse my brevity.

God forever bless you, my dear wife, that you may enjoy yourself and return early to your ever devoted friend and ever loving husband, is the prayer of

Thomas B. Laighton

This letter reveals an accord which Celia was never to attain in her own marriage.

A house in Newtonville was chosen for their new home, but Mr. Thaxter, senior, who was doubtless helping to finance the purchase, decided that the price was too high and the idea was abandoned. Fortunately for Celia and the children, her friends at Newburyport again offered the Mill House and the young Thaxters gladly accepted. Here they spent a second happy winter.

It was not until five years after their marriage that Levi Thaxter acquired a house of his own. The land on the corner of Nevada and California Streets in Newtonville, Massachusetts, was probably given him by his father. California Street was a long boulevard bordered by maple trees, and Nevada Street, crossing it, ran down to the Charles River.

From the back windows of the new house a lovely view of the river could be seen, and in another direction lay the hills of Waltham. Between house and river, a small bridge crossed a little glen, in sight of which was a rolling dam and grist mill, similar to the one at Newburyport.

It was to the Charles River that Celia looked wistfully, as it nearly encircled the town and flowed on past Watertown, past Cambridge, finally to empty into the sea at Boston Harbor. The river was navigable the whole way and played its own part in the life of the new family who, in the winter of 1855-56, came to live beside it.

At this time Celia was twenty-one years old.

She furnished the new home with some of the furniture sent from Levi's cottage at Appledore, and some good pieces given her by the Thaxter family. She was an exemplary housekeeper, well trained as she had been by her mother, and her husband pronounced her "virtuous," which to her was worth all her trying. "But sometimes it's a great bore being exemplary," she once wrote.

She felt it almost against her conscience to write letters, except on Sunday. But on that day, after a morning visit to church, she delighted in opening her heart to her friends and family. To Lizzie Hoxie, at Artichoke Mill, she painted a picture of life in their new home:

> I am happy as the day is long and the children are perfect gardens of paradise, and Levi is beautiful, gentle, good, unselfish as mortal men can be! We have a splendid time and such good evenings, that sometimes we do not go to bed until eleven! We draw the table up to the roaring fire and I take my work, and Levi reads to me; first he read

CELIA THAXTER ABOUT 1856, WITH JOHN AND KARL

DAUGHTERS OF CEDRIC: MARGARET AND RUTH

LEVI LINCOLN THAXTER AND SON ROLAND

Aurora (and you're an abominable woman for not thinking it the beautifulest book ever written), then Dred. . . . Next to Dred we read Dr. Kane's books, the two volumes of the Arctic Expedition. . . full of beautiful pictures taken on the spot by Dr. Kane himself. . . Now we are reading Ruskin's last volume of Modern Painters, and I declare I can't tell what we have the best times ever, for we sometimes lose ourselves in wonder and admiration at him, and then shout with mirth over his impatient sarcasm, his downrightness . . . and fall into a great feeling of reverence occasionally. . . and say how true are Margie's ideas of the highest art because she follows nature so nobly and faithfully, — that is high art according to him; very few people do it faithfully. You don't know how entirely happy we are to be together again, with both children; it seems as if we had found each other anew and never were so substantially happy before. . . . Aren't we very happy to be able to hear Theodore Parker? The sermon I heard this afternoon was wonderful . . . He described the rapture of a father when his firstborn son is put into his arms so truly, so carried away by his own feelings, that he was transfigured. He looked a god standing with outspread arms before us all, instead of the stern, middle-aged man that walked up to the reading-desk an hour before. And yet he never had a child! . . . Was it so perfect for the very reason that the rapture is denied him? . . . He moves people to tears and to laughter . . . makes them quail under the weight of their own sins and shows them then where is strength and hope and comfort . . . I don't see what I have done that the Lord has given me so great a delight among other delights as hearing and seeing and knowing this man . . . I was so glad to hear how comfortable you are in the dear little Mill. Levi thinks that a walk on the Artichoke would put climax on his state of bliss. Beautiful little river! . . . Is Myra still with you? If she is . . . do not tell her how I swear at her every day I wear the dress she made for me, for it is continually giving out in all directions, and the wrists have taken up their position just below my elbows, whence they stubbornly refuse to stir.

This was a precious period, with her own home and family; it fulfilled long-cherished dreams for Celia, and was the brightest time since barefoot days at the lighthouse — before she knew the word responsibility. Later she looked back sadly, wishing she could recapture that lost tranquility.

Her brother Cedric wrote her at that time somewhat wistfully: "I am glad you have at last settled in your little house. Have you a pussy yet? We wish we could send you one of ours, and a fresh fish for a chowder!"

Her father did send five dollars to buy a bedstead — a modest sum, but it showed the fond parents were always thinking of their daughter and her well-being.

Now came a whole year spent away from her beloved islands, which depressed Celia. Also she missed her friends at the Mill and in another letter to Lizzie Hoxie wrote:

. . . To think of your asking such a question as "Do I care about Charlotte Bronte"! As if I did not care everything I am capable of caring of anything! As if Levi and I had not read her books with rapture, and hadn't looked forward to the publishing of Mrs. Gaskell's books as one of the most interesting things that could happen; as if we didn't lament her loss to the world every year of our lives! Oh, Lizzie! I'm ashamed that you know so little of your friends . . . How nice they are making "Putnam's," aren't they? We have had one extract from a letter of Baynard Taylor's, a spirited reindeer performance . . . My heart is full of you all this delicious spring weather. Tell Mammy I think the Whittier poem is one of the sweetest and freshest I ever saw of his. Give my best love to all . . . do beg them to write. Ever . . . your poor little helpless foolish
Celia

Celia now had a vegetable garden to care for, but as the season continued, the large amounts of fruit and vegetables got ahead of her and she wrote wearily that she spent her time lugging tomatoes to all her friends — racing to eat up her produce before it decayed. She longed for a small part of the time "which elegant young ladies fritter away." Her own washing Celia did by hand, of course, and became "tired to death, as Karl and John played out of doors and got dirtier than the whole dictionary can express." Small wonder that her patience took flight and left her feeling "forlorn, ugly and harried." She wrote:

> . . . It seems as if the weary load of things one makes out to do with such an expenditure of strength, nerves and patience, goes for naught! No matter of notice is taken of all that is accomplished, but if one little thing is left undone, what a hue and cry is raised!

Little by little she began to recognize the growing anxiety that was to be hers for the rest of her life.

> . . . We've had no sickness to speak of, yet, and I humbly trust in Providence we may get through the winter without any very horrid time. John is splendidly well and comfortable and comforting and delightful. Karly, I think, is getting less nervous than he was. I try very hard to let him alone, but he is so mischievous that I can't help visiting him with small thunder occasionally, also spanks. Poor little spud! he is very loving and sometimes very sweet and gentle.

Levi had to spend much time in Watertown with his aging parents, who were neither of them well and had no one in the house but servants for companionship, since both daughters had married and left home. Mary Thaxter married Judge Samuel Ellery Jennison; Lucy Thaxter married Captain Beniah Titcomb. Celia was anxious for them, as she would be later about her own parents, to whom she would always hasten if they were ill.

In the year 1858 everything seemed at low ebb with the Thaxters. The country was having a financial panic and Celia wrote rather pathetically to her friend, Mrs. Hoxie, in Newburyport:

> . . . Are you any worse for the hard times? We're not; not having anything to lose, we've lost nothing, and having no risks run, and nothing to do with anybody or anything

in the way of getting a living, we're no better nor worse
than before the panic.

In spite of all the drudgery Celia dreamed of a "little
Celia" but "she is *non est.* I sigh for her and the children
sigh in chorus."

As Christmas approached she was tempted to hang up
her stocking, but she feared St. Nicholas would overlook
it, although all she really needed was "a present of cloth to
make Levi six shirts." This was the little seasprite who more
than anything hated to sew patchwork! Now those days
seemed far behind her except when she found a moment
to devour books. She read Dante while she peeled squash
and fitted other reading in as best she could between household tasks.

In January 1858, her brother Cedric, now eighteen, made
his first visit to his sister. Her house, the view of hills and
valleys on one side, the expanse of the river Charles and
fine mansions on the other, all impressed him. The frost
on the trees — he had never seen trees — seemed the most
beautiful sight he had ever beheld. All this was as new to
him, as had been Oscar's trip to the mainland when he was
fifteen, and saw his first horse and trees. On his return
home, Cedric wrote Celia that he had stopped off at Portsmouth to visit a large English steamer in the Navy Yard,
which was there for repairs in drydock. Not knowing his
way, he had walked behind an old wagon, heavily loaded
and pulled by a decrepit horse, and the trip had taken
nearly all day; but he had been so interested at sight of the
high steamer that it had made him dizzy. He wrote also
that he had found the walls of the little playhouse which
they had built together, and now he thought how, long
ago (really only nine years), Celia used to reach into the
deep pools for the green mosses and how, when they first
came to Appledore they played in the wonderful fairy-
land which they called Neptune's Hall, and found fairy
rings in the grass.

As spring advanced bringing warm days, Celia grew ever more homesick, and wrote her mother how much she needed to see and talk to her. Eliza with great difficulty replied explaining to her daughter that letter-writing was extremely hard for her, since she had never had the advantage of as much education as her husband. In a cramped but precise hand she wrote:

> . . . I am very worried about you and your coming confinement. You will be careful, won't you, dear. Do not reach up or start sudden or do any heavy or hard work . . . By what you say of your feeling, it should be a little girl. I long to talk it all over. Try to come to the Island and bring the children. Father is quite lame and I don't feel I ought to leave him for any length of time, but I shall try to come in the fall when I can stay two weeks. Father invites you all to come here. You must for my sake. Come early. I long to see the children. John must help his Dom make a sponge cake. I have made bed ticks, curtains, carpets, sofa coverings, cushions for the house this winter. . . . I feel I am growing old fast! Kiss the boys, your devoted mother,
>
> Eliza Laighton.

The devoted mother would have loved to visit her daughter and share in the care of the little boys and the demands of the sometimes impatient husband, who was not proving in any way to be a support. But Eliza always stayed by the side of Thomas. Celia remained in Newtonville where the baby was born on August 28, 1858. He was not the desired little daughter but a third son! Celia again wrote Lizzie Hoxie:

> . . . Now baby and his brothers are in bed and asleep and I feel like being in bed and asleep too, too sleepy to have any ideas left. How charmingly Nanny's letter was written! — She may look forward to a very big letter all to herself very soon. I wish I could see her. I know how beautiful it is at the mill, how beautiful in every way. Somehow "crude" is the word to express this place. It seems to me at the world's end — lonely, un-get-at-able, uninterest-

ing, not one beloved, friendly face within reach, no
children for ours to play with; but might be a great deal
worse too. I don't wish to be ungrateful, the Lord preserve
us! With such a baby too! Lizzie, I'm fairly in raptures
with this baby; never was in raptures before, always thought
small of my own goslings, but this baby smiles the very
heart out of my breast. He is too angelical for words to
give any idea of him. Isn't it funny that he should be such
a jolly sweet little pleasant creature when his Mamma
was always so glum before he came? And he hasn't a
name! Levi wants to call him David, but I despise it, and
Roland, which is the only other name he will listen to, isn't
satisfactory either. Dear me! if had only been a girl
there would have been no difficulty in naming him . . . I
wish I could shake my own family off for a week and
come and help.you wash dishes and mend stockings and
admire Neddy. Tell Margie we've got a new set of silver,
New Year's present from grandmother (Thaxter), very
solid, very heavy, very handsome, very horrid to take care
of, have to keep drumming up girls about it and going
around with a nasty bit of wash-leather rubbing here and
rubbing there. Give me my iron jug and iron spoon, say I
with Mr. Thoreau. Susy Dabney gave Karly "Wee Willie
Winkie's" nursery songs, and it is so charming.

We take the semi-weekly "Tribune" and think of you.
Isn't "Minister's Wooing" killing good.

Roland was the name finally decided upon, chosen from
the lines "Childe Roland to the Dark Tower came," by Robert Browning. The youngest son who was such a jolly little
creature was in after years a very scholarly man.

Her husband's love of poetry had always been an inspiration for Celia and in the lonely moments of her busy life,
she found in it an infinite source of satisfaction and relaxation from all her trials. She read to herself Robert Browning's *Men and Women*. These poems greatly appealed to
her, and gave Celia her first insight into the work of the
English poet who was to mean so much to her husband.
His wife's appreciation of his reading of Browning's longer

poems may have given Levi the first thought of reading to
larger audiences, which he was to do with great success
twenty years later. In due time Celia wrote to Browning
that his more obscure poems then and always, seemed clear
to Thaxter's keen, well-trained mind. Celia however enjoyed
more the singing rhythm of Alfred, Lord Tennyson, and
she often used to quote from his poems as she went about
her daily tasks. Soon young John also was roaring out, "The
splendour falls on castle walls . . . " from beginning to end,
then "Half a league — half a league — half a league onward
. . . " In a different vein the homely, idealistic poems of
Whittier gave Celia great comfort

During Roland's first winter, the many callers and invitations which were added to Celia's daily routine, wore her
out. How she would have loved to be lulled to rest by the
sound of the waves! But her brood must be tended and fed.
One day she greatly astonished her maid, who overheard
Mrs. Thaxter exclaim, while cutting up a fish for dinner:

> Blessed old haddock with your lilac skin all striped with
> black and your lovely old intelligent countenance, can't you
> tell me the last news from the salt sea, or did you leave it
> too long ago?

Always part of herself was back with the seagulls, the
waves, and the scarlet pimpernel. The returning fishing
boats, with all the memories of childhood hours and dear
faces lived in her imagination. She looked out of the window to the sunset behind the black hills and to the river
running toward the sea, and hardly knowing what she did,
she too made a poem. Wishing to share any new emotion
with her parents and brothers, and to keep them in touch
with her feelings, she copied the verses and slipped them into a letter to Cedric. Delighted, as were all on the island,
Cedric wrote enthusiastically to his sister, "I intend to keep
the poem as long as I live!"

Celia's career as a poet had begun.

8

FIRST POEM
1860 - 1862

IT WAS eight years since Levi Thaxter and Celia Laighton had exchanged their vows that September day on the Isles of Shoals. Although she sometimes called herself "not a good child," when she wrote her mother, she had grown into a woman who had "lived to learn in Life's hard school . . . "

In the years since their marriage, her husband had continued to disregard the necessity for some regular occupation which would make an established living for his family. This inadequacy, added to his emotional terror of the place she held so dear, were contributing factors in Celia's need for emancipation. Her parents had learned to be independent at their remote lighthouse. Celia now showed she was made of the same stern stuff.

The hot summer of 1859 was passed mostly at Newtonville. Celia found herself constantly picturing the old view from the cliff on White Island, and sniffing the air for the tang of salt. She looked at the Charles River flowing past her window, and desperately wished to follow it to the sea and the little group of islands where she had left part of her heart. The urge for self-expression and her lonely homesickness had woven themselves into verses which she had characteristically sent first to Cedric at Appledore.

She was heartened by his delight with the little poem, and his intention to keep it. At last one evening, seated by the fire in their cozy sitting-room, Celia shyly handed a sheet of paper to her husband. Levi was used to reading poems by those whose works were well-known and praised by the public, and she felt he would probably think little of her attempt. To her surprise, once she had his attention, he read the poem carefully and pronounced it good. Instead of returning the yellow paper, he folded it and placed it in his pocket. She was, of course, pleased that her former school teacher cared enough to want to keep the verses and she quietly continued her mending.

In those days Celia's husband often entertained his college classmates and literary friends· at the Newtonville home. The young woman whom Hawthorne had found "to have the manners of a lady," now manifested a greater eagerness to keep up with all that was being talked of and written in the current publications. She always read and enjoyed the Atlantic Monthly, a new magazine published by Ticknor and Fields, the first editor of which was Levi's friend, James Russell Lowell. She found it full of interesting and informative material.

One cold February morning in 1860, the March copy of the Atlantic arrived at Celia's door. She seized it eagerly and for a few moments stopped what she was doing, to scan the pages, knowing that when evening came the head of the family would demand first reading of the periodical. In her haste she did not linger over The German University, The Professor's Story or Gymnastics, but on arriving at page 302, her eye was caught by an unsigned poem entitled *Land-locked.* Wondering if she were seeing correctly, she began to read.

There it was, her little poem full of her longing for the sea, in print in the Atlantic Monthly, famous for its reviews and literary notes. Levi had thought enough of her poem to show it to James Russell Lowell. Without a word to the author, Mr. Lowell had given it a title and printed it exactly as it had been handed to him by Celia's husband. The poem appeared with no signature, according to the custom of the time.

The goal for which so many authors aim, usually attained

only after years of effort and disappointment, had been reached by Celia Thaxter in a single bound. She was elated beyond measure, and Levi must have been very proud. She waited eagerly to hear what the family on the Shoals would say of her poem's publication. Letters came slowly but finally the envelope addressed in Cedric's handwriting arrived. He wrote:

> . . . While Bocky and I were working out in the barn, Mr. Folsom came rushing out with the Atlantic Monthly for March and pointed triumphantly at a poem. I recognized it in an instant as the one of which I had a duplicate in my desk. Mother is delighted. Mr. Folsom read it to her, and she cried like a child. I don't know why she did! I am sure everything is for the best. . .

They were pleased, and that was enough for Celia.

Urged on by her husband and Mr. Lowell, Celia began to write more poems about the sea and her early memories connected with it. The following season she and Karl visited Appledore in the early summer, but she missed her husband, who had stayed at home with the younger boys. In her poem *Off Shore,* she recalled the moonlight night of his courtship when the little boat rocked beneath them and the moon sent "silver sparkles down." (See page 246)

The line, "Sweet sounds on rocky shores the distant rote," brought a question from James T. Fields, new editor of the Atlantic Monthly, when some time afterwards she sent the poem to him for his "dissecting knife." Her letter insisting on the use of the word rote is interesting enough to those not familiar with the sound of the sea, but especially so to those who are.

> . . . Did you really mean to mark out the r in rote and substitute n, making the word note? Then I think you are not familiar with the word rote. It means the sound of the sea on the rocks, it is very sweet and suggestive, that word, I cannot possibly spare that. It is all right, you will find it in Worcester's Dictionary. I find many people are unfamiliar with it, but it is much used at sea. The islanders at the

Shoals can tell their whereabouts in the densest fog or the darkest night by the rote of the different islands and the mainland, so nicely educated is their sense of hearing. No matter how dark it is, they can judge with curious accuracy the distance between them and the sound, whether the breaking waves are gentle or furious, whether they break on the long sand beaches or the shore or the ragged rocks of the Islands and each island, each small isolated rock has its own peculiar rote, different from the rest. Woe to the boatman who hears on a wild night, close at hand, the rote of the long ledges of Duck Island, the long sunken ledges, that is a terrible sound but the sound is inexpressibly delicious in a calm, so remote, you know. (or rather you don't know, but I hope I shall make you hear it some time) so sweet, like a murmur in a dream. "Sweet sounds on rocky shores and distant rote." Please let it remain rote, if anybody should chance to read it, and reading, understand it not, there is the Dictionary with a full and pleasant explanation of its meaning.

A new world opened for Celia Thaxter with this unexpected outlet for her emotions. The literary friends who visited the Thaxter home, became more and more interested in Celia for her own sake. She was not only a good hostess, as well as a busy mother and housewife, but she was becoming a successful poet.

This was an age of greatness, of men and women striving to express themselves by means of the printed page. Through the enthusiastic sponsorship of James T. Fields and his wife, Annie, whose home was a center for artists, Celia was given every opportunity to hear and meet the foremost literary figures of the day. Inspired by them, poems flowed from her pen whenever she could find a few moments in which to write. A letter to Mr. Fields dated September 23, 1861, probably referring to her poem *Seaward*, reveals her absorption in her new activity:

Mr. Fields:

I thank you very much for the kind things you said about my little poem, and am grateful for the trouble you took in looking it over and making suggestions. I am sorry I could not act upon them all. I am not good at making alterations. The only merit of my small productions lies in their straightforward simplicity, and when that bloom is rubbed off by the effort to better them, they lose what little good they originally possessed.

I'm afraid you will not think the unconscious quotation from the "Ancient Mariner" remedied by the mere transposition of words, but I cannot alter it satisfactorily and say what I wish. If the first and fifth verses do not seem to you too objectionable, pray let them pass.

I'm sorry its name is not as felicitous as Land-locked, which Mr. Lowell christened.

Pray pardon me for trespassing on your valuable time, and believe me,

Gratefully yours,
C. Thaxter

In another letter to Fields, Celia begged him to remember "I have never corrected a proof in my life, but I am going to learn!" She sent her proofs gladly to her editor, who continued to be delighted with her work and to ask for more of her verses, which she managed to evolve among the pots and kettles.

Another early poem, *Expectation,* reflects her disappointment that her husband let her go alone to the islands. She longed for his companionship there and felt that the chill wind of autumn had somehow entered their lives. The poem is full of the wistfulness that appears in so much of her later verse. "Who dares to question Time, what it may bring?" For the present at least, time seemed to be bringing personal recognition to Celia.

These were the years of the war between the States, but the terror and the tumult seem to have left the Thaxter family largely untouched. Karl and John loved to drill and beat each other with barrel staves. They melted up good pewter plates to make play bullets while their mother was in church listening to Mr. Weiss preach his striking sermons on slavery. Celia tried writing a poem entitled Minute

Guns, but realized, herself, that it lacked the descriptive quality of her other poems, the subjects of which were the things with which she was best acquainted — the sea, birds and flowers.

Appledore, September 4, 1862

My Dear Mr. Fields:

Thanks for your note, I am just as sorry as I can be, that you can't come — "April, 1863"? Why, by that time, every man, woman and child will be drained out of the veins of the nation and lost in war! Do you expect to be alive in April 1863? I don't. Very faintly the spent wave of terrible news reached us here in this remote nook, till yesterday. A note from Mr. Weiss brought it all horribly in sight. What carnage, what endless suffering! It is hard to realize when the delicious days go by, one after one, so still and full of peace. I never saw more perfect days, full of all loveliness, the islands never seemed so charming before!

I think you are entirely right, about my rhymes. I should hardly have sent them, but you had surprised me by liking other things and it seemed possible you might these . . . I am afraid, I never put my heart into anything that doesn't belong to the sea.

She continued writing with much success about the things she knew. The poem for which she is best remembered, which has a universal appeal to old and young alike, is the *Sandpiper,* which she wrote in September 1862, but which was not published until March of 1864. (See page 251)

Twilight, Watching, Wherefore and *Spaniards' Graves* were all sent to Mr. Fields for his criticism, but she seldom changed a word from her first copy. As time went on Mr. Fields began asking her to write something in prose about her islands. This frightened her. Verses spun themselves while she went about her household tasks, but to write the story of her life as he suggested seemed a task beyond her. How could she tell it, "being still alive?" she asked, but he continued to urge her.

October 25, 1862, Newtonville

. . . I'm sorry I've as yet no prosaic manuscript for you,

patience for a little longer. Meanwhile here are some verses which have been evolved among the pots and kettles, to which you're welcome, if they're good enough for you. Verses can grow where prose can't. "While greasy Joan doth keel the pot!" The rhymes in my head are all that keep me alive, I do believe, lifting me in half unconscious condition over the ashes heap, so that I don't half realize how dry and dusty it is! I have had no servant at all, for a whole week, by a combination of hideous circumstances. I wish you'd tell Annie that I have had infinite satisfaction and refreshments out of her tickets already, and forget all weariness and perplexity on the crest of a breaker of earthly bliss while Emerson discourses . . . Just as soon as this family is settled for the winter, so that every wheel doesn't creak in despair, I will begin the papers . . .

Actually it was not until the spring of 1869 that she began the series of articles which were collected under the title *Among the Isles of Shoals*.

Her readers began to wonder how Celia Thaxter looked. Was she young, old, fair or brunette? "She is a most beautiful creature, still very young, with a slender figure, and exquisite perfection of feature," wrote Elizabeth Stuart Phelps.

Annie Fields wrote begging for a photograph. Celia was glad to comply with this request and had several pictures taken for her public, her friends and family. Without vanity, she was frankly aware of her own good looks, and realized that she had a classical profile. In all her best photographs, in the portrait painted by Otto Grundmann, and in the well-known picture taken of her in her garden, her pose is either three-quarter or complete profile. Celia Thaxter's head was always held high and her blue eyes had the far-seeing look of one who has often gazed over water. She had always a vivid color and in both youth and middle age was considered very beautiful. Her sensitive mouth was tell-tale of the hardships which early made her set her jaws firmly, but her ringing, jubilant laugh was said to be almost boisterous in its heartiness.

9

LIFE ON THE CHARLES
AND BUSY DAYS AT APPLEDORE
1862 - 1866

WITH THEIR own home in Massachusetts, for the next few years, instead of enjoying long summers in Levi's South Cottage, Celia and the children made only brief visits to Appledore in the spring and fall, spending the remainder of the year at Newtonville. To be deprived of a long stay in her island home was a great cross to Celia. The children's small illnesses, with her own minor ups and downs, and an increasing worry over her first born, all tended to make the days in Newtonville pass slowly.

The summer after she had written her first poem found her a tired, anxious "drudge," as she expressed it, but whenever possible she continued to write poetry. Because she missed them so much she also wrote long, vivid and humorous letters to family and friends. In the spring of 1861 she wrote her brother Oscar:

> . . .It seems to me, my dear brother, that I once possessed a father — will you tell me what has become of him? For since I bade him a tender farewell in the rain last September, never a word has he spoken to me. It would be agreeable to receive a faint token from him occasionally, but I dare say there are plenty of reasons why he doesn't write, and I'm sure he doesn't forget his daughter, and if you boys write, why it is all that is necessary to be sure, but you don't tell me anything about him — is he pretty well? The children have just gone to bed and are yelling like

67

so many wild Indians upstairs, and tearing the bed-
clothes into ribbons I should think by the sound. I remember when you and Cedy used to cut just such capers. I just
called John "Bocky" at breakfast this morning. The chicks
are all wild about the carpentering. They all stand and
stare and admire the performances. Roland rushes around
as big as anybody, and has his remarks to make on all subjects. We tried to walk to Watertown to meet Levi and the
other boys this afternoon, but the rain came down when we
reached the bridge, and I caught the little fellow up in
my arms and wrapped him up in my cloak and carried him
all the way up California Street from which feat I haven't
yet recovered. We saw a frog by the roadside, stretching
its legs and blinking its eyes and the rain fell on its shiny
green back. Lony's little talk about it was so sweet and
cunning. Once or twice he stepped on my dress and to
hear him apologize, "dear Mamma, I didn't mean to step
on your dress." was too killing. If you ask him what he
is, he says, "Papa's pretty little boy" with a little conscious
look that is irresistibly funny. . . .

Monday night. If I was sleepy as one cat last night,
I'm equal to six full grown tabbies tonight and can't keep
my eyes open — have to take a little nap after every other
word! But hasn't this been a delicious day! And oh, the
sunset! Not a cloud in all the sky and such heavenly pink
light in the east and when the twilight gathered, such
wonderful green sky in the west! I couldn't bear to take
my eyes off it, but Karl teased me to play backgammon and
Lony wanted me to read Mother Goose, and John wished me
to repeat his ballads — they were clamorous — still I
stood at the window, Tennyson-haunted, and said to myself "dip down upon the northern shore, O sweet New Year,
delaying long." The heavenly peace of the sky entered into
my spirit. That color in the sky preaches sermons to me.
And the children beseige me. Round I turn — "can trouble
live in April days? or sadness in the summer months?" I
requested to know. About that they evidently couldn't
satisfy me. So I undressed Lony — he sat up till very late
tonight because he walked to the bridge and back and was
tired, and had a long nap this noon. I rocked him in my

JAMES T. FIELDS

ANNIE FIELDS

arms and crooned "He dowlot, Uncle Cedy", out of Mother
Goose, and many many little songs the children like. John
stood at my shoulder and listened, every now and then saying, "Oh how I like that, Mama," and Lony with his doll
hugged tight looked so lovely, so "shut up in measureless
content," that it was a treat to behold. And still the little
fellow begged for "one more" and "one more," and still I
sung, till at last I put him, all rosy and sleepy and lovely
into his little bed, murmuring drowsily about "hey, dowlot, Uncle Bocky," and Blue Beach and Fossom and C., and
then there was John's ballads to hear and he has lost a tooth
and lisps like a sentimental young lady, and I laughed to
hear him sound his s — heavens what's the plural? S's?
Ask Mr. Folsom if that is right. In the midst of his recita-
tions Lony called out, having waked up (probably from
hearing his Mama laugh), "Mama, Lony's all wrong side out
— please come fix Lony!" A slightly alarming statement
if true, but that made me laugh still more . . , His nightgown had got twisted tight around him. I smoothed him
and his wee bed afresh. "Let me kiss you once before you
go," he said. Perhaps I did! Then Karly and I played in-
definite backgammon and now they're all asleep — all but
Karl and he's quiet. And Levi has gone to hear "Martha"
tonight, Flotow's opera, he invited me to go and I declined.
He has taken Ellen Robbins and I believe they are going
to sit in the gallery. Tomorrow D.V. we shall go to hear
"Lucia di Lammermoor" and I haven't a flutter of anticipa-
tion, not a sentiment of satisfaction in the idea but I'll tell
you in what I do take satisfaction — Tomorrow is the day
of the Emerson lecture, you know, and from there I shall
quietly stay put, curled up in the corner of the sofa with
my work all the rest of the day and shall not have to stir
till Levi comes to call for me to go to the theatre. For I
believe I am tired, and inclined to sing with the Lotus-
Eaters, "We have had enough of action and of motion we"
and "there is no joy but calm." I am lazy I suppose but
these two weeks have been so busy. . . . .

Levi is mean. I share all my letters with him and I find
he doesn't, one in twenty, with me. I read yours aloud to
him, dear boys, but I believe I shan't, any more!

Tell mother the long lock of yellow hair that did hang
down and extinguish Lony's organs of vision lies here on my
desk, close by this paper. A day or two ago he was playing
about with his lovely countenance utterly blinded by it, and
I looked at him and soliloquized, "Three bairns have I seen
growing up to boyhood with that lock of hair putting out
their bonnie e'en — with two I have endured it. Can I
with this? I have a right in that child — he belongs to
me by every right. What if that lock should be shorn?
Would the skies fall? Then we should catch larks." Thus
moralizing, I snatched the scissors, "Hither! O son of my
affection," quoth I, "hither, beautiful buxom boy," and while
he looked amazed with his two cheeks like carnations and his
blue eyes wide, I slipped the shining steel along his "snowy
brow" and lo! the deed was done!! The sky fell not, neither
did the earth yawn, not even a far off peal of thunder chilled
my nerves, and the little face looker more celestial than
before with the hair straight, a la Sir Joshua Reynolds, over
the forehead. But when his papa did discover it, "an angry
man was he, I wot." At first I said I had as much right in
Lony as he, but then said to myself "Least said soonest
mended" — so wisely held my peace and felt very sorry I
had done it, because he said, "You knew I particularly wished
not to have it done." I did know and was sorry, because
after all, what was the use? The two others had lived
through it and not gone blind and I wasn't a good child
— was I? Don't tell me I was, because I was not good and
I know it. But Lony looks enchantingly pretty and I don't
think I care any longer.

Good night dear ones and write — pray write to your

Own little
Sister

Winter passed with an ever-growing circle of guests,
which made hard work for Celia who had only insufficient,
incapable help. Now and then her routine was relieved as
by the Emerson lectures to which Annie Fields had sent
tickets.

Before the next busy hotel season at Appledore began,
Celia took Roland on a visit to her parents for a breath of

the sea air, to carry her through the long hot summer in Newtonville.

To Elizabeth Hoxie, Celia describes in detail the long trip home . . . up at four in the morning, to catch a fishing boat sailing to Portsmouth, she reports how the breeze died and she and Roland, instead of reaching the city in an hour or two, did not board the train for Boston until ten o'clock that morning. She was completely tired out when, after a two-hour train trip, her husband met her in Boston, triumphantly reporting that arrangements had been made for them to row home up the Charles River from Cambridge to Newtonville. Celia and Lony, and all the bags and baskets were stowed in a large rowboat, where the two other boys, John Weiss and George Folsom stood ready to take turns with the rowing. As they wound along the river, past Cambridge and Watertown, children and oarsmen feasted on all the goodies prepared by Grandma Laighton's loving hands. They devoured the "beautiful fresh loaves of bread, the lumps of fresh butter, a great huge plank of sponge cake and a huge leaf of plum cake, a great many corned mackerel, splendid salt fish, and two lovely, indeed I may say, heavenly jars of fresh potted lobster." Celia described herself as a "travel-stained Cleopatra, observed by four admiring masculine bipeds opposite — I don't include Lony; he only set store by me in a general way." After the July sun had set, they reached the landing at Newtonville, and unloaded the weary passengers.

During the summer the Thaxter family looked forward to days which they could spend on the river and planned on Sundays to entertain their guests in that way. Celia's friendship with James and Annie Fields was growing fast. She invited them to come for "a day among the lily pads and spikes of purple pickerel weed." They explored a brook and loaded the boat with flowers and altogether had a charming time. Returning to the little house friends were regaled with ice cream churned in the new freezer, a gift from Levi.

A freezer which really and truly freezes in five minutes, and will freeze in four, a small quantity . . . and the reason I am writing to you tonight is because I am afraid to go to bed after a big plateful flavored with strawberries freshly mashed up in it and sherry wine, a jolly mixture I assure you!)

Now almost every poem Celia sent to The Atlantic Monthly, Youth's Companion or St. Nicholas Magazine was gladly accepted. She received five to fifteen dollars for each poem, and with this little nest egg she was able at last to hire a good maid at thirteen dollars a month! She also purchased a sewing machine, which was a great necessity, as she made all the shirts for the growing boys and "there were vile old trousers to be patched, enough to make the spirit of mortal quail."

When Levi gave her a piano, a source of undreamed of pleasure was opened to Celia, who in early years had little or no opportunity to hear or know good music. His friends often came in the evening and played to the family. Celia, in her poem *Mozart at the Fireside,* gives a picture of the listeners.

Listening quietly to the music or to their father reading aloud was an early part of the training of the little boys. Their father demanded perfect silence, so Celia thought of many plans to keep three little pairs of hands busy. They all learned plain knitting and made yards and yards of reins, and knit garters for their grandmother. Then they picked over baskets full of barberries for jam. The best idea of all was the making of a wonderful patchwork quilt. Celia cut out squares of gay gingham, and the boys' stubby fingers painstakingly sewed them into blocks of four each. Finally all these were put together and lined by Celia. She found it easy to tell which squares belonged to which boy, as the thread of Karl's patches was slightly gray because he forgot to wash his hands; John's squares were puckery because of his impatience to finish; but Roland's work was almost perfect.

Oscar and Cedric wrote their sister faithfully almost every week in the winter of 1862-63 and were full of descriptions of the new middle house which was being built to enlarge the original Appledore House. The building had a central hall or parlor, twelve feet high, below which, after much digging and removal of rock, room was made for a huge cistern sixteen feet long, fifteen feet wide and six feet deep. All the earth removed was carefully spread and seeded down to make a lawn. The painters stayed at work through the winter and by the time the building was completed four thousand dollars had been spent. Cedric and Oscar feared they never would have boarders enough to fill the new house and pay for it!

The fame of this first summer resort hotel on the New England coast had spread far and wide. So great a number of persons were coming that all rooms had to be engaged far in advance. The establishment owned a horse and wagon just to carry from dock to door, the numerous trunks brought out by each family of guests. A tremendous amount of supplies had to be brought to the islands by sail boat, transferred to a flat-bottom barge, and then be transported over the steep path to the hotel - a huge undertaking.

During the winter Thomas Laighton had suffered paralytic strokes which kept him housed for nine weeks, and from which he never fully recovered. When spring came and it was time to change quarters from winter cottage to the new hotel building, his sons rolled him in a chair. Cedric wrote his sister how the leg of the chair broke on the way, but because of Thomas' well-known stubborn determination, the move was successfully accomplished. Eliza Laighton felt that she could not walk either, because of her neuralgia, so her sons placed her ample form in a wheelbarrow and wheeled her to her new residence. Celia, after hearing of their ill health, wrote from Newtonville suggesting that a teaspoonful of lemon juice taken every hour would be a harmless remedy for neuralgia, and the best thing for rheumatism.

In the summer of 1863 an increasing interest in ornithology decided Levi to plan a journey down East in Maine to observe the water birds on the island of Grand Manan; an extraordinary choice from Celia's point of view. To her, one could not ask for any other spot on earth so satisfying as the Isles of Shoals in summer. But with Levi's departure she took her sons and gladly occupied the North Cottage on Appledore. All three boys were busy rowing, fishing, sailing and swimming. But most of all they ate enormously and learned to love the life on the islands as their mother and her brothers had done, Now, however, at Appledore there was no longer the solitude which the children of the former generation had known.

In Celia's letters to three friends she gives a new picture of the changed conditions on her island. Instead of a small congenial group on Appledore, as described by Hawthorne in the first days of her marriage, the number of guests had now increased to two hundred and fifty or more, made up of many of the Thaxters' friends, well-to-do or curious persons and self-centered invalids seeking health. The staff was often inadequate, and Celia found herself filling in wherever she was needed, from hostess to pastry-cook. The weeks of her twenty-eighth summer developed into a sort of nightmare.

To Kate Field she wrote:

August 10, 1863

. . . Thank you for your letter . . . what fun it must be to do just what one likes and nothing, if one chooses. But in the first place I have three ruffians to take care of in the shape of my dear and innocent offspring. In the next place I am staying with my mama and papa and the latter has had a paralytic stroke which renders him nearly helpless, so that it is my duty and my pleasure to be ready at his call. Then we keep house and have only one small Irish handmaiden, so that the greater part of the work falls on me. Then there are 300 souls, "bodies" I mean, to be fed at the hotel and one kitchen establishment hardly sufficient so that Mother and I vary the scene by making every other day a bushel or two of doughnuts and several stacks of sponge cakes for the benefit of the unwashed — the moment humanity gets beyond the coast line it throws off all the restraints of civilization and the raids upon this household of Thomas and Richard and Henry and their families would hardly be credited. I could a tale unfold, but I forbear. The fact is I seldom if ever get one free hour during the day. I wish, I'm sure, they'd all stay away, except my yellow bearded norsemen, my blessed brothers twain. Today Gen. Ruica who was staying here, being father's particular friend (I'm sorry, but my respected papa is the most horrible copperhead) took it into his head to depart, and, as I heard him asking anxiously for me, into the entry I stepped carrying a big pan of cake into which my arms had been plunged to the elbows in butter and sugar and flour and spice and currants and things . . .

Ten days later she wrote to Mary Lawson, a Newtonville neighbor:

. . . You have no idea how busy I have been all summer — so busy that I have sometimes been discouraged almost, having no time to myself at all. It has been a very busy season here, and tho we do not live in the hotel, we are so near that it overflows us and the pressure of people and circumstances is so heavy that we suffer much sometimes, and think no peace to be had. When there are two hundred and fifty people in so small a space you can't get rid of them. . . . .

The hotel season was over in September. When her boys were sent home to school, Celia begged Levi to be allowed to stay one more week. The hard summer months had been so busy for her that she had lost health, strength and spirit. She treasured the few peaceful hours that came now, when she and her brother Cedric could row and sail together.

To Elizabeth Whittier, she wrote September 1, 1863:

. . . I am almost alone here, the crowd has thinned to two tables full of people, all my immediate family are gone. Mr. Thaxter came from Mt. Desert last Saturday and this Wednesday morning went home with our two youngest boys, so I am left alone with Karl — and it is so lovely to be alone — (not that I'm not proud of my family!) I've had such a long siege of people. I almost grow to dislike the aspect of the human shape divine in a perfectly whole-sale manner. If people would only let an unoffending Christian alone! But when an unknown creature in petticoats comes up to me and inquires if I am the "Rose of the Isles," a decided loathing of my kind possesses my soul. Dear friend forgive my intolerance and uncharitableness, if you had passed through as much of that sort of thing as I have you, even you, I think would lose patience. Well, it's all over now, heaven be praised! and I am left here for one golden week almost alone. The island blooms bright with golden-rod, tell Mr. Whittier, tossing all its shining plumes in every wind that blows. What a lovely name the country people have for asters, "frost flowers" they call them. It is so suggestive. The last wild rose died long ago, so I wear frost flowers and golden-rod. How sweet it is to think that next year's roses will bloom just as fair, if we only have patience to wait for them, just as bright and fragrant as the dear darlings of this summer. I please myself think-ing of inland flowers, — the river banks flame with cardin-als, and the gentians prepare to blossom. I'm in no hurry to see them, one long breath of this cold salt breeze is worth them all to me, one long look over these cold, plung-ing, sparkling waves more refreshing than all of the mellow autumn landscape, sweeter even than "the happy autumn fields," for always the waves are talking of "the days that are no more."

To Lucy Larcom, Sunday, September 6, 1863:

. . . I have had such a hard time this summer, so different from the splendid time I generally have — losing strength and flesh and spirits instead of gaining all, which is what people come for, you know. So I have had the loveliest week, rowing and sailing with Cedric, taking blissful lonely walks, listening and resting. Sometimes peeping out of the corner of my eye at a dreamy sail afar off, or a floating gull, fair and white in the sunshine, or watching the play of color on the changing water, or a flitting peep piping its sweet, plaintive note, flying hither and thither. Dear me, what a good time I have had, gathering driftwood and sketching and picking up shells and seaweed and things, and hunting mushrooms and being deliciously lazy and carefree generally! I wish you could have been here too! We had some splendid surf a week or two ago and we had such fun down on the eastern rocks, watching the cold plunging seas roll in and thunder against the rocks and rise in clouds of spray, to fall in numberless little foamy white cascades down the irregular surfaces. In one or two places it was churned into creamy masses of trembling foam which the wind tore apart and sent flying over our heads like flocks of frightened birds — the children played with it taking up great flakes in their hands — the coloring was so curious and misty. I wish you could have seen it, so many cold, slaty blues and purples about. A man-of-war, the Marion, beating about the bay, looked like a tall column of black canvass, her weather-beaten sails perfectly black, being wet through and all her spars and hull and masts marked in ink. She was quite a solemn spectacle — but the emerald breakers were a feast to our eyes — such a living, crystal green!

This morning Cedric took me to White Island and there it was heavenly. It was the fairest, bluest morning that ever rose, believe me, everything so light and bright in the ever-near sunshine. We spread our little spritsail and flitted across — it was so beautiful, the water so cool and clear, the faint wind so perfectly delicious with its sea-scents. Every sail on the horizon filled me with a kind of inexpressable joy. I'm sure I don't know why, but they always do. We stayed there all morning and went to all our dear old haunts and wished I could go back and live there forever. I found the wild pink morning glory still growing and blossoming profusely, though everywhere the golden-rod waved and nodded and the sweet asters bloomed, the seasons yet are so strangely mixed here, the housatonia is blossoming thickly all over the island now, though the rosehaws have turned scarlet and sumach bushes flame with the touch of autumn.

Always, Celia loved and warmth and sunshine. In sharp contrast she dreaded the approach of winter and wrote later from Newtonville in the autumn of the same year, to Annie Fields:

> . . . Now the leaves are falling, dry and sere after the sudden frost. It looks pinched and cold outdoors and the wind whistles and we cluster about the fire and tell stories to the children as if it were midwinter. I cannot tell you how I dread the cold. Were I only a stork or a swallow! I would fly away from the fields, locked up hard and fast with the snow stark-still-glaring, spread over all for months and months! It takes all my philosophy to stand it and keep my equilibrium. I long for the light of life, and ever shifting color and ever the delicious sound of the faithful old sea, sometimes more in winter than in summer! No frost or snow can extinguish it.

Celia did not guess that for the next twelve years, she would spend some part of every winter beside that "faithful old sea" on the bleak islands, or that she was never to have a winter where there was warmth; always she must face each successive season of cold and snow.

While still at home in Newtonville that winter, making her own bread, and writing poems when she could, she heard from her brother Cedric at Appledore that they were "running short of supplies, not a drop of rum, whiskey or brandy and only a little sherry wine and claret left!" He kept himself awake while watching at the sickbeds of his parents by reading Charles Dickens', *Our Mutual Friend*. He reported his mother also had fallen ill with a severe attack of pleurisy and "kept groaning piteously," and his father seemed "not likely to live a fortnight and suffered greatly."

When this news reached Celia in Massachusetts she longed to go to the island, but she wrote a friend:

. . . They want me, and I want them, God knows, but other people hold me fast here! I trust to get away in March and all my blood stirs to think of it.

Soon Cedric wrote again, asking "how soon could she get away without unreasonable disarrangement of her family?" for "father is taking no nourishment and growing weaker every day."

After that letter, nothing could stop Celia from going down at once to Appledore. She stayed until the middle of April, then feeling it her duty to return home, she left, although she knew that her father could not recover and that the situation would only grow worse.

Eliza Laighton's unselfish devotion to her husband was touching and beautiful until the end, which came within a few weeks of Celia's departure. She had followed Thomas without question to his chosen exile, endured the rigors of island life happily, and made his home bright and comfortable in spite of isolation. She had always encouraged his new ventures. Without her, his hotel and his very existence could never have achieved such remarkable success.

On a spring day, May 16, 1866, Thomas Laighton's children laid him to rest on the island which had been his refuge, his home, and place of successful business for twenty-seven years. But for his choice of this ocean stronghold, the story of his daughter Celia would indeed have been a different one.

10

THE WAVES OF CELIA'S LIFE
1866 - 1872

THIRTY-ONE years old when her father died, Celia's life had not flowed along peacefully like a quiet stream; it course was more like the tides of the sea which ebb and flow and beat against the rocks. There were many waves, each one distinct in itself, seeming to rise high and then fall to a great depth, in rapid and ever changing succession.

It was to be Celia's fate that no single year was spent quietly at home in one spot. At a time when travel was slow and difficult, she was forever journeying from Massachusetts to the Isles of Shoals and back. What writing she was able to do was squeezed in between her other pressing and often vastly varied duties.

At the close of the summer after Thomas Laighton's death, Celia took her mother on a trip to New Hampshire where they stayed at Glenn House in the White Mountains. She thought a change of scene would cheer her mother, and both women were thrilled with their first sight of a mountain. At Tip Top House on Mount Washington, where they went for a day, Mrs. Laighton was overcome by the altitude - she had lived at sea level all her life - and had to be revived by brandy before they could return to the hotel. This was undoubtedly the first time Mrs. Laighton had stayed in a hotel (other than her own) and it must have been a strange feeling for this simple woman to be the guest, rather than the hostess.

During that first winter following their father's death, free of the care of him, Oscar and Cedric took turns visiting their sister, seeing the city of Boston, where Oscar attended the opera for the first time.

Although the brothers enjoyed the diversions of the city and seeing their sister and her family, they felt they must return soon to the islands. To watch over Appledore, the boats, the farm and livestock had so far required the continual presence of the Laighton family. The Shoals were not only their home but also the site where everything they owned and loved was situated. This valuable property must be watched over and guarded from storm damage.

Sixty miles away, on the outskirts of Boston, was the home of Celia and Levi. Here the winters were full of interest and fresh contacts. Though circumstances were to separate their lives eventually, they were able for a few winters to enjoy together the advantages of the Boston season. They were especially fortunate in being among those who attended Ralph Waldo Emerson's "Conversations", the "Saturday Club", and best of all, they were frequent guests at 148 Charles Street, the home of James and Annie Fields.

Celia wrote a brief note to Mr. Fields on January 6, 1867, enclosing her latest poem:

. . . Please say to Annie, with my love that we had a most charming time last night. It was a real delight to see Mr. Dickens and to have one's idea of an individual so completely realized.

This occasion is described in Annie Field's own diary, and quoted in Memories of a Hostess by M. A. DeWolfe Howe:

January 5, 1867

Sunday night dinner went off brilliantly. Longfellow, Appleton, Mr. and Mrs. Thaxter came to meet "the chief" (Dickens) and ourselves. Unfortunately there was one empty seat which Rowse, the artist, had promised to fill, but was ill at the last and could not — curiously enough we had asked Osgood, Miss Putnam, and Mr. Gay besides, all kept away by accident when they would have given their eyes to come. In the course of the day Dickens had been to see, with O.W.H., (Oliver Wendell Holmes) the ground of the Parkman murder which has lately been so clearly described by Sir Emerson Tennent in All the Year Round.

Dr. Webster, a man known to all Boston, had murdered the equally well-known Mr. Parkman and attempted to conceal the evidence of the crime by burning the body. He was later tried and sentenced to be hanged. Annie Fields' diary goes on:

> . . . . In the evening the talk turned naturally enough that way, when, after much surmise with regard to the previous life of the man, Mr. Longfellow looked up and with an assured, clear tone, said: "Now I have a story to tell! A year or two before this event took place Dr. Webster invited a party of gentlemen to a dinner at his house, I believe, to meet some foreigner who was interested in science. The doctor himself was a chemist, and after dinner he had a large bowl placed in the centre of the table with some chemical mixture in it which he set on fire after turning the lamp low. A lurid light came from the bowl which caused a livid look upon the faces of those who sat around the table, and while all were observing the ghastly effect, Dr. Webster rose, and, pulling a bit of rope from somewhere about his person, put it around his neck, reached over the bowl to heighten the effect, hung it on one side, and lolled his tongue to give the appearance of a man who had been hanged! ! ! The whole scene was terrible and ghastly in the extreme, and, remembering in the light of what followed, had a prescience frightful to contemplate."
>
> Appleton did not talk as much as usual, and we were rather glad; but Mrs. Thaxter's stories took strong hold on Dickens' fancy, and he told me afterward that when he awakened in the night he thought of her.

On another occasion, April 6, 1867, when the Thaxters met with Mr. Dickens at the Fields', the dinner guests

included the poet Longfellow and his daughter Alice, the
artist William Morris Hunt and his wife, the essayist Ralph
Waldo Emerson and his daughter Ellen, also Dr. Oliver
Wendell Holmes. Celia Thaxter easily and simply took
her place in this distinguished company, and her husband
must indeed have been very proud of the lighthouse
keeper's daughter, his former pupil, who was now the
much sought after "Rose of the Island". The guests did
not rise from the table until eleven P. M. Celia had
planned to stay in town, but Levi had missed his last train
home, as had Mr. Longfellow. They walked out to Cambridge together and then Levi walked on to Newtonville,
getting home about two o'clock in the morning! He said
he had had such a spendid time that he did not mind the
long walk.

The Thaxters entertained frequently but simply. Everyone enjoyed being asked to the friendly home in Newtonville. Both host and hostess talked well and had a keen
sense of appreciation and ready wit. Husband and wife
hardly realized that these years were probably the fullest
and richest for them together.

It was after her first meeting with Dickens that Celia
attempted prose for the first time. She wrote Mary Mapes
Dodge, editor of Young Folks:

> Newtonville, January 14, 1867
> . . . Do you want this very minute literary effort for the
> Young Folks? Or are you overrun with things of this sort?
> I have many little stories to tell of various birds and beasts
> and if you like I will send them. Please let me know and
> will you not do me the favor to point out any great im-
> perfections which may affect my production, for I'm entire-
> ly unused to writing prose, and feel as if I didn't know how
> to use the King's English. . . . I hope to go to see Mr.
> Whittier next week, can I take any message for you?
>   Affectionately and respectfully yours,
>   Celia Thaxter

The summer of 1867 Celia and Karl spent at Appledore,

although at first she did not expect to go. Levi stayed home, the younger boys with him part of the time. Together the three would tramp about the countryside with their guns and flower cases, pursuing natural history studies with enthusiasm. Grandmother Laighton treasured a photograph of a pair of mighty hunters, father and son, in rubber boots and old clothes, carrying guns with a powder horn slung over the shoulder of each. Levi's piercing eyes and heavy beard made a striking contrast to sober little Roland, aged nine, holding his father's hand. Celia, in a letter to Mary Lawson, described one of Roland's personal hunting adventures.

> April 6, 1867
> Roland went out in the lane and shot a cat nearly as big as himself and came in with it by the tail — as old as Methuselah and as calm as a clock!

In February, 1868, Celia left home to make her first long winter visit at the Shoals, leaving Levi and the children with an Irish girl, Katy, to take care of them in the Newtonville house.

An emergency in the kitchen at the hotel in the summer of 1868 made it necessary for Celia again to leave Newtonville and spend her time helping her family in their endeavors to keep their often exacting guests happy and well fed. To her friend, Kate Field, she wrote, August 21, 1868:

> . . . I have been engulfed in the pastry room half and sometimes more than half of every day, for the cooks still disappoint us and I could not but flee to my mother's rescue. — For the rest of the day I am good for nothing, man delights me not — nor woman either — but the time is nearly passed and each day it grows less hard. The fog! You might chop it as an axe chops a log.

John Greenlief Whittier was a frequent guest and Celia always looked forward to his coming and regretted when his visits were curtailed. She wrote Annie Fields:

CELIA THAXTER 1872

Levi Lincoln Thaxter and son Roland, 1869

. . . Mr. Whittier came Saturday and went Monday afternoon, I could only see him in the afternoon and too tired to do anything but lie on the sofa and be profoundly stupid.

I don't hear from Levi, but expect to see him any day, then the dear man says he will take home the children, open the house, and I may stay here a week, all alone, that's too lovely to hope for. I am afraid I shall think I mustn't, it is such a blissful prospect. . . .

Life was full of different problems as soon as she returned to Newtonville. Celia wrote Mary Lawson, telling of six weeks of minor illnesses of the children, then two weeks in bed herself. After Christmas, Levi suffered his first serious attack of illness. Celia laid aside all her literary work to nurse him. The doctor declared that he must go to a warmer climate and in February 1869, Levi set out for Florida, accompanied by John, who was now thirteen, and Roland, only nine, with their school books and camping outfit. All three carried guns in the hope of adding to the collections of birds found on the Atlantic Coast. There seemed to be no possibility of Celia and Karl accompanying them, and following their departure, Celia sought her family in their winter solitude, taking with her Karl, from whom she was never parted.

Her mother's sunny kitchen was bright with plants and there was a good man and woman to help, but there was always plenty to do in advance of the recurring summer season at the hotel. Curtains and bed tickings had to be made which kept Eliza Laighton busy sewing. Celia, however, found time at last for the writing of the articles for the Atlantic. Many of her best poems were also written in these surroundings. She did not dream that all or part of the next eight winters would be spent on the Isles of Shoals but so it was to be. There she found herself "imprisoned as completely as if we were in the Bastille. The northwest wind mounting guard, and mail only once a fortnight!"

But in the lonely solitude of the islands Celia wrote of

the wind and sea and her memories of long ago. The process of sending the poems to papers and magazines was very slow because of infrequent mails, and correcting proof seemed to take forever. But The Atlantic published almost every poem she sent and her readers became increasingly eager for any verses from her pen.

More and more people came to see her and the islands, which she described. The summer of 1870 was an especially successful one for the Appledore House. Many distinguished and some very wealthy people came and thoroughly enjoyed the peace and quiet and the invigorating air; all wished to return next season and bring their friends.

As it became more and more apparent that her eldest son was very nervous and a decided problem, an addition to the household was made. A young Hungarian boy, Ignatius Grossman, about fifteen years old, came to live with the Thaxters and attended the Friends' School with Karl. "We have taken him for good," Celia wrote, "he is a lovely boy and a great comfort." But all was not to be smooth sailing. Celia wrote to Annie on December 4, 1870:

> . . . I have been going through an ordeal such as never fell to my lot before. Mr. T. has been dangerously sick with rheumatism which again settled in stomach and about the heart. I hardly dare to think he is out of danger yet, but hope for the best. The physician's fiat is exile for us, as soon as Mr. T. is well enough he must flee for his life to a milder climate. The thought of leaving New England desolates me. . . . Alas for my poor manuscript. . . . I shall hate to go away from here more than I can tell.

And again to Annie -

> . . . I don't see but we have got to become a kind of human Shuttle Cock and Battle-dores — for Levi must go South in the winter because of his rheumatic heart and fly north to escepe fever and ague in the summer.

This well described the next few years. However, a great amount of her best writing was done at this time. While Levi and Roland made a second southern trip. John now in high school, stayed with friends in Dedham. Karl went again with his mother to the islands.

These southern trips were a strain on the family exchequer, but Levi's nomadic way of life precluded Celia's accompanying him, while the care of Karl and her loyalty to her mother called her to return to the island on her husband's departure. Her worries never ceased, as this letter written one winter somewhat later well shows.

. . . If the far-off continent did not hold so much that is precious to me I should not get so vexed with wind and waves. I miss my boys, so much I can't bear to think of it! It is truly remote, unfriendly solitary. Last night I had a shock that nearly stopped the beating of my heart. When I left home I told my husband if he ever wanted me, if anyone were very ill, or anything, to telegraph to Captain Rand of the steamtug Clara Bateman in Portsmouth, and he would come for me in any weather. At 10 o'clock just as we had gone to bed, I heard through the hoarse breathing of the gale, the long low melancholy peal of a steamer's whistle! Heavens, I was up in a moment. No one heard it except myself. I threw something over me and pushed up the window and leaned far out into the fury of the storm. The wind cuffed and buffeted my defenseless head and the snow melted on my face. Through the cannonading of the billows, and all the confusion of sounds came again that long, sad moan, like a cry for help, for human succor or divine aid. Nearer and nearer it came every moment louder and louder, till at last it passed by and went wandering to the eastward, uncertain of the way. I was sure at first it was the Clara come for me, and hardly dared breathe until I no longer heard the startling sound.

Only to Annie and Whittier did Celia open her heart with confessions of her worries.

Life would have been more simple for Celia if the Thaxters and their sons had occupied a cottage at the

Shoals each summer, but because of his accident and the resulting dislike of the boat trip, Levi remained either in Newtonville, where his cronies, Folsom, Weiss, Hunt and others often joined him in his bachelor hall existence; or made journeys down the coast of Maine with John and Roland.

The summer of 1871 was a very happy one for Celia, with Mr. Whittier and many other dear friends visiting the islands. She wrote busily and then read and discussed her poems with her friends. *All's Well, Tryst, The Hag of Star,* and the *Ballard of Heartbreak Hill* were among the poems of this period. Mr. William Dean Howells, then editor of the Atlantic magazine, accepted some but rejected others. He suggested that she write poems with a little more human interest. This she tried with the poem *For Thoughts,* telling of an incident connected with a charming amethyst locket in the shape of a pansy flower - "gift of an unknown admirer" - she told her family! (This was one of her few pieces of jewelry and it is still treasured by the author.)

> A pansy on his breast she laid,
> Splendid, and dark with Tyrian dyes;
> "Take it, 'tis like your tender eyes
> Deep as the midnight heaven," she said.

Celia was now at the height of her womanhood. C. T. Young, the writer, describes her:

> Celia Thaxter was, I sometimes think, the most beautiful woman I ever saw, not the most splendid nor the most regular in feature, but the most graceful, the most easy, the most complete — with the suggestion of perfect physical adequacy and mental health in every look and motion. She abounded in life, it was like breathing a new life to look at her.

Little wonder all the guests on Appledore sought to meet and know her.

In the autumn, October, 1871, Levi, feeling better after a summer in northern Maine, decided to try a winter in the north again. The house in Newtonville was repapered and painted and the Thaxters once more enjoyed a few months of being all together and handy to the cultural activities of Boston. Celia delighted in the music and theatre. She looked forward eagerly to a visit from her brother Cedric and her mother, but Christmas came and went and they still delayed. When at last they did arrive Mrs. Laighton stayed until spring.

The *Poems* were very well received by Mr. Whittier and others. Celia enjoyed to the fullest the pleasures and stimulation of city life with all its literary and social contacts. She was inspired to create some of her best work.

The summer of 1872 was a very good one and the season ended with money in everyone's pockets. For almost the first time Celia was able to spend money a little more freely. She arranged to have John and Roland take lessons at the Conservatory of Music in Boston. Thereafter Roland's fiddle would wail from the attic and John, at the piano, respond from the lower story, while Celia, writing between them, was glad to hear the sounds of activity and able to write that "Mr. Thaxter is rather better than he was." She also had a maid who "kept everything like wax" and was so good that Celia expected "her to go up in a cloud of smoke any minute." She wrote her brother Cedric in February that she had pretty nearly everything ready for the publication of *Among the Isles of Shoals.* It was to have illustrations by Whittier's friend Fenn, and to be printed by James R. Osgood and Company, 1873. With this book, as with her *Poems,* she was given much careful assistance by her husband.

In January, 1873, Celia made her mother a short visit and engaged a Norwegian girl from Smutty-nose as companion for the next two months. This girl, Karen,

stayed until Celia's next visit in March, when she returned
to her family on Smutty-nose. Celia and Karl who had
only come for a visit stayed on, leaving Levi and the
other boys in Newtonville, with a housekeeper. This
woman became increasingly unsatisfactory and in May,
Levi sent for his wife. Annie Fields in her own Diary
paints a sad picture of the situation.

Tuesday, May 20, 1873

Went to Newtonville in the afternoon to find Celia Thaxter.
Rang the bell of both front and back door without reply.
Walked in and found a deserted looking house, with "House
for Sale" placarding the doors. Presently I saw a boy whom
I recognized at once as her youngest, Roland, coming
towards me. He greeted me with a frank laughing face, like
his mother's though he did not know me; he asked me polite-
ly to walk into the parlor and sit down, as he was just going
to fetch her from the station. Will you take me back? I said.
O Yes! he replied — so I went in and sat down to wait. The
piano was open where the young men had been practicing.
There were good books on the table and interesting sketches
on the walls — but the stripped look of a barren house
where no woman has been to care for it lovingly for months,
was on everything — and Celia does so much to make it
beautiful when she is there. I am sure they must feel the
difference. She reached home from the islands the previous
evening. . . . Mrs. Laighton, Celia's mother is too ill for
her to leave and she is evidently penetrated with anxiety to
return, especially as her mother's own servant was obliged
to come with her to get clothes for the summer. Celia had
been in town all day with this maid, her first duty, in order
to get the girl back to the island as soon as possible. In the
meantime Mr. T. decides to rent the house for the summer.
Ah! poor Celia! This was her first home when she was
brought away from her islands to begin their married life.
She has suffered much under the roof, yet all her married
joys have been here too, and I know she must suffer to see
this forlorn shell — only too emblematic of their love.

Back on the island the next winter Celia cried out how

she missed her boys, from whom she would not be able to hear for weeks at a time, and describes the desolation:

. . . You would not know the place. All the boats are housed, not one on the moorings . . . the dike removed that keeps the water in the basin of the upper cove, floating wharf towed into the basin and fastened with chains, not a settee on the wind-swept chilly piazzas; the music room, piled sky high with sails, traps, the "carved" eagle descending from his perch on the house top, even the vane taken down, everything double reefed for the hurricane in store. It is truly "remote, unfriended" solitary, "slow," but nothing to what it will be when the snow makes a bitter shroud for us. . . . Twenty weeks of blustering between us and spring. But I wouldn't mind if we could have mail once a week . . . I have taken the plants (in my mother's room) in hand and really the desert blossoms like the rose, ten windows full . . . a passion flower running round the top . . . roses, geraniums, clouds of pink oxalis, Abultilon and callas in bloom. Polly hangs in one window . . . She has learned my unfortunate laugh and keeps it up from morning till night, peal upon peal . . . it is irresistable.

In this bleakness and loneliness Celia's winters were to be spent as her mother's health became increasingly precarious. For the next four years the tides of Celia's life ebbed to this lonely desolation during the seemingly endless winter, but with the song of the first song sparrow, they turned to sweep back, to life and beauty.

Celia wrote to a friend, Mr. Fox, March 19, 1874:

. . . I don't think I shall rejoice more if I ever chance to see the angel Gabriel's plumes of burning gold. . . . I found his dear little tracks all about my little garden. . . . What bliss! Today we have been swathed in a warm fog, the snow falls off, the spring seems possible!

Again on June 16, 1874 -

. . . I have not seen one lilac spike, not one apple blossom, this year, but I'd rather have the sandpipers if I can't have both. . . I am . . . content with what I have. I don't envy you a bit . . . They are cutting the grass on the lawn today and the air is so sweet with land and sea scents!

Friends, flowers, painting, music, all was gay and interesting and beautiful for a very few weeks. Then came again the divided duties. Celia felt, as between the two homes, she was absolutely indispensible at the Shoals, so for the next four winters, all exceptionally severe ones, she spent most of her time in the midst of the roaring waves. While Levi nursed his own health and feelings of neglect, the house became shabby and the neighborhood in Newtonville depressing. His own parents were dead, as was his sister, Mary Jennison. His sister Lucy's husband, the sea captain Beniah Titcomb, had sailed away, leaving Lucy in London, he was never heard of again. Shortage of funds at length brought her back to Boston, where she continued her vigil and .took over care of her brother from time to time.

11

A MEMORABLE MURDER
1873

IN SEPTEMBER, 1871, a small group of Norwegians settled on the south end of Appledore. One of the families, the Ingebertsons, became tenants of the Laightons and moved into Levi's South Cottage, about half a mile over the hill from the hotel buildings and the barns of the family. Ingebertson planted a fine garden and also went fishing. He had several daughters all of whom were at some time in the employ of the Laightons. Celia felt a great interest in these people; to her they were especially dear and her sympathy drew them to her as if they were her own. She wrote her *Spinning Song, Lars, Karen, Thora* and several other poems about these people. Soon more of these Norwegian fisherman brought their wives and took up their residence on Smutty-nose Island.

On the night of March 5, 1873, a celebrated double murder was committed there. The only winter inhabitants were John Hontvet and his wife, Marie, Ivan Christiansen and his beautiful young bride, Anethe, and Karen, Ivan's sister, who had been Eliza Laighton's companion until Celia arrived in March. On the day mentioned, after a particularly good catch, John and Ivan headed for Portsmouth to sell their fish and get more bait, leaving the three young women alone. During their absence, Louis Wagner, a drifter who had been befriended by the family, apparently rowed to the island from Portsmouth and bludgeoned two of the women to death with

93

an axe. He sought, unsuccessfully, to kill the third. A
horrified Celia described the event to her friend, Elizabeth
Peirce.

. . . You know I suppose from the newspapers of the horrible
murder at Smutty-nose. Those dear lovely Norwegian people
had a settlement. Ivan and Anethe had been married but a
year and only came from Larvik, Norway last fall. Anethe,
everybody says, was a regular fair beauty, young and strong,
with splendid thick yellow hair, so long she could sit on it.
Both husbands, John and Ivan, were devotedly fond of their
wives and their little home was so bright, happy, neat and
delightful that they never ceased congratulating themselves
upon having found such a place to live.

Louis Wagner, the Prussian devil who committed the
murder, had lived with this family all summer and they had
been most kind to him. In the winter he had drifted to
Portsmouth where he had a room and for months had been
working at nothing in particular! Tuesday March 5 being
a fine still day, the two husbands went to Portsmouth to
sell their fish, leaving the three women in the cottage on
Smutty-nose as they had done before, and as the women on
Appledore are often left. These women had been heavenly
good to Wagner and nursed him in sickness and supposed
him to be a friend; all of which he did not choose to remember. Reaching Portsmouth, the men met Louis and asked
him to come baiting trawls with them. He pretended assent,
but knowing the three women had been left alone and thinking Karen . . . had money with her, he took a dory and
rowed twelve miles out here in the calm night lit by a young
moon, landed on Smutty a little after midnight, broke into
the house in the dark and hacked and hewed those poor
women till he killed two of them by sheer force of blows,
chopping off Anethe's ear and smashing her skull. She had
twenty wounds where he had blundered at her haphazard,
in the dark! Marie told me all about it. She heard him first
at Karen, rushed to see what was the matter, got three blows
herself and a bruise on the jaw from a chair he flung at her
when she fled, fastening the door behind her, into Anethe's
room. She shook and roused the poor girl out of the deep

heavy sleep of youth, and throwing some clothes over her, made her get out of the window, Louis thundering at the door all the time to get in. In vain Marie cried "Run, run, Anethe, for your life!" Utterly bewildered and dazed, poor little Anethe cried, "I cannot move one step," and with that Louis came crashing out of the house round the corner, and Marie saw him kill Anethe with many blows, felling her to the earth. She rushed back to Karen and tried to pull her out of the house, begging her to come and save herself, but poor Karen, half dead with blows, cried only "I too tired," and Louis coming back, Marie leaped from the other window and ran for her life. He struck at her with the axe as she leaped and drove it deep into the window ledge. Having to finish Karen, he delayed long enough for poor Marie to get off among the rocks. The little dog, Ringa, was barking wildly all the time. He followed Marie and was really the means of saving her life, but for him she would have crept under one of the old fish-houses to hide, but she knew his barking would betray her. Next day the devil's bloody footsteps were found all round the old buildings where he had searched for her everywhere. Barefooted, in her nightgown, over the snow and ice and rough rocks she fled with the little Ringa, down to the uttermost end of the island, crept into a hole and hid. The moon was just setting as she went; and there she stayed till morning, and dared not move till the sun was high, hugging Ringa to keep herself alive.

Wagner meanwhile finished Karen by strangling her, and sought Marie in vain. Then he searched for the money, found only $15.00 and a few buttons in an old purse, completely missing over two hundred dollars which were hidden between the sheets in the linen closet!

Realizing that he must have nourishment before attempting the long row back to the mainland, Wagner cooked himself a meal and ate it, with the two dead women at his feet. He then apparently took his boat and rowed back to Portsmouth, "arriving at Rye in the first sweet tranquil blush of dawn, a creature accursed, a blot on the face of the day."

With the rising of the morning sun Marie, on her torn feet crawled round to Malaga Island, opposite Ingebertsen's house. She signaled and screamed till at last they saw her. When Ingebertsen rowed over for her, he was astonished to find her in nightdress, bruised and blood-stained, with her feet bleeding and frozen. Ingebertsen asked, over and over, "Who has done it?" All Marie could answer was: "Louis, Louis, Louis." The fisherman rowed her to his house on Appledore and sent word to the Laightons. Celia went over to see her. Marie clasped her hands, crying "Oh, I so glad to see you! Oh, I so glad I saved my life!" Poor thing, she tried hard to save the others!

The two husbands arrived home just after Marie had been taken to Ingebertsen's. When they went into their own home and beheld the terrible sight, they came reeling out immediately and fell flat in the snow. A watch had to be set over Ivan lest he should destroy himself.

Celia continues:

> . . . You can't imagine how shocked and solemnized we have all been. Oscar walks up and down, now ejaculating, "Oh poor, poor things, and Anethe so beautiful, so beautiful!" Karen was quite one of the family here; it was she of whom I wrote the little *Spinning Ballad,* you know. Now I'm afraid these dear people will all be frightened away from here and no more will come.

When the murderer reached Portsmouth, he bought a new suit of clothes and then took the train to Boston, but as soon as the news of the event was known on the mainland he was quickly apprehended and brought back to Portsmouth, where an angry mob was with difficulty restrained from lynching him as he was taken from the railroad station to the jail. He was later turned over to the authorities in the state of Maine for trial, since Smuttynose, the scene of the murder, is under the jurisdiction of that state. Wagner was tried and sentenced to death.

Then, because of his sudden pious protestations and because there were people who did not believe it was humanly possible for him to have made the long row to the Shoals and back in one night, he was granted a reprieve. After a new trial he was convicted and sentenced to hang for first degree murder. Wagner was the last man to be hung in the state of Maine. Only a few months later the new law doing away with capital punishment in the state went into effect.

Celia Thaxter had been so close to the whole affair that she felt it her duty "to do her little best" to see that the "murderer should be put in a place of safety, or receive the just punishment for his fiendish crime." She stayed in Portsmouth some time and carefully reread all the files of newspapers on the matter. Then she wrote the story which she later published under the title of A *Memorable Murder*. Immediately after the execution, she wrote to Annie and James T. Fields, asking them to tell her if she had "offended against the good taste" or "proprieties of existence" in telling the story. "The subject was a delicate one to handle," she wrote, "so notorious, so ghastly and dreadful! I would not dare to send it to Howells, without asking Mr. Fields first." Hurd and Houghton offered her $125 for the manuscript and $10 for every page over twelve. Her account was published by them in the summer of 1875.

This tale has often been rewritten as a famous murder, but never with the vividness of Celia's version. Under the same title it was published ten years later by Scribner's Sons in the third volume of "Stories by American Authors", a little book now very hard to find. It is still well worth reading. Celia stressed the fact that the new tholl pins (oar locks) in the stolen craft were almost paper thin when the boat was found, showing the terrible effort expended by the murderer in that twenty mile row in a single night. Other details brought out at the trial added more color to the story than the records of the State of

Maine Court of Justice show. Among them was the fact that when Wagner paid his fare on the train he drew out, with a handful of change, some buttons which matched those in Marie's sewing basket.

Lawrence Hutton refers to Celia's description as "one of the most vivid bits of prose in American literature." Mr. Whittier wrote on March 25, 1873, soon after the event:

> . . . I often think of you all in connection with the island tragedy. The imagination of man never conceived anything more dreadful than its grim reality. What a weird, awful interest will for all time vest that island. It will be haunted by the murdered women and in future midnights the light of Wagner's lantern will glimmer along the shore in search of another victim.

But the double murder was by no means the only tragedy which struck at these simple, uncomplaining people. Sometimes it seemed all they could do was keep alive. One particularly severe winter, they were caught without fire or food, excepting flour, and although the Laighton family tried to send supplies, it was impossible because of a roaring snowstorm. Help from Portsmouth seemed further off than ever. The sea was a hideous spectacle of tormented water, the cold was intolerable and no boat could bridge the churning foam of only a few hundred feet between Appledore and Smutty-nose. At last, in despair, one of the fishermen tried to reach Portsmouth. He was nine hours in an open boat in the wintry sea, beating to town against wind and tide, with only a woman passenger in the boat with him. He made it, reaching safety more dead than alive, but he was able to mail the fifty letters Celia had entrusted to him.

In another few days, March 26, there was a wreck on Duck Island. It was twenty-four hours before the settlers knew there were survivors. Then a fleet of small boats went out to salvage driftwood. One young man, Hans, with his little brother, "a morsel of a child", made several trips, but when he was bringing in his last load a squall broke and Hans and the boy and the heavy laden tiny boat disappeared! All other boats had gotten in but young Hans was a landlubber, with no real idea of how to handle a boat. The father and sisters, Minna and Ovidia, were almost beside themselves. Celia wrote:

> The sea was black and white as death with horrible long billows that break and roar aloud, Their only hope was to steer for the continent and there was great danger of the poor little tender boy freezing to death . . . My brothers walked the floor up and down, up and down, the storm raged cruel, inexorable, unmerciful, bitter. The father, poor Bernt, worked doggedly all morning, all the time weeping bitterly. Word came at last they had been saved only because they had picked up a broad firkin from the wreck with which they bailed desperately while flying before the gale. At last they had reached shore at the mouth of the Piscataqua River.

It was doubtless the result of experiences like these, and another which Celia retold in her poem, *Lars,* where two young men were blown in an open boat two hundred miles out to sea, and one died of exposure while the other flew on toward an almost certain similar death, that affected the sanity of several of the colony. First, old Ingebertsen became violently insane and had to be taken ashore to an asylum. In October, 1879, Celia heard that Annie Ingebertsen suffered long periods of complete prostration, and spent her days weeping bitterly. Having lived on the mainland as maids for several years, when they again had to endure the winters in lonely isolation, two of the girls broke under the strain. On December 13, 1882, Celia was telegraphed to in Boston from the Shoals telling of a terrible blow which had befallen Minna Berntsen's two sisters. Arriving at Portsmouth, Celia took Dr. Parsons out to the islands in the boat which had come for her. They found that Annie was dead and Ovidia raving mad. The homesickness and loneliness had overwhelmed them. Ovidia was quieted by means of keeping her under ether all the way by boat and train to Boston where they were met by Levi, with a letter from Dr. Bowditch, and a carriage. Her brother Hans drove with them right to the insane asylum in Somerville. During the drive the girl never stopped screaming a minute, but they left her among kind people who said professional medical care was the only hope for her recovery. Only two years before the two girls had kept house for Levi during Celia's winter with her mother. The thought of the insane asylum always haunted Celia in her fear that Karl's fits of temper and melancholy might sometime make it necessary to place him there also.

SMUTTY-NOSE ISLAND 1870 MID OCEAN HOUSE—
HALEY'S COTTAGE—HONVET (MURDER) HOUSE—
WAREHOUSES AND DOCK
(*Taken over Malaga Island*)

APPLEDORE HOTEL ABOUT 1880

CELIA THAXTER AND HER MOTHER ELIZA LAIGHTON

GOSPORT HARBOR FROM STAR ISLAND
THE YEAR OF THE GREAT RACE, 1873

12

POOR'S HOTEL ON STAR ISLAND
1872 - 1876

THE APPLEDORE House had been a going concern for eighteen years, when, after the death of their father in 1866, Oscar, then twenty-seven, and Cedric, twenty-six, took over the full responsibility. With so little knowledge of how people lived in the world outside their island, it was remarkable that these two young men knew how to make the guests comfortable and happy. The young hosts were genial, obliging and handsome, with an eye for the ladies, and an inborn courtesy and hospitality more ingratiating than the brusque manner of their quick-tempered father. Mrs. Laighton, always the inspiration and guiding spirit of the family, had early learned to "look well to the ways of her household, be it large or small." Her well-tried receipts were used in the hotel menus and many of them were collected in Mrs. Parlos' Cook Book, a stand-by of the day.

In 1870 the Laighton brothers, because of their increased business had decided to enlarge the hotel. For the sum of $4,000, they bought out the part of Appledore Island which Celia had inherited from her father. After another most successful summer they decided on a second addition and again turned to Celia. Her brother-in-law, Samuel Jennison, advised that if she made the loan of $2,300 more, they must pay 7% interest, which they agreed to do. Work was started before the summer guests

101

had all left the island for the brothers felt a need of haste. On the mainland they could see, at York Beach in southern Maine, a new ninety-room hotel being built, with which they must compete! Workmen came, stayed all fall on the island and rushed to complete the outside work before snow. Their cousin, Chris Rymes of Portsmouth, sent them $300 worth of hardware for the new annex. Many rocks were cleared away, and a large water cistern installed. Gas pipes were run all over the buildings for the gas which was manufactured in their own plant for lighting.

The Appledore House, being the first resort hotel from Eastport, Maine to Nantucket, Massachusetts, had become famous throughout New England and had developed into a popular and fashionable summer resort. Families of means closed their city houses and journeyed to the Isles of Shoals to spend the summer.

A page from an early ledger reads:

	Account of Julian Hawthorne	
July 27	sailing to Rye	$4.00
"	2 cigars	.30
" 29	rowboat	.50
	3 extra dinners	3.00
	board one week	7.00

That was the year young Hawthorne calmly departed from the Shoals to row to Newburyport.

The articles which were published in the Atlantic Monthly in 1869 and 1870 had stimulated greater interest in the New England archipelago which Celia Thaxter described. These articles, comprising the book *Among the Isles of Shoals*, were also printed in a fifty cent edition, as a guide book to be sold in railroad stations.

Celia, because she lived near the city, was asked to buy many articles for the new building at the best possible prices in Boston. When the newly enlarged dining-room needed wallpaper, carpeting, furniture, curtains and many other things, she was expected to procure them and arrange for shipment to the islands. Even her mother became extravagant and sent Celia $100, asking her daughter to go to Boston and buy her two and a half yards of the best lace for her cap and the largest corset available. Celia also sent a sewing machine, which she knew would be a great help in making many things which her mother had previously made by hand. Once she was even asked for three hundred young chicks "to be bought for not more than 15c each", to be shipped out on the Lone Star, the sailboat which was the Laightons' only passenger boat. Fulfilling this multitude of requests exhausted Celia and left her little time for her own daily tasks and obligations, and the writing of her poems.

The Laightons had always been extremely careful whom they accepted as guests, with the result that a congenial and delightful company assembled each summer, who were content to stay for weeks, enjoying the wonderful fresh sea air, and the quiet of the place. The two hundred or more guests joined fishing and sailing parties during the day, and the fascination of visiting and exploring the other islands in the group was unending. The daily menus were simple but wholesome and well-cooked - much seafood, varied by occasional lamb and chickens raised on the island, fresh vegetables. Reservations for rooms had to be made far in advance. A group of musicians played for concerts or dancing and came each season. They occupied a building behind the hotel known as the Band House.

Among the guests who visited Appledore in 1871 was a man named John R. Poor. He saw the success which the Laighton brothers were making of their summer hotel and cottages, and decided to compete with them. He went over to Star Island and found that the remaining fishermen in the village of Gosport were a rather pitiable and worthless lot, and the small Gosport House, where visitors were accommodated, was in a bad state of disrepair. He offered to buy the houses and the whole island, including the Meeting House and Gosport House. His price must have seemed good to the owners, as they sold out and moved en masse to Portsmouth. Some of them always regretted their exile, and for years spoke wistfully of those island homes.

In the winter of 1872 Mr. Poor built a rival hotel on Star Island, at a cost of $35,000. He called it the Oceanic Hotel. He hoped to surpass the Laightons on Appledore. Poor was a great promoter; he advertised far and wide, stating especially that he had a fine landing pier. He also advertised that he had engaged a well-known caterer, Mr. G. G. Mead of Boston. Then he sent word to all the yacht clubs up and down the coast, inviting the members to bring their yachts and participate in a Grand Regatta to be held in August 1873.

The thirteen mile race took the course out around Boon Island, off York, and back to Star Island. Excitement was great, and the yacht America was the winner.

Poor hoped this event would add greatly to his prestige. However so many noisy and objectionable people came to the new Oceanic Hotel, the more discriminating guests moved to the Appledore House where the atmosphere continued one of refinement and culture. Although the Appledore was usually filled to capacity, the Laightons certainly gained from the new publicity given the Off Shore Islands.

The hotels carried on a lively competition. Two steamers left Portsmouth simultaneously and raced to the islands with their passengers. A little launch made half-hourly trips between Star and Appledore for those who wished to visit and explore.

In 1873, the Laighton brothers built their long-needed landing pier. A fleet of small pleasure boats from both islands could be hired by guests for sport and pleasure. For two successful seasons the rival establishments continued to operate side by side.

As we have seen, the Laighton family watched over the Appledore House through the long, dreary months of winter, much more carefully than Mr. Poor ever supervised his hotel after the guests and help had all left. At the end of the summer season of 1874, the Oceanic Hotel and several adjoining dwellings on Star Island were burned to the ground. Nothing daunted, Poor decided to rebuild in a slightly different position. For the new hotel he was able to utilize some of the old buildings which remained standing. He was a man of considerable means - his family packaged Stickney and Poor's spices - so he did not shrink from the tremendous cost of procuring materials and labor from the mainland for the reconstruction.

The season after the rebuilding went badly. There was much fog and cold weather, and the less resourceful guests at the Oceanic Hotel were not happy. Many reservations were cancelled. Despite the fact that he had a measure of success, Poor became discouraged. Suddenly he offered to sell the whole establishment to the Laighton brothers for the amount which he had orginally paid for Star Island.

The brothers were still in debt to the bank for their improvements, the pier and the purchase of a steamer. Christopher Rymes, however, agreed to invest in the venture with them and they made a deal with Mr. Poor for $100,000. This was a large sum to raise, and it was against the better judgment of Mrs. Laighton and of Cedric, always the more practical business man of the brothers. Notwithstanding, the Oceanic was bought in 1875. The purchase was made only about a year before the death of Mrs. Laighton, at a time when she was really ill, and unable to take her accustomed place as the head of the establishments. Mr. Harry Marvin, who had first served as a messenger boy and then stayed through the winter months, became clerk at the Appledore, and his association with the business continued many years. The Oceanic office was the special care of Cedric, assisted by a young man named John Warden, from the Parker House in Boston.

This acquisition and enlargement of their business was the first really unwise move which the Laighton brothers had made. The cost of upkeep of two such large plants, in a spot every wind of summer or winter could cause great damage, was enormous! There was a very short season, three months at best which added to the transportation problems, made expenses prohibitive. When their own vegetable garden, hens and chickens, flock of sheep and the abundant fish were almost sufficient to supply the needs of the first hotel, money could be saved to show a profitable operation. But for the two establishments, perishable supplies had to be bought in great quantities, and at high cost transported to the islands. Also, although ice was cut on Appledore, refrigeration was meager. A week of fog could discourage less hardy souls from coming, or staying on at the fog-bound islands. However, for another twenty to twenty-five years the two hotels were to flourish, and it has been said that the success of the Statler Hotel chain was due to a study of the Laighton methods. Though the Appledore is gone, the Oceanic, now owned by the Star Island Corporation, still continues to be open to guests and is the site of an annual religious conference during the summer months. Conferences are held on Star Island at the present time from June 15th until after Labor Day, two boats going daily to the Island and back. Many people enjoy picnicking and sightseeing there.

Celia, for many years, handled all the correspondence connected with reservations, and a variety of new duties were added; as her mother's role diminished, her own and her brothers' responsibilities increased. In a letter to William Dean Howells, she explains how to reach the islands:

> . . . The best way to make the journey to the Shoals is to start from the Eastern Depot in Boston, on the 3:15 train

arriving at Portsmouth about 6 o'clock in the evening. The little steamer which connects with the arrival of the train will bring you across to us in an hour, with the sunset behind you, if the night is clear. If you prefer you could start at 8:30 a. m. reaching Portsmouth at 10:30 and get here by noon, but the afternoon journey is pleasantest. . . . Do come early in the season, because after July Fourth every corner of the Islands will be crowded full, so that there will not be a single nook in which I can find a place for you. The rush of the traveling public is· tremendous. From early July until September, there is a chaos of humanity let loose upon Appledore.

She tells of one day when ninety persons had to return to the mainland, as there were no sleeping accommodations. She also mentions that with five hundred persons collected in so small a space it was hard to find solitude. But with the coming of each September, like the swallows, the visitors all left the island. Then Celia,, loving the quiet and the beauty of the autumn days, always tried to linger a few weeks, to catch her breath in the tranquility of Indian summer. She wrote once:

. . . The crowd has thinned out and it is lovely to be alone, after I had such a siege of people all summer. I almost grew to dislike the human form. . . .

It was difficult for her to take up the duties of life in Newtonville after the excitement and adulation accorded her on the island. It was a let-down to return to the many family problems, and to the manifold household tasks she was required to do there herself. It was understandable, on the other hand, that her husband might, although he chose not to share in the summer life, become somewhat resentful of his wife's part in the midst of it.

13

ISOLATION AND HEARTBREAK
1874 - 1877

AFTER THE health of her husband became precarious, necessitating family separations of husband and wife, mother and younger sons, Celia turned with desperate longing to the four persons who were dearest to her. Above all there was her mother, whom she adored with a love more than filial. Next there was her eldest son who, because of his unfortunate mental and physical disabilities, was her constant care and cause for worry. And then there were her brothers. With Karl she went to Appledore where they were to spend the greater part of eight winters, sharing the months of loneliness with the family there.

Celia felt the isolation more than they, lacking the interests, pleasures and inspirations of life near Boston. This was a period when that city was at the peak of intellectual and literary blooming. For a short while Celia had tasted the sweets of association with the fine minds of men and women of letters. She had heard great actors and musicians. She had earned a place for herself among these cultured and gifted people. Now to have only the winter waves to watch, separating her from those inspiring human contacts, was to feel deprived. Her letters to her two dearest friends, Annie Fields and Whittier, reveal over and over her consuming desire to communicate what she felt and thought, her intense need for their understanding.

She spent New Year's weekend, 1874, at home in Newtonville, looking for a servant to take back to the Shoals. She decided at length that Annie and Ovidia Berntsen were everything she could desire in the way of help.

In January 1874, Celia sent a new poem to Mr. Ward, editor of The Independent, who made some suggestions. She replied:

> . . . I am truly obliged to you for your suggestions about the poem *With the Tide*. I have altered it in every particular which you so kindly pointed out. Sorry to have been so careless — I was entirely unconscious of the alliteration till you spoke of it.

It was unusual for Celia to be willing to change her lines, especially to eliminate alliteration. She was very fond of this form of writing, as it seemed to suggest the murmur of the sea about which she so often wrote. This time she was evidently eager to please Mr. Ward, and she succeeded so well that a few years later he had seventy of her accepted poems on hand at one time, and so could not purchase her *Memorable Murder.*

Celia pointed out to him that he had best not address her to Newtonville, but Appledore, Isles of Shoals, Off Portsmouth, N. H.

> . . . We are obliged to write out the address in full, as many letters go to Appledore, England, and come back if at all, after months of travel. In January, we have mail only once in ten days, so this must account for the delay in sending you the corrected poem which I would so gladly put into the Post Office tomorrow, did not nine miles of howling, wintry sea roll between me and the continent. . . . Such a state of things seems preposterous in this nineteenth century and only fifty-four miles from Boston!

But for the infrequently delivered letters, the family would have lost all contact with the outside world and all touch with the lives of friends.

The winter months over and summer come once again, Annie Fields' diary describes:

. . . another brilliant group at Appledore, in the Thaxter parlor, where the Republic of France was discussed one day and Robert Browning's poems the next. Mrs. Laighton, like a full moon in her silk dress and jewels, sat with them at tea. The jokes between James T. Fields and John Weiss amused the old lady greatly.

This was the summer when Celia's new and enlarged volume of poems went on the market. James Fields wrote her, and his praise was precious.

> 148 Charles St.
> June 8, 1874

Dear Celia,

I have been in Hanover talking to the boys and did not return until Saturday, so I could not get a look at your new edition last week. But this morning I rose up at 5 o'clock and sat over against the bay and read your poems one and all, straight through. Of course I know nearly all the poems there, but now I know them as a book of lyrics. Just what this little note is written for is to express what I feel to be an unchallengeable fact: that you can now take your place among the singers: high up in the beautiful ranks. It seems to me that no collection of Modern Poems can be considered excellent, either in England or at home, without some of your perfect pieces. I am rejoiced at your success and proud of your assured fame. You too are bringing consolation and beauty into a world which sorely needs all the good things. With Annie's love and mine to you and your dear mother,

> J. T. F.

Celia wrote Annie in the fall of 1874:

> Newtonville

. . . Soon my family will be entirely scattered. Levi and Roland on their sea voyage. John to Mexico with young Burnett. Karl at work somewhere. Then, if my dear mother keeps well, I shall stay awhile in Boston before going back to her for the terrible winter. I have promised the Eichbergs and Carrie Hedge and Parkie, each a little visit and shall hope to linger for a "sweet brief space" under your

most lovely and blessed roof, you dearest woman, before
I fly away to the lonely snows of Appledore. You must tell
me when you come back, what time will be most con-
venient for you, for I can't accept your grand-ducal invitation for half the winter, you beautiful dear! . . .

I have seen William Hunt, saying that he had been
living near Newburyport with Tuckerman and his mother
and sister, close to the Marquands and Curzons, all summer.
Hunt hasn't drank or smoked or taken tea or coffee even,
since last spring! He shows the good effects of it. O
Annie, I pity him so. He is charming. He is trying to find
a new studio with a north light . . .

Mr. Whittier sympathized with Celia in the change from
a busy summer to a winter of loneliness saying "it must be
very hard for flesh and blood to bear" - and indeed it was.

John's trip with Burnett fell through, but Levi and Roland
set off for the West Indies. Celia wrote Annie:

Shoals, Nov. 22, '74

Dearest Annie,

Many thanks for your cheering note. One came from
Karl also, saying he should be in Portsmouth tomorrow,
so I suppose the voyage is given up. I have sent one of the
Norwegians across the sea for him. I feel very thankful
that anxiety is removed. Now he will stay here with me.
I am very grateful for your sympathy. . . .

Karl was now twenty-two years old but was really unable
to take his place in the world. His father became angry
if the situation were referred to in any way; but Celia was
genuinely thankful when Karl gave up his job and joined
her at the Shoals. In the same letter she continues, referring
to her constant worry over her eldest son:

. . . I only mention to you alone out of the fullness of my
despair. Despair! It is a large word, but sometimes I really
feel as if it environed me. If I could get away from myself, but that is what solitude inflicts on us all and makes
us feel morbid and melancholy. Good heavens, the idea
of ever coming to that! To write morbid in connection

with my name! I'm ashamed of myself! I am growing old! When I have word of Mr. T's departure, I shall go home as if I were a leaden statue. Mary Parkman writes she has a ticket for me to hear the Fifth symphony on Dec. 2. I feel as though I might see the door of heaven was a little ajar and snatch one little glimpse of infinite comfort. I shall try.

In January 1875, Celia, having closed the Newtonville house, turned her face Shoalsward. A very severe storm forced her to stay over in Portsmouth with her friends, the DeNormandie family, in their handsome brick house on State Street. When Oscar came for her in the Lone Star, he was a whole day making his way through thick snow and floating ice. Another furious storm followed immediately, and as Celia had promised to attend the performance of Eichberg's operetta, Sir Marmaduke, to be given in Portsmouth in a week, she decided to stay over. In all she spent three very pleasant weeks in the city of her birth, the longest visit she had made since she left the town thirty-six years before! She enjoyed receiving letters daily. One of them told that — "her spouse was just starting with mules and a guide for a trip inland (in Jamaica) to see what he could see."

All the Eichbergs came down to see the fun, all the little town of Portsmouth was quite excited over the operetta. "Isn't it larks! Just think of dissipated me!" she wrote. The operetta went off well; the Eichbergs took tea with the DeNormandies and the two families enjoyed each other greatly, much to Celia's delight.

She also made the most of her time as usual. It was at this time that she went to the office of the Chronicle to study over the back files of the Wagner murder case. Then she visited Marie, the woman who escaped, and had a chance to question her. This research enabled Celia to finish her story of the memorable murder.

During this visit in Portsmouth, Celia was also asked

to read before a highly intellectual ladies' club, the Eclectic Society. After this event she wrote a letter to Annie at midnight, full of natural excitement over her success - "I read like a Trojan - it was larks!" On another evening she went to a "swell" dinner at George Haven's handsome mansion on Congress Street. Here among other beautiful antique furniture, she saw chairs, the "first cousins" to some of Annie's, she wrote gaily.

These festivities over, Celia sailed out again to Appledore. After having been away two months she found her mother well, but worn with the cold and hardships of winter. She wrote to Annie:

Feb. 11, 1875
. . . Having the fiercest kind of weather — water smoking in the bitter temperature day after day. The wafts of vapor made me think of the wild gray locks streaming in the wind, of some maniac foaming in the mouth in fury! Bitter, bitter is the only word for it. It is all we can do to keep alive! It wears on Mother! How ghastly it is, no pen of mine can ever tell. . . .

February 23, 1875
. . . You don't know how hard it has been to keep alive while the arctic wind blows over us. Today is the first token of relenting we have seen, for the first time we see the mainland on the water instead of lifted above it by the hideous cold, blurred and ghastly! Now the eves drip — Oh pleasant sound. . .

The chickadees called "Phoebe, Phoebe" and windows blazed with crocuses.

Shoals, March 14, 1875
. . . It is worth while to endure the winter with patient abhorrence to be so rejoiced at the first whisper of spring! . . . The carpenters will soon begin work on the enlarging of the kitchen which really isn't big enough for this caravansary. Mr. Thaxter writes he has had enough of the tropics and is on his way home!

March 26, 1875

. . . Ever since I got back to the Shoals I have been busy,
making ugly flannel shirts for Karl — which I hate to do —
but I can't buy such as I want, ready made. Besides, think
of getting 3 shirts, 3 pr. drawers, and 2 nightdresses, all
for $5.00 by making them one's self! . . . Night before
last a large vessel went ashore on Duck Island. The Capt.
and one man were drowned the rest of the crew picked
up and taken to Portsmouth. . .

Her husband and son came home earlier than expected
because Roland had had fever. Celia returned to Newtonville to open the house and stayed until summer took her
back to Appledore.

She found her brothers delighted with the new steamer,
The Appledore, which made two round trips daily to connect with Boston trains.

Celia wrote to John Weiss the summer of 1875:

. . . I am going tò Montpelier, to visit a lady there who has
been begging me to go for nearly 20 years. I have never
travelled so far before.

She was entranced with the views from the mountains,
which she described:

. . . The hills were like the sea, a combination of large
swell and "chop" crossing against the sky, and mountains
seemed to be heaved up like petrified waves! . . . there were
trees bigger than I ever dreamed they could grow! . . .

Celia stayed in Newtonville that fall, and on November
13th was busy making a new bonnet for Christmas. She had
a wonderful visit with the Fields in Boston, until February
18, 1876 when she again turned her steps toward the Shoals.
Karl met her in Ipswich with beautiful flowers. She waited
at the DeNormandies' until her brother could take her out
to the island in the yacht Mollie,

Shoals, Feb., 1876

. . . it blew so fresh that we could not land on the front
of the Island but had to lay under the lee at the eastward.

The Islands were white with snow in the blue water, and the sun glared down like a lidless, flaming eye upon the ghastly snow, ice and rushing sea. . . But in the house a summer of blooming plants and singing birds. My mother was so glad to see me and delighted with all the little things you sent her. . . Already I feel a million miles out of sight of land. O! Annie, what a beautiful time I had with you! How good you were to me. How can I ever thank you! . . .

Celia plunged into the writing of a new manuscript *Sea Sorrow* (a book about wrecks and disasters, begun but never finished) and had written forty pages when on March 4, 1876, she wrote to Annie:

. . . I would give anything to read to you and James this account of various wrecks and perils and sadness connected with winter at the Shoals — am writing in hope of earning black gowns enough to clothe myself next summer; if Howells won't have it, I shall send it to Harper or Scribner. . .

She wrote again on March 8, 1876:

. . . It is Lent, you see, and because the pious cannot eat meat, the fishing trade is brisk and so we have mail almost every day! . . . Mr. Howells returned my M.S. Wants me to set my constructive faculty to work on it. Du Lieber Gott! — if one hasn't any — one must live without new gowns! If one could only be as economical as Mr. Emerson's aunt, who wore her shroud alike for life and death!

March 14, 1876
. . . Thank you for your letter. Also had one from Florida. When I get one of those, I feel like saying: — "Leave hope behind all ye who enter here." Yet it is one of the best of men who writes! Oh Annie, if it were only possible to go back and pick up the thread of one's life anew. — Could I be 10 years old again — I would climb to my lighthouse top and set at defiance anything in the shape of man. How inexorably sadness grasps us. How the waters of bitterness almost close over our heads and desperate endurance is the only thing left us. I fight to keep my

head above water, to find something to thank heaven for
and I am grateful for good food shelter, for any kindness that falls to my lot, for my mother's freedom from
pain — I hold on to these things with all my might.

April 4, 1876

. . . Were you disgusted at me Dearest Sweet Saint Annie
— because I said my springs of cheerfulness were broken
forever and for aye within my mental and moral machinery?
It was only in fun! But I die 20,000 deaths of anguish
and anxiety over my unfortunate boy (Karl) in Ipswich,
from whom I have heard not one syllable since I came home.
Always he makes an undercurrent of misery and anxiety
deep down among the very sources of my being. But I
never mean to talk. —

All our heads are reeling with gas. The wind blows
the fire out of the stove or fireplace — gas, flames, ashes,
even brands and coal! We sit in all our outer garments.
I am in deadly terror lest my poor mother should take cold.
Oscar says: "Let's go sit in the barn with the cows." The
chimney of the student lamp just cracked where a snow-
flake blew against it! What will become of us? Good night,
sweet Saint.

They lived through it somehow. Celia worked on steadily,
writing, painting, covering a sofa and chairs with some
brown and yellow brocade sent from Boston by a friend.

Although she did not realize it, the winter of 1876-77 was
the last Celia Thaxter was to spend on the Isles of Shoals.
She wondered what she would have done during those long
months, had not someone suggested that she try to paint.
After a few sketches she attempted the hand painting of
china, which was very popular at that period. Little pitchers
and vases were backgrounds, on which Celia was able to
show her great love of nature, and all its beauties. Her
first results were quite successful and she wrote joyfully
to Mr. Whittier that "a new world opens to me, although
I have not yet had a lesson. I feel it in me, I know I can
do it, and I know I can do it well, for I realize what a
resource it will be for me." Mr. William Morris Hunt, the

THE PRESENT STAR ISLAND OCEANIC HOTEL

VIEW OF STAR ISLAND FROM APPLEDORE

APPLEDORE HOTEL

AND

COTTAGES NOW STANDING

Celia in her garden 1887

OLE BULL

artist and portrait painter, told her, "You are not afraid, therefore you will be able to do anything." As the years went on, her painting of china, and the illustrating of her books of poems brought her a tidy income. She used different designs which she painted on tiles, plates and cups, and bowls, while her mother slept and the wind howled. She painted birds, butterflies, lizards, flowers, grasses, and leaves, a Japanese lady, and her own seaweeds.

Due to her mother's now severe illness Celia hardly left her side through the fall of 1876. She described her household to Annie:

> . . . Up at six o'clock every morning, often before, laying plans for dinner for a family of eleven. I attend to all the house-keeping, since my mother has been sick, helped by my sweet little Norwegian girls. . . . . I make the dessert and lay everything in train for the noonday meal, so I may paint every minute of daylight that I can steal. I take my cup of coffee, then arrange my cooking and sit down at my desk with a student lamp to write till the winter sun rises. I write as fast as I can, not to take sunshine from my painting. We have breakfast at eight, when my brothers come down and the day begins for the rest of the household also.

The year 1877 was to bring Celia the greatest sorrow of her life.

Jan. 7, 1877

Dear beautiful Annie:

Oh what a week of fury! We manage to keep alive through the sting of the cold, but it has made poor mother so sick, so full of aches and pains, she is full of misery more than half the time. But she has been sitting up an hour or two today. How is your mother? I hope she does not suffer! Thank your fortunate stars you are not on a desolate island, the butt of the kicks and cuffs of the elements — alone to battle with unforseen emergencies — but are in the centre of civilization with friends, advice and sympathy and apothecary shops! Oh Annie the days are twelve minutes longer! I keep busy every minute — I am just wild to think of the music I can't hear. How I think of your sumptuous beautiful room! How warm! How the fairy lights sparkle across Back Bay. I wonder if there is any such nice place in Heaven? Do write to my forlornness.

Jan. 17, 1877

. . . Mail for the first time in 7 days. Yes, I was ill, coughed at night and tired all the time, etc. the doctor said I had spent too much vital force through the summer — he ordered quinine and my utter cessation of banting! I am rather ashamed of being ill — so did not tell you. . . I am writing nothing. I haven't an idea in my stupid head — gibbering idiocy would set in if it were not for my china painting. . .

Celia found great joy in her painting, although like everything else there were great difficulties in procuring supplies — all the paints, the plates, cups and tiles, which must be shipped by rail and boat from the city. Fragile china did not always withstand the rough seas.

. . . Last night came your box from the express. Mother is so pleased, she sipped her cordial and nibbled fascinating cookies and is delighted with the yellow dish and tray.

Oscar has gotten some East Lake furniture for her room. This is the sixteenth day of serene tranquil weather. I am writing before the sunrise but the sky is beginning to glow.

Feb. 24, 1877

. . . I long to see everybody and the beautiful, dear city, which always brims over with delight for me! The splendid new silk gown I had made last autumn hangs in Emily DeNormandie's closet in Portsmouth. I had it on just once!

Mar. 2, 1877

. . . We were just able to toss the mail bag on to a passing fishing smack today. — Mary Parkman sent me $50 worth of bliss, condensed in a small paintbox. — Mr. T. sent a paragraph from The Advertiser marked with sable dashes stating that I "married the first man who came to the Shoals for shooting and fishing!" I wish all the fools dead — myself among them   C.

Later:

Mar. 22, 1877

. . . I have painted 114 pieces of china this winter. a great deal of immensely careful and elaborate work. We have had another terrific storm — I dread to hear of the disasters! I am growing old and decrepit fast — I hate the pictures I paint — I hate the poems and I hate myself for perpetrating either.

In April 1877, Celia had a short visit in the city, heard the Niebelungen Lied - "frightfully magnificent!" - and brought back strawberries, lettuce and radishes to her mother from Annie, also many pieces of china to paint. She wrote April 21:

. . . The beautiful cherry brandy has been such a pleasure to my dear mother, but every breath is a moan! If I could only see you every week and clasp your hand and look into your faithful beautiful eyes, everything would be easier to bear . . .

April 29:

. . . Had a telegram from Mr. Thaxter, saying he was on his way back, so I rushed to Newtonville, wrestled with the furnace fire and began cooking when my brother telegraphed from Shoals "Mother very ill. Come at once."

Celia dropped everything and rushed by the next train to Portsmouth, where her brother met her, The Clara Bateman towed them to the Shoals at midnight. "Found Mother out of danger, but weak and voiceless. . ."

By May 1st, worn out at last, Eliza Laighton consented to let Celia go to Portsmouth and bring back Dr. Parsons. He gave her some medication but could stay only a few hours, He was hopeful about her mother and said there was no need for the illness to be fatal, with incessant care and proper remedies. He said he should, of course, see the patient every day.

Poor Celia at last had to admit:

... I have such a dreadful backache leaning over the low bed so often and so long — it just kills me! But now I can face the music! But one of the maids had a sore throat which the Dr. pronounced diptheria! There's one piece of joyful news. Our boatman Charlie Hart is coming soon and I can come and go in the Molly.

As the season advanced, she wrote:

Appledore, May 16, 1877

... I am so tired I think I must fall to pieces! In 3 weeks Minna can be spared from the housekeeping, but I haven't the heart to call her now. I spent one night in Portsmouth and it was like heaven!

To her son John, in West Virginia, she wrote:

Appledore, June 11, 1877

Dearest John —

"Dom" has been so sick! She is just as helpless as a baby — but she is more comfortable. — Don't let it be so long again that you do not write. I don't want to scold you — I was only grieved!

On August 15, Celia wrote Annie, mentioning a few people at the hotel, but said she spent her time in her mother's room, painting jars. Appleton Brown gave her a few lessons, and also painted a picture of her piazza and the sea beyond her garden.

Celia was shocked when she wrote: "They have to give Mother opium which they had been fighting. I am too sad to write - The winter terror draws near and I am full of dread!"

Before the steamer stopped its regular runs, Oscar and Cedric rented the Trudy House, 29 State Street, Portsmouth, so that "dear Dommy Laighton" could be moved back to the city. This was a difficult journey, because of the old lady's helpless condition and ample proportions.

Once on shore, a nurse was obtained to share the long

hours. Celia, when off duty, found relaxation in galloping on horseback over the countryside for two hours each day. Much of the time at her mother's bedside, she painted. Thanks to a few lessons, she now had orders to paint jugs at $10.00 and two panels for a Japanese screen for which she received $50.00 each. This all helped to fill in the long hours of watching and waiting.

Eliza Laighton was seventy years old. In the nearly forty years since she had followed her husband, his islands had been her home. She had cared for and tended her eccentric, quick-tempered mate, until she saw his dream of an hotel come true, and she had almost never left his side until his death. Later she would not leave her sons alone on their desolate, rocky isle. For years she listened to the sea lulling her to sleep or buffeting the rocks, until she was nearly blown from bed.

Always Celia gave complete devotion to her mother. Now watching by the bedside of the dying woman, she wrote Annie Fields:

> Portsmouth, Nov. 14, 1877
> . . . My eyes are stiff with weeping and watching, my beautiful dear mother is sinking away, and we are heart-broken beyond bearing. It seems I must go too, I cannot let her go alone! She lies looking like an angel, talking and babbling of green fields, clinging to us. Almost I perish in the grasp of grief. What do I care for this world without her! If I could but go too. . . .

Before her death Eliza was able to say to her sons: "Be good to Sister! She has had a hard life!"

All three of her children, Celia, Oscar and Cedric, were with their mother "when her beautiful spirit faded out of their lives forever." Celia and little Minna, the maid, did everything that was necessary and made her comely for her coffin. The daughter called for bright flowers and placed them on the pillow, where her mother "lay like a lily flower, her snow white hair under her white cap of delicate lace,

and her sweet tired hands folded at rest. All was as she
would have wished."

Again, in November, thirty-eight years after her first
voyage, they carried Eliza Rymes Laighton back to the Isles
of Shoals. She was buried beside her husband, Thomas, on
Appledore Island. Celia, with Rev. DeNormandie, read
the service. Karl and Ed Caswell, friend and helper of
lighthouse days, Minna and Ovidia Berntsen, joined Oscar
and Cedric in their sorrow beside the grave.

14

READJUSTMENTS
1877 - 1880

THE READJUSTMENTS for the Thaxter family, who had been separated so often and for such long periods, were extremely difficult. After her mother's death, which nearly broke Celia's heart, she was tempted to remain in the little house in Portsmouth which her brothers had rented. All the household tasks were well cared for by Minna and Ovidia Berntsen, who made all cozy and comfortable for the sad brothers and their sister. At her mother's bedside, Celia had filled every daylight hour with her writing and painting, and now there were many verses and sketches begun which she would be glad to have the leisure to finish. She had little desire to return to Newtonville because, since she had been absent, the house had lost the look and feeling of home.

For so long she and her husband had led separate lives, mentally and physically, that they now had little chance of regaining any kind of sympathetic companionship. Her boys had grown from children to young men. Both Karl and John were ready to go to work. Although poor Karl was now twenty-six, he was always seeking some job which he could do and be paid. John, at twenty-four years, was definitely interested in farming and had lived with the Burnetts in Southborough. Now he was an assistant on a large estate in West Virginia. Roland, who was now twenty, begged her to come home, saying she should remember "everyone has had more of you than I, who feel as if I had never had a mother;"

This plea demanded her return to the now forlorn and shabby house in Newtonville, where all was so changed from those happy days eighteen years before, when the young Thaxters first had a home of their very own. She wrote to Annie, November 1877:

> . . . My brothers do not care for Thanksgiving, but my boys do. My only hope and comfort are my boys at home. To them I am dear, to them I am welcome, and I can cheer and make them comfortable. It seems to be forever my lot to be between two inclinations or duties!

Levi felt that with Celia at home, it was unnecessary to employ help. He expected his wife to cook, clean and scrub as in the old days, before her position as poet and hostess had become established. During the summer months at the hotel, or even in the weary winter days in her parents' island home, she had been busy either nursing, or with creative accomplishments. She had never been afraid of hard work, but begrudged time spent on the daily household tasks, which she could use to far greater advantage writing or painting. She wrote Annie Fields thanking her for a concert which they had attended together in Boston, hearing the famous Modjeska, and described one day's program at home:

> March 7, 1878
> . . . First I made a pudding and did other cooking, then went for a scamper on horseback for two hours in the country. Home again, I wrote a sonnet to *Modjeska,* (See Page 268) whose singing I enjoyed with you. Then I painted a small cup for an order; and felt the day went better than usual, so before going to bed I made brown bread and buns!

"Life is but a dream at best!" she sighed, but was grateful to her many loving Boston friends who did all in their power to entertain and cheer her by inviting her to lectures, concerts, theatres where she saw Fanny Kemble in the Merchant of Venice, and Charlotte Cushman, the actress, who was a frequent visitor on Appledore. Celia found the trip from Newtonville into the city difficult for evening engagements, so that if Levi did not escort her she often arranged to spend the night in Boston. After attending a concert with her friends the Eichbergs she wrote sadly: "I am so thankful for a night away — in spite of my dear Roland" — but after five days in Newtonville . . .

> . . . I wonder, what are any of us made for? I wish I could fall asleep and have done with the weariness of this world. I long to come to stay with you but Sunday I must be in Newtonville with my dear tyrant, Roland, when he is at home.

However as winter progressed Mrs. Augustus Hemenway, always a very generous benefactress, made it possible for Celia to ride regularly at the Cambridge Riding School and the exercise was good for her mind and body. Invitations came for the opera with the Julius Eichbergs, for an evening of reading with Mrs. Sargent. Celia had a new gown made for such occasions, which she proudly described as "a most imperial gown, of black cashmere and silk and satin, with a sweeping train!" It was in this gown that the artist Otto Grundmann painted a life sized portrait of her. The handsome face tells its tale of sadness, but with determination she still lifts her well shaped head "above the clouds and looks to the future."

She threw herself heartily into whatever she did. Elizabeth Stewart Phelps said:

> Celia was always sure of a welcome, and was the best of company — everyone wanted her. Hearty, wholesome, she rose through a decorous drawing room like a breeze from her own island waves. She was never afraid to be herself. Her vigorous physique had much to do with this, for she had her share of the sorrows of life.

It was an extremely severe winter and Roland, who had

spent so many previous ones in a warmer climate, became quite ill. Celia nursed him until Lucy Titcomb, her sister-in-law, returned home and then she went to spend a few days with Annie in Boston. But when she returned home to Newtonville she wrote Annie on March 6, 1878:

> . . . Came home to find house in confusion, the Dr. just gone — Roland looking so ill — just recovering from a severe malarial chill. Poor Levi was all alone and had to leave Roland, and rush for the Dr. . . . Ich bin sehr traurig — Meine liebe Annie! I must get a saddle for this horse of ours and ride out of doors or I shall perish with the blues!

By the middle of April, she made a visit to Appledore, and from there she wrote her second son:

> Appledore, April 12, 1878
>
> Dear John:
>
> I cannot tell you how forlorn and miserably sad it is here without dear Dom, and I have been busy looking over and sorting her possessions, stowing away and locking up her little treasures, some of which I remember when I was a very little girl, and it all gives me such a heartache. . . .
>
> I think of you so gladly, dear, doing what you like to do and being busy and happy. It is a great comfort to know all is well with you. I have not heard a word from home since I left it, but trust all is well there. I am thinking of going back the first of the week. I dreaded to come, now I dread to go and leave these poor fellows again (Oscar and Cedric). . .
>
> I have been putting the cottage in order and my garden. It looks very bright and charming. I suppose I shall be here at least part of the summer for papa says he is going away somewhere, he isn't quite sure where. I hope he and Lony will be here part of the time at least.

It was on April 21 that she wrote Annie of an unusual migration of birds stopping on Appledore as if especially to cheer her:

> . . . The song sparrows fill the house, they fly into the

great rambling empty place and sing, oh how they sing! The sweetest songs, all day and about all night — if they see a ray of light from moon or star or human candle, they lift up their delicious voices and proclaim the same. We open the windows to let them out, but they make their way within again almost immediately. I never knew them to do so before, there are so many of them, they fairly have taken the island by storm, even in this pouring rainstorm they are chorusing as if the sun were shining its brightest. They are a blessing. I believe I should perish of melancholy without them.

I have been at work without cessation since I came, putting things in order in my own domain and sorting and arranging and locking up my dear mother's possessions. . .

It is all so lonely, so lonely — the boys are so forlorn. . .

To Annie on April 16, from the DeNormandie's in Portsmouth, Celia wrote:

. . . In all my fortnight's absence, it is another heartache, not to have had one word from Newtonville, although I have written several times. The world is so changed and sad!

But her buoyant spirit conquered and two days later from Newtonville, she wrote happily to Annie:

. . . Isn't the weather divine? How the birds sing!

Then later, from Boston to John:

May 6, 1878

Dear John,

I came to spend a most lovely Sunday with the Fields. Mr. Eichberg played his violin and Mr. Liberling, Professor Grundmann, Appleton Brown and Rob Weiss were here and we had a jolly supper and it was very charming! I left Lony at home rather quaking and expecting the arrival of a man to rent the house for the summer. Roland doesn't want to be tossed out in such a short space of time — but he will go somewhere as soon as his exams are over — to the Shoals I hope and Papa too. Karl and I will probably go soon, he is the limpest object just as soon as

it grows hot. Only the Shoals puts the starch in him!
Did you thank Papa for your boots? I beg you won't forget to do it! This is a poor scrawl to show you that I love
you darling. Do let me see that you love me too and write
to your

Mum

May 29, 1878, Newtonville

Dearest John,

Did I tell you the State of Maine has been selling all
the islands along the coast and has written Uncles Oscar
and Cedric about selling the Shoals . . . Now isn't even
the possibility of such a thing too bad! We had a lot of
company on Sunday. Mr. Eichberg came on the Worcester R.R. Prof. Grundmann was driven out in a festive
beach wagon by Mrs. Fields and Rob Weiss and his friend
Parsons also came. It was all very jolly. Papa seems very
well for him. We are all so glad!

Back at the Shoals she wrote to John:

Appledore, June 2, 1878

. . . Karl steered the steam launch for Miss Parkman and
me. I miss Dom so I am ready to perish, but it is beautiful here. There is one poor young man named Claude
Kettle, who came early to try and find relief from hay
fever — what was it ever made for!

This morning the floating wharf has been towed out
of Portsmouth by the little steamer Appledore — a crowd
of men are busy adjusting it — Polly hangs on the piazza
and calls and whistles so you can hear her half a mile
away — we have a great fire in the open stove.

Celia went back to Newtonville on June 17, "very
anxious about Roland's Harvard entrance exams," but she
took time to give John a bit of motherly advice:

. . . The season opened well at the Shoals, although the
weather had been dreadful. But there are lots of nice
people. All the Bowditches and Dr. Bowditch and his
wife and daughter — they take twelve rooms for the summer and that is quite a nest egg to begin with. Karl has
set up his printing press and hopes to do all the printing
for both houses — if only he does, he will earn something

. . . Dear John, why don't you thank your father for your books? My dearest, don't neglect the little civilities of life — it will be so bare and ungracious if you do. They cost you nothing and they win you more love than a great many things that seem more important. Take the word of my greater experience and believe me that you will miss something beautiful out of it if you do not gratefully and promptly acknowledge the kindness of your friends and your father's loving thought. Don't be angry with your mother, who loves you dearly.

The summer which followed was one of the best of Celia's later life.

Shoals, July 11, 1878

Dearest Annie,

Summer is summer as of old and all the world is kind to me. Only I am working very hard, there is such a sun on my studio! Up at five and at it every morning wishing I had a dozen hands.

Isn't it good my Roland passed his college examinations with honors in Latin and Greek. He is here and I am trying to keep him, that he may grow well and strong. Alice Wellington was here yesterday, pleased with the success of her first book *The Ring of Amethyst.* Claire Erskine Clement is also here very nice and jolly.

Oh Annie, Mr. Paine's playing is such a comfort to me! Lifts me right up out of the mud and dust of the way. He brings new things and as it were, teaches my ignorance, playing over and over and saying "here, listen", and "there" — it is heavenly! He has set a song of mine to music. (See page 271)

She urged Appleton Brown to come quickly:

Appledore, July 22, 1878

. . . Where are you? Paine is playing Beethoven sonatas morning, noon and night in my little parlor, divinely! He makes a business of making them known to me, think of that! Comes and says, "Shall I play you the Opus 90?" — and another and another until I don't know where I am, It is too beautiful and you ought to be enjoying it too . . .

Never had I such heaven on earth before — I never imagined it. I paint and paint in my corner and life is intoxicating. I am emerging out of all my clouds by help of it.

Ninety people had to be sent away this noon. Mr. Whittier has just gone away.

One month later she wrote:

Shoals, Aug. 21, 1878

. . . I am thinking of you every hour dear Annie, but the time to write never comes — for I am so busy and get so tired. 6 hours sleep in the 24. I don't know what demon of toil possesses me — Yesterday the music stopped, the Paines went away after six weeks. Never was so kind a man! When I said, "How shall I thank you?" he answered, "Only let me go on playing" — although he never meant to play a note all summer. My eyes shut with weariness — I never saw so many nice people together, and I shall be so glad to see you. . .

All too soon the season was over. She wrote Annie:

September 4, 1878

. . . I have had a heavenly summer and now there are all sorts of perplexities — but nothing can rob me of the beautiful hours I have had, I have yielded to everybody, at last about printing a new volume of poems, which I want to ask Mr. Fields about.

This was the collection called *Driftweed*. Many of the poems have a melancholy touch because they had been written during the last years of her mother's illness. To James T. Fields:

Newtonville, Nov. 12, 1878

Dear friend:

Let me keep the title *Driftweed*. Don't you see it is more than a name and signifies something, namely — as the water is God to the seaweeds, making them to live out of the cold and dark bottom of the sea, and as the sun is God to the land weeds making them grow out of barren, "bare-blown rock," so is our God, to our barren lives. And as these little verses are weeds that sprang out of the rock and never knew cultivation. Don't you know I never went to school? I can fancy you smiling and saying to yourself that there is little need of telling you that.

Celia's personal popularity was so great at the time that the new book sold well. She added to the value by taking orders for special copies, in which she painted about ten delicate water color sketches appropriate to the poem on the page. For these volumes she later received as much as $25.00 apiece and they are now outstanding collectors' items.

It is little wonder that when she could spend her time with such creative accomplishment she could not tolerate giving much to household tasks which could be done by a paid servant. She wrote from the Shoals on November 4, 1878 to Annie:

> . . . My place is in that dear, despairing Newtonville but . . . I have but one thought, to go and live in Sufferance as I did last winter. But my work? . . . I am poor, perplexed but loving
>
> Celia

Life again seemed everywhere very sad with "the worst heartache at home in Newtonville." All summer Celia Thaxter, the successful authoress, was looked up to and admired by a host of friends and made the center of a life which had outgrown "the trinity of the soapkettle, the ashcan and the cook stove" to which her husband somewhat jealously seemed to wish to condemn her! Celia was shocked at her own use of the word "morbid" in describing her feelings to Annie Fields. Now, after years when she had led such a constantly changing existence, given the opportunity to settle down, a routine of domesticity seemed intolerable to her.

All five members of the Thaxter family spent the summer of 1879 in Celia's cottage at Appledore. Levi overcame his reluctance and returned to the Shoals primarily because of

the presence there of his life-long friend, the artist William
Morris Hunt, who was ill in mind and body.

Celia wrote to Annie Fields:

Shoals, June 24, 1879

My dearest,

Is James Fields getting strong again? Tell me a little,
Oh, and will you tell the dear lovely Langs my delight in
my piano. They are the dearest, kindest, most charming
people in the world!

My garden waxes mightily! How is yours? Every time
I look at my growing things I think of you.

Mr. Thaxter and Roland came last night to my joy —
I expect John soon. The new resident physician, Dr. Daven-
port and his wife are charming (and will be most helpful).
I work, work, work! It is all my joy! It is not yet six
o'clock a. m. and I am writing for the early boat, which
sends a warning whistle from afar!

She showed her sympathy to Annie during Mr. Fields'
illness:

July 19, 1879

My dearest,

Every day, almost every hour I have thought of you.
How is James Fields? Will you not send me word . . . .

Just think of our having William Hunt here, just shuddered back from the dreadful verge, so attenuated so pathetic!
He and his sister, and his brother and his man Carter, all,
all housed beneath this cottage roof, and I hope and trust
the air is going to do everything for him!

Poor dear fellow — there is nobody I pity so much!
Mr. Thaxter is here, next door to Hunt's room. I really
couldn't believe my senses last night when I found myself
walking up the piazza between them (Hunt and Levi)
with an arm of each — it was the most delightful thing
that could happen to me! Truly we never know what the
gods have in store for us, and that truth should finally
prevail, is worth fighting for against the stream, with many
years of all the striving. I told Hunt to consider my little
den his property. He said "You dear child, you don't know
what a sick weak good-for-nothing I am — fit only for

OSCAR LAIGHTON IN HIS EIGHTIES

KARL THAXTER WITH AN UNKNOWN FRIEND

OFFICE, APPLEDORE HOTEL

DOCKS AT APPLEDORE

CELIA THAXTER, 1878
(*Portrait by Otto Grundman*)

my bed." — But he eats and sleeps better and yesterday rowed a little.

Celia's happiness was soon turned to grief again, however. On a dark rainy afternoon Hunt restlessly went in and out of the cottage and past the window where Celia was painting. She called him in and begged him to sit by the fire until the weather cleared. After a few minutes he again wandered out into the storm and disappeared. He hated to be followed and each of his friends thought him to be in a different place. When, after two hours, he had not returned they all became worried and a search was organized. It was Celia's fate to find him — face down in the little pond on the north side of the island, where the wild roses dropped their petals. She called his sister, who was nearby, but because of Jane Hunt's complete deafness, she could not make herself heard. When at last help did come, they carried Hunt's "beautiful dripping length," his gold watch chain swinging, to that piazza where he had sat looking at the flowers and listening to the music. They rubbed and rubbed, to no avail; although there was very little water in his lungs; he had been dead for hours. (Note: See Celia T.'s collected Letters.)

The shock of this tragedy broke up the happy company which his presence had created, and cast a gloom over the remainder of the summer. In the fall, his friends prepared a memorial exhibition of his work at the Boston Art Museum which was largely attended, even his estranged wife and children being present. Masses of bright flowers were placed beside the self-portrait which he had given Levi, whose portrait he had also painted, which now hangs in Eliot Hall at Harvard, a gift of the Roland Thaxter family.

The peaceful atmosphere at the Shoals had temporarily relaxed the Thaxter family tensions. They had been brought together by an eagerness to restore their old friend to health but the family unity ended with the artist's death. Now seemed the time to make a decision, long-discussed, about leaving the house in Newtonville. The various interests of the family members seemed to indicate a change of headquarters, so the house was put up for sale.

John, a handsome young man of twenty-four, had returned from his apprenticeship at farming and overseeing in West Virginia. He spent a carefree and delightful summer on Appledore and became convinced that an outdoor life, near the Isles of Shoals, was the one for him. He urged his father to find some place where he could engage in farming, which would also serve as the family home and headquarters. They searched the shores of Maine, and New Hampshire's short seacoast, and at last narrowed the choice down to two — the Governor Benning Wentworth estate on Little Harbor, near Portsmouth, and the old Cutts Farm at Brave Boat Harbor in Kittery Point, Maine.

Both places were an easy sail from the Isles of Shoals. The Wentworth estate was the more accessible, but the beautiful residence of the former Royal Governor was far too large for their needs, and had no view of the open ocean. The final decision, therefore, was made in favor of the 150 acre farm belonging to the Cutts family.

This farm had been originally inherited by the brothers, Richard and Robert Cutts, whose father had come to Kittery from the Isles of Shoals. Their mother, the Widow Cutts, had taken as her second husband a Captain Francis Champernowne. He was an Englishman who had sailed across the seas from Devonshire to take possession of a tract of land which had been deeded to his uncle, Sir Fernando Gorges, by King James I. It was described as "a grant of 500 acres by the waterside, that runneth towards Braveboat Harbour."

It was this same spot which charmed the Thaxter family. The estate had woods, plenty of cleared fields and good pastures well-fenced by stone walls, and rocky shoreline. Near the house was the little graveyard where Captain Champernowne was buried in 1683, in a simple grave marked only by a cairn of stones. Celia described perfectly the setting and surrounding view:

A low wall over which the roses shed
Their perfumed petals, shuts the quiet dead
Apart a little, and the tiny square
Stands in the broad and laughing field so fair
And gay green vines climb over rough stone wall
And all about the wild birds flit and call,
And but a stone's throw southward the blue sea
Rolls sparkling in and sings incessantly!

In a Kittery Churchyard

Unfortunately Levi Thaxter, having purchased the Cutts
Farm at a very low figure, decided that it was easier to
tear down the old house and rebuild than to repair the
somewhat dilapidated structure then standing. This was the
second house on the same site, the first one built by Captain
Champernowne having been destroyed by fire.

During the rebuilding of the farmhouse, John camped out
in a little shack near the sandy beach, called Sea Point. The
farm was extremely isolated, although it had been occupied
for over two centuries. A small creek, named Chauncey for
a Cutts son-in-law, encircled the two islands now known as
Cutts and Gerrish Islands. This creek enabled passage by
small boat from Portsmouth to Brave Boat Harbor at high
tide, a distance of eight miles. When the Thaxters first
bought the farm, this long sail or row was the best way of
reaching the place. Chauncey Creek was narrow and
shallow. At one point first a ford, and then later, a small
bridge, permitted dwellers on Cutts Island to drive or ride to
the mainland, but this difficult access greatly complicated
trips to the village of Kittery or the city of Portsmouth.
The small harbor lay at the northeastern end of the property and divided the township of Kittery from that of
York. The New Road along Chauncey Creek, and the
bridge onto Cutts Island, were not built until several
years after the arrival of the Thaxter family. In the first
years of their occupancy, Celia often wrote of the two
and a half mile trudge which one of her sons must take to

the post office, where a stage brought the mail to Kittery Point. There were steam cars running from Boston only as far as Portsmouth then. The trip from the Isles of Shoals to the farm was best by boat direct to Brave Boat Harbor, although the seas were sometimes very rough. Celia wrote to Annie:

> Shoals, March 2, 1880
>
> . . . Tell J. T. (Field) they spilled me overboard in the stiffish gale of wind — I did not go over my head — but I was not benefited by the briney bath! It is lovely, lovely here like a sea of sapphires and emeralds, flashing to the sky; the bluebirds and robins are singing, but the rose tufted grosbeaks have made a wreck of my gold and purple crocuses — I expect to go home to Newtonville next week — where there is a whirlwind of business. . .

In the spring of 1880 the Newtonville house was sold at auction and the Thaxter family moved permanently to Maine. It was not a period of simple architecture, and the new house had a mansard roof and dormer windows. It was roomy and comfortable, the three large chimneys made possible six fireplaces, assuring plenty of heat in the most severe weather. The third floor was given over to Roland, with many shelves built under the eaves to hold his collections of butterflies and moths. All the windows framed unusually beautiful views. In one direction there were pastures and pine woods, and in the other fields stretching to the seashore. Beyond the crescent of sandy beach, the Isles of Shoals lay on the horizon. From Appledore on a clear day, the farmhouse and huge tree could be plainly seen. Every night White Island Lighthouse sent a friendly beam across the water toward the farm, making the two homes seem very close.

Celia wrote many letters to John, now living in the new house but faced with many problems.

> Newtonville, April 13, 1880
>
> Dear Old John,
>   I send you bread and lobster receipts. Have written

Uncle Oscar I will go out to the Shoals Mon. April 26 and as soon as I can, I will go to Cutts Island and see you and if there is anything I can do for you and cook you a lot of things and show Mrs. Call perhaps. Isn't there any place I could sleep a night or two perhaps? Mr. Dolby and son are closeted with Pa in the green parlor this very moment. Papa showed me a plan of the lean-to shanty which looks very fascinating. Dear boy, you shall have some new neckties. Life isn't long enough to turn old ones upside down. Send word to your

Mum

Newtonville, April 19, 1880

. . . I can't come down till after the 26th — I wish it weren't so far and remote, so it would be possible to get there and back more easily! I sent some things by Papa and I wish I were going with him. Pa will tell you all the news, Glad you went to the DeNormandie's. Miss Jane Hunt gave me $25.00 for you to buy a calf or something for the farm! She gave the same to each of you boys for anything you like best. Folsom is here and sends love, so does Karl — I think about you all the time!

Celia's last letter from Newtonville was to Mrs. William Dean Howells, dated April 24, 1880.

On April 29 she describes her rough passage to the Shoals:

Dearest John,

I hope you got home safely with your load, and will send me word. We had a devil of a time getting out, yesterday. It was so tremendous I was seasick! I don't know when such a thing has happened to me before! The Pinafore stood right up on her bow and then on her stern, the sea washed from end to end and my feet and hands were numb with cold. My feet were plunged above my overshoes in salt water all the time. Everything smashed that could be smashed, including the glass cover of Karl's clock, for boxes and baggage plunged wildly and in all directions. When I got here I could hardly stand, I was so used up. I will send a bundle of seeds and lots of sweet peas and they ought to go right into the ground. Uncle Oscar is

trying out and steaming and boiling all the bones of the
White Whale, and is going to have it set up! Such an
undertaking!

May 2. Still no chance to send mail. I tried to flash a
light to you yesterday at 5 o'clock, from Portsmouth to Agamenticus along the shore. Did anyone look? I am longing to hear from you, Lony and Papa. I hope to see Karl
today. I wish you would put a word on a postal to tell me
how you are and if you have got a horse yet and if Papa is
there? — Uncle Oscar means if it really pleasant Sunday,
to sail over to Brave Boat Harbor for he knows the way
now and wants so much to see the place. Of course I will
come if I am here.

In each letter Celia continued to ask John if he had
gotten a horse, which seemed one of the first necessities
of existence in such a remote place as the Kittery farm.
She also worried about the departures of a succession of
women who had been hired to cook for the hard-working
young farmer, his father and younger brother.

Sadly she writes May 12, 1880:

. . . I have never seen poor Karl so daft. I think he is
going to lose what little mind he had, poor unfortunate
fellow. It is too dreadful — Thank the Lord that you have
got your wits and the Cutts farm, dear John, and have
your chance in the world, which poor Karl never can
have. I pity him so, I don't know what to do. . . I am sending a large covered basket of painted china to Mrs. Saf-
ford and I will send it from Portsmouth by the Stage.
There is a plaque to hang up and a pitcher with daisies
and a vase with seaweed and a little plate with poppies.
I hope they get it, for there was as much as twenty-five
dollars worth at least!

From time to time John sailed over to Appledore for a
day or night during the summer season. He was the darling of all the young girls, among whom was a demure
and pretty girl from Worcester, Massachusetts, there with
her invalid mother, Mrs. Stoddard. Mary Gertrude Stoddard was fascinated by and devoted to Celia, who in

turn became very fond of her. It was Celia who introduced her to John at dinner. Though no one suspected it at the time, this was to have great effect on the young farmer's whole future!

After the hotel closed, Celia went to the farm at Kittery Point, to find the house helter skelter. She and Minna worked like fiends to make everything as comfortable as possible for John and Karl, who were to spend the winter there. Roland, at Harvard, would be living in Cambridge. Levi expected to give some public readings during the winter and planned to divide his time between his sister Lucy's home in Boston and occasional visits to the farm. For the first time, Celia appeared to be free.

15

EUROPEAN DAYS
1880 - 1881

THE YEAR following Hunt's death brought great changes, not only to the Thaxters, but to the Laighton brothers as well. Both Cedric and Oscar fell deeply in love, Cedric to become engaged to Julia Stowell. Oscar was not so fortunate. Each year since the opening of the Appledore House, the bearded young viking had found a new sweetheart, with the arrival of the summer guests. He would adore each in turn, and be desolated when she left in the autumn. He wrote impassioned verses to them, one by one. In the year 1880, however, came the love of his life, in the person of Lucy Darby, daughter of a wealthy merchant from Salem. Unfortunately, though the young people were greatly attached, her stern and ambitious parent wrote his daughter to beware of entanglements at the Isles of Shoals as they had other plans for her. This was a crushing disappointment to Oscar and, as he wrote on a later date, his "health broke" and he "wished only to die".

He suffered a complete nervous breakdown. A trip to Europe was advised for him as the best possible cure. He could well afford to go, thanks to the prospering hotel business. Kind friends, knowing Celia's love of and interest in the beauties of the Old World, urged her to go with him. They even offered to assist with the financing.

She wrote Annie Fields:

Shoals, Aug. 2, 1880

. . . I am so busy. It is really settled that Oscar and I
are to go abroad — I can't quite take in the possibility when
I hear people talking of it as if it were all settled. It is
much too good to be true. Mr. Thaxter has been here
for a few days. He thinks it would be a fine thing for me
to go! —

For me, I have one idea — to paint — I am beset and
do not breathe, yet I enjoy all things, while Paine and
Eichberg play together like two angels.

Passage was secured from Boston on the Batavia, of
the Cunard Line, for a sailing early in October. Before
her departure, Celia went to the farm to do everything
she could to insure the comfort of her husband and sons
there during her absence. Just before sailing, however,
brother and sister spent a few days at the Parker House.

When the last whistle had blown and the ship was
pulling out, Oscar spied Lucy, waving her shawl from
the dock. He went wild, to the great excitement of the
passengers, and was with difficulty restrained from climbing over the rail to swim back to the girl he loved.

Celia, who had often watched ships disappearing over
the horizon line, was now, herself, to cross that vast expanse of ocean. She wrote Annie of the voyage:

Oct. 8th, 7th day out, 1880

. . . Incarcerated in the bowels of this remarkable fish!
. . . Here we are, "midmost the beating of steely sea" and
such a time as we have had of it! For we ran the first
night into a raging, roaring, ranting, tearing, dry easter.
Rough? I believe you! My brother wanted "to see how
she behaved in a storm." Well, he had his wish, and quite
enough of it, without a moment's delay. Oh, she pitched
like a maniac and she rolled like a drunken elephant; at every
plunge her propellor was bare to the blast, and made her
shake and quiver like an aspen, or better, like the variations
on the violin in the Kreutzer sonata. My brother stormed up
and down, like the jolly mariner he is, but I — I lay very low
indeed, I assure you, and right quiet I kept, nor dared I move

an eyelash for three days. Then I emerged and Captain Moreland tucked me under his arm and rushed me up and down the deck until I got used to its angle of 45 degrees, and since then I stay on the deck all the time. But it's very nasty indeed. Yesterday the captain called the sailors to lash me and my chair to the iron railing under the lee of one of the life-boats, where they rigged a canvas to keep off the flying water, and they lashed my bag to the chair . . . The first six hours were heavenly calm, two song sparrows followed the vessel till almost out of sight of land, one dear bird came and lit close to me on a rope, clinging with his slender feet, panting, as much as to say, "Really, I'm all out of breath, but I had to come after you, comrade, to say good-by." Wasn't it sweet? I was so delighted. No other bird would have so moved me . . .

I am the only lady cabin passenger on board this time, and the dear Capt. is having an easy time of it. There are not more than thirty steerage passengers. But down in the hold there are three thousand five hundred barrels of apples and you can smell them powerfully through the huge ventilators on deck. . .

The Capt. had come way aft here to my cubby-hole under the life-boat to "take the sun." Seven compasses on board this boat and a man at each; and the man at the wheel his solemn, motionless level eyelids are most impressive. He sees nothing but that compass night and day.

Once on shore the brother and sister were interested in all they saw. Celia wrote Annie from the Red Horse Inn in Stratford-on-Avon:

Oct. 15th, 1880, Friday
. . . We reached Liverpool Tuesday morning. Monday night (when we were to sight Fastnet Light) I was up at two o'clock. Pitch-dark of course, but the bosun was piping like a whole wood full of robins up on deck, and the mariners made night vocal with yo-ho-hoing. . . . . . "Well, such an early bird as you I have never had on board," the Capt. said. On deck it was black as Erebus, a vast chill, with a fresh wind always ahead. But we sat on the great metal sarcophagus covered with canvas (that the bath

water is heated in) between the smokestack and the
Capt.'s cabin, with our feet over the cook's big range, where
fires were still burning, and it was very comfortable,
especially as they brought us hot coffee at once; and then
we watched the rockets sent up from our ship and the answering signals from the invisible shore, and it was so nice
to think how the telegram would speed across the world and
you would all read, "The Batavia is in!" and think of us.
Such a glorious dawn at last! such a heavenly sunrise and
the Irish coast, divine in color and new, strange shapes; the
hurrying sea, all pea-cock blue and green; and the most
extraordinary craft flying about with delicious dull-red sails
that I sketched all day. . . . When we landed at Liverpool
(and Oscar and I nearly turned a double somersault with
amusement at a Bobby to say nothing of forty thousand
other things all at once) the Capt. went with us through
the custom house and they didn't even open our things
and then took us to the big Exchange which was quite a
sight, and then sent his own private attendant round the
town with us and we went to St. George's Hall and to the
Art exhibition. . . . While we sat about a hundred work-
house children — girls — came up for a lark, and anything so sweet and clean and pretty I had never seen. Cheeks
like carnations, and bright eyes and smooth shining hair,
and the nicest little costume of dark blue, and each with
a white straw bonnet of old-time shape, with dark-blue
ribbon crosses over the top and tied under the chin, all
alike, as if they had been turned out of a machine by the
gross. I can't tell you how we enjoyed it. Then the good
Capt. met us and took us down to Roby to dine with him,
and wasn't it just like a chapter out of Dickens, oh my!
— "Rosina Cottage", just at the back of the station, all
smothered in green things and full of yellow-haired children,
papa's slippers warming before the fire, and an atmosphere
of unmitigated loving-kindness pervading the whole place.
Oh, how they worshipped each other! . . . Next morning
was bright and sunny. We went up on the old Roman
wall around the city, and oh, what a morning we had!
We loitered all around that wall, two miles, and every
step was charming. The lookout, near and far, was so en-

chanting. You know it all, of course, but everything is so
new to us, and every smallest detail, even to the shape
and color of every brick, so different and strange. . . A man
with a donkey came down a side street, the donkey laden
apparently with some loosely tied sacks of coals, and the
man, oh such a long, lank, ungainly, big-jointed creature,
his battered cap pulled over his carrot-head, where the
stiff tow locks stuck out all round, and such an undescribable
costume! His hands were stuck in his pockets and whether
school kept or not he did not care a tuppence, but up the
sunny road he stumped crying continually what sounded
to me like "Troubles! Troubles!" . . . We started for Stratford at 2:00, and didn't enter Chester town at all! But
we saw enough to stay with us all our lives. We must
allow more time for places in future. Our journey here
was one series of pleasures. When we got to Wolverton
we said, "This must be Birmingham," for we thought there
couldn't be more smoke; but Bloomsbury was thicker yet;
and when we arrived in Birmingham, O. said, "this is
surely H. — itself!" and it did look like it. Smoke and
flame everwhere and the blackness of darkness. . .

I am hopelessly in love with the English girls.   Oh,
their sweet seriousness, their dove-like eyes, their lovely
contours, their fresh, delicious color, their smiling mouths,
with such grave and noble curves, their modest mien, and
flocks of them everywhere, a feast to the eyes, a refreshment
to the soul! It is worth coming to England only to see
them. At Stratford it was dark. . . . As for the Red Horse
Inn, it is too charming to be believed. We had our supper
in a cozy coffee-room by ourselves, and Oscar sat in
Washington Irving's chair, if you please and it was all
heavenly. . . .

. . . I light my candle and from a corner of this big
curtained feather bed with damask sheets, that dewlap
Falstaff talked about, while Stratford is slowly coming to
its senses this fine morning. . . .

From Stratford they went to Paris for a week of bitter
cold, then to Brussels where they saw the lace workers
and on down the Rhine to the great cathedral at Cologne.

They traveled to Dusseldorf, where Heine was born, on to Frankfort, birthplace of Goethe, and then Heidelberg where they were delighted with the University and its students. After visiting the spa at Baden-Baden, they journeyed south to Basel, where Celia was thrilled to look west to France and east across the Rhine into Germany. From Schaffhausen, where Celia thought the falls of the Rhine "perfectly beautiful," they went south to Zurich and then to Lucerne, where the lion sculptured on the face of the cliff greatly impressed her. At Bern she was amused by all the bears; at Freeburg they heard the glorious organ and found it a fascinating place. At Geneva they caught their first and only glimpse of the Alps, since at Lucerne the Rigi was lost in thick mist and at Bern the Jungfrau wrapped itself in heavy clouds. At last, however, Mont Blanc emerged clear at sunset "rosy snow in the high blue and we looked at it a whole half hour." Since their time was so short they could not arrange for any mountain climbing, but the majesty and immobility of Mont Blanc deeply impressed Celia and Oscar, so used to the ever-changing wide stretches of ocean. The great plains between Turin and Milan were "like a beautiful garden, cultivated to the last inch."

From Milan she wrote again to Annie:

. . . I saw a priest the living image of John Whittier, and one who looked like my Roland. — Oh the pathos of it all! Every face a study! Such devotion, such love and sorrow and fearful hope — everywhere there is but one cry to which my heart responds — "Lord, have mercy upon us" helpless and defenseless that we are.

To her cousin, Albert Laighton, she described the glories of Venice

Nov. 21, 1880

. . . Nothing I had heard or read or seen of photographs, etc., prepared me for Venice. We came into it in a great glory of full moonlight, after a long ride in the express train from Milan, and I can't tell you how strange it seemed to emerge from the dark station after the rush and rattle of the train, into the cool quiet moonlight on the stone steps, where the gondolas were drawn up waiting for passengers (they are the hacks of the place), each black graceful boat with its glow-worm lamp, everybody talking the delicious language that sounded like music; all the white marble palaces and statues gleaming in the moonlight and lights from vessels at anchor, and bridges and houses throwing trails of gold across the glassy water. The gondolas are the most comfortable things in the world, with cushioned spring seats and high backs to rest against, the motion is delightful and the gondolier the most graceful creature, he can't help being so, to give the proper stroke to his oar he must throw himself into a beautiful posture. It is a sleight of hand, something utterly different from anything we do with oars. The gondolas are supremely elegant, black, with fine carving, many of them, and brass ornaments, sea-horses or dragons on each side the middle of the boat . . . It was pleasant after the jar of the train to glide away through the mysterious streets without a sound, except the quiet dip of the oars, to our hotel (which had been an old palace) with water washing its white marble steps. People go about in gondolas; the street bands do the loveliest serenades, with guitars, etc. every night. As we went we heard the most beautiful singing rise from a distance; the lovely Italian voices singing the lovely Italian language in the soft air, it was like a dream and I thought I must wake every moment. We have had a beautiful week here all too good to be true, and tonight we go to Bologna on the way to Florence.

Annie had news of the journey to Florence:

Florence, Nov. 24

. . . We came to Florence from Bologna yesterday, through the Apennines. We started at 7 o'clock in the morning so as to be able to see the view. We went through 80 tunnels between here and Bologna — that railroad is perfectly astonishing. The engines they have to tug you up and down the mountains are colossal, tremendous machines. When we came through the Mt. Cenis from Aixles-Bains to Turin we had one to push, and one to pull the train; we entered the tunnel in dark, dull weather and emerged into the most superb clear blue and golden weather on the other side, with the mountain peaks dazzling white with snow all about us high up in the stainless sky. . . . . . . We met some delightful people in Venice, Mr. and Mrs. John Field, who, seeing my name on a letter, came and introduced themselves, being Americans and the same people are here now, and it is charming to know some pleasant people who know all the ropes, they have been abroad seven years. I wish you could see the great bowl of delicious pink roses they have just sent me tonight. They grow here out of doors everywhere, blossom here all winter. This IS such a beautiful place. The Arno, swollen by the last rains, rushes a broad flood beneath my windows, but it isn't like the clear green Rhine or Rhone. The stone pines and olive trees are so picturesque and beautiful. The city is a great treasure house of pictures and statues and all sorts of precious things. We have been through the Uffizi Gallery this morning but it would take a week to look at the things at least. I always try to go through the market in the different places because you get a better idea of the life of the people that way than any other. The unaccustomed sights, for instance the baskets of oranges and lemons on the branches from which they grew, with the splendid glossy green fragrant leaves; the big rich pomegranates, cracked open, full of rubies and garnets inside their tawny yellow rinds; the olives in strange shaped jars, the heaps of seeds from the stone pine, something like hazel nuts; the green figs, the barrels of shining sardines all symmetrically arranged; cinnamon cakes, rolls and yards of bread; cooking going on everywhere, chestnuts boiling and roasting, corn meal hasty pudding making, which they call polenta, soup stewing, all out in the street. . .

Celia did not like Naples much. She wrote Annie, December 8:

. . . God made Naples the divinest place. Men have converted it into a pigsty of unspeakable squalor. The best thing that could happen to it would be to have Vesuvius roll a league or so of red-hot lava over it and sweep away or bury it deep, like Herculaneum and Pompeii, and end it some way. North Street in Boston is clean and sweet and wholesome to it. It isn't one street, it is the whole great swarming town. We ride through miles of it to get any place. Up on the heights are palaces and fine houses, and an approximately clean street, where carriages and toilettes rival the Champs Elysees, but, ye gods! the whole town along the sea border! No drainage, everything in the streets; no windows to the houses; no human creature who ever combed their hair or washed their faces since they were born; ten thousand million billion filthy babies! O, it is a race of vermin, rats are clean, beetles, spiders, any vile thing that creeps is better. Like monkeys they sit and investigate each other for unmentionable horrors. They need only tails. There is not a ray of joy or decency in the place; the only cheerful element in Naples is the all-pervading flea! King Humbert and Margherita are in their yellow-pink palace. Great Heaven! can they not find some way to turn the whole Mediterranean in on their nasty city! . . .

Our hotel is high up above the smells. Before us lies Capri, melting in sapphire and amethyst. The Mediterranean is wondrous; it is like the Arabian Nights. Tongue can't tell its color, — its greens, blues, purples, its lambent light. It's not like water; it's like leaping, liquid, prismatic flame all about its delicious islands. Its very substance is colored, as if you dripped the fine brilliant blue color we have for washing clothes, you know, into a cup of water; it doesn't owe alone its marvelous effects to reflection from the sky. We see Vesuvius smoking away, the broad, red-hot band of lava down its black side. Just this moment it is splendid, its great dark mass heaved high against the crystal-pure sunrise sky; not a cloud in the whole heaven except the mountain's own long, floating plume that trails across the sky from east to west, and catches all the faint rose-tints of the coming sun . . . O heavens, Florence! The Arno rushed under our windows. Oscar liked that, we stayed four or five days, every instant full. . .

Then we came to Rome, Vedder sent me such heavenly

CELIA THAXTER 1875

JOHN GREENLEAF WHITTIER

flowers, first evening, then he came himself and was charming. We stayed a week in Rome and, thank heaven we are going back there again. O the Campagna! Annie, if I had time to talk! But the daisies! I thought of you every minute, 1st day of December I gathered violets, and I went to the grave of Keats. I can't tell you with what a feeling I dropped over the ashes of his heart the most perfect rose it has ever been my lot to behold, one from Vedder's bouquet, every flower of which an artist's eye selected. I send you a violet leaf from Shelley's not far away. I scattered some daisies over Shelley's, someone had been before me to both places, and a spike of clustered, fragrant narcissus flowers, waxen white, was lying on each grave.

. . . Friday we spent the whole day in Pompeii, that is, it took us the whole day to drive there through Portici and Resina, and go through the only half-buried city and back at six in evening. It was breathlessly interesting; the excavations still going on; something new revealed every moment. . . No end of Roman ruins and Greek traces, the vast remains of an ancient city all along the coast, to Lake Avernus and down the black fearful descent to Hades and into the cave of the Cumæn Sibyl. That was fearful, we never meant to do it, but before we knew it we were in that almost perpendicular passage just wide enough for us to move, pitch black, and down we went interminably; suddenly we came to black water and the guides, without a moment's warning, seized and carried us through it up to their waists, and deposited us on a narrow shelf in the cave of the Sibyl, when we broke into such shouts of laughter that why we didn't crack the mountain I don't know, and they must have heard us down in the brimstone lake a little further below. The guides were aghast. . .

Sunday we went up to the top of Vesuvius, and burned our shoes on the hot lava; Monday to Capri; yesterday to Herculaneum, and to the most marvelous, exquisite aquariums here on the Mediterranean border. Oh, such dreams of beauty! Such colors and delicate shapes of weed, coral, anemone, and myriad undreamed-of things! and fearful octopus swimming about, the most dreadful creatures I

have ever seen. Today we go to the Museum. In Florence
I moused till I found your Dante's fresco on the wall,
and brought away a photo of it. Saw "Sassa di Dante" in
the square, written on the wall below which the small
iron bench used to be, where he liked to sit, near Giotto's
lovely Campanile; saw his house with the sweet inscription
over the door. Went all over Michaelangelo's house; oh,
wasn't that interesting! Saw his old paint brushes, writing
desk, sword, plans of St. Peter's, etc., manuscripts. . . .

On Christmas Eve she thought fondly of home and
friends, and wrote again:

Genoa, Xmas Eve, 1880

. . . We left Rome Sunday and reached Pisa at night, spent
Monday there and Tuesday morning came here to beautiful Genoa. "Genoa la Superbe" well may it be called! I
sent a note by mail to Mrs. Clarke Wed. morning and then
we went out to the Palazzo Rosso and saw the Van Dycks,
heavens, how splendid they are! And to Palazzo Andrea
Doria which was most interesting, lying on the edge of
the Mediterannean, with its gardens, and terraces a mass
of crimson and pink roses, violets, heliotrope and all kinds
of lovely flowers sloping to the sea, and all its treasures
shown us by such a proud and comical and delightful re-
tainer who took me by the shoulders and sat me mildly but
firmly down in the magnificent throne chair in which the
1st Napoleon had sat, and all the dukes of Genoa had been
crowned. . .

Celia and Oscar were invited for Christmas Eve dinner
at the villa of her recently widowed friend, Mrs. Cowden
Clarke who had spent so many summers at Appledore,
and her brother Mr. Alfred Novello.

. . . Little Mrs. Clarke, the prettiest, sweetest, daintiest
creature imaginable, Sabilla Novello in sable velvet, homely
and nice, Portia and Valeria, the two nieces, fine, noble,
handsome, delightful looking girls, a little quiet English
friend staying with them, and an Italian maestro, sweet and
intense, they were playing at two grand pianos, so I begged
them to go on . . . As I sat and listened I had an oppor-

tunity of taking in the room and its details. . . After the
music was done the maestro departed, and then we had a
long charming talk, it was about you principally, I wonder
if your ears burned! I had taken along your little book,
I knew of course they would have it but wasn't sure that
it might not have reached them by some chance and the
Fields and Vedders to whom I took it in Rome were so
charmed with it. Soon as the sun set we all went downstairs into the dining room because it was warmer. . . After
dinner which was so gay! Sabilla taking the head and carving, her mother at the other end opposite, and dear little
lovely Mrs. Clarke by me at the side like a guest. Could
I but tell you about her cap! Such a mesh of cobweb lace,
frostwork caught and fixed, and a little lustrous satin bow,
white as moonlight over her forehead, a little rosette, like a
flower, not a bow. After dinner we went into her library
and by the open fire, talked and told stories and had
such a beautiful time . . . and they begged me so to
stay over Xmas. Then I determined to make Oscar go
to dine at Villa Novello as they had begged me, but
when I opened fire on my brother, he said he would die
first before he would go, nothing would tempt him.
And he was so unhappy about it that I was in despair,
however I worked at him all day till at last with wrath and
woe and despair he gave in. "But what do they care to see
me" he cried, "how ridiculous it is! I shall be miserable
and they too." To which I only answered "you will see,"
and instead of moping in his room in the hotel over a
nasty book, Oscar had an evening he will never forget
in his life, and never wished to leave the place he so hated
to enter. They bro't in the great Xmas pudding for us to
stir, and made us promise to come and eat it next
day, and my brother absolutely stayed in Genoa another
day on purpose to go to the Villa Novello again! Such a
Xmas! He said he never had such a beautiful Xmas in his
life and it did him a world of good. . . . Sweet Mrs. Clarke
put on her most wonderful Point d'Aguille to please Oscar
who has a passion for lace and he watched Valeria's fair
fingers making lace on a crimson cushion, and altogether he
was in heaven, and they praised his verses and petted him

generally, for I gave them the verses by way of introduction. And oh the dinner! the pudding sprouting holly and mistletoe! The toasts we drank! "To all we love in both worlds," said sweet Mrs. Clarke and then finished Oscar entirely by proposing "Cedric's health" — never was anything like it in the wide world!

. . . Dear friends, now it is four o'clock in the morning of Xmas day and I go on. Genoa hasn't slept any all night as nearly as I can judge for I have been conscious with every striking hour of music in the streets, singing and instruments, chiming bells and gay guitars, a most melodious medley! "TIS the gayest place! . . . .

Mentone, Dec. 31, 1880

. . . We are going to Monaco in a few hours, we see its high cliff from here, it is only a little way. How I hate to leave this bright little room of mine with its great window opening like two doors on the blooming garden and the summer sea, the armchair in the recess of the window and the table with all my writing traps and books. Oh to stay here in quiet and write! But I suppose I'm an ungrateful pig not to rejoice over what I've had instead of lamenting that I must go home so soon. . . O there's nothing so beautiful in its way as an olive, so graceful, so elegant, so classic, one might say! Do keep everything to show me about the little book, no wonder you have letters, it is beautiful! . . .

I'm sorry to go back so soon, but I'm grateful for this experience which has pushed my horizon out in all directions immeasurably! I'm so delighted to hear Mr. T. succeeds so well! Thank you for all your kindness.

While Celia was in Rome she dined with her old friend T. B. Aldrich and the artist Elihu Vedder. During dinner the talk turned to the spirit life after death. Later both Vedder and Aldrich each in his own medium expressed their ideas. The artist's sketch was of the meeting of two draped figures, while the poet wrote:

> Somewhere in desolate windswept space
> In Twilight Land — in No Man's Land —

Two hurrying shapes met face to face,
And bade each other stand.
"And who are you?" cried one, agape,
Shuddering in the glooming light.
"I know not," said the second shape,
"I only died last night!"

Mr. Vedder gave Celia his pencil drawing and later she wrote asking Mr. Aldrich to copy his "wonderful dreadful poem" on a piece of paper the correct dimensions to place under the sketch for framing.

Lyons, Jan. 13, 1881

. . . It was bad to turn our backs on the sweet south this morning to leave the olive trees and stone pines behind. (I love them like human things!) to come up here and find ice in thin sheets in the little streamlets, snow scattered here and there, no more flowers, alas! to come into the winter in one day! We are to stay here a day, then to Dijon a day to break the long pull to Paris, — a few days in Paris, then to London, where I am going to try to find all your friends, Annie dear, and bring you the last news of them. . . .

O the unaccustomed pinch of the cold this morning! The first thing I see out of the window is a string of horses with all their tails done up in incorrigible hard knots, dragging cart loads of ice. . . .

Levi's friend, Mr. James Gordon Clarke, turned up unexpectedly at their hotel in Lyons and was very kind — took Celia everywhere and showed her everything and they discussed Annie Field's new book, *Under the Olives*. From Lyons, Celia and Oscar went back to Paris. Here Oscar had a taste of night life. When an old man he still vividly recalled being taken by a friendly hotel-keeper, after Celia was safely in bed, "to see some sort of a show — where there were many beautiful girls who did not have much of any clothes on!" Brother and sister also paid a visit to the Opera to hear Melba sing, and Oscar had to wear his "infernal dress suit" made in London, which, once back at the hotel, he "tore off, rolled it into a tight bundle, tied it with a long shoe string, and as the clock on the Cathedral St. Germain struck two, cautiously opened the window, looked down on the dimly lighted boulevard and with a glow of ecstasy, hurled the demoralizing fabrication with all my might to the pavement fifty feet below!" This sturdy islander longed for his pea jacket and oil skins!

Their last stop was London. Celia went into raptures over Ellen Terry in The Cup. She was entertained by Robert Browning, to whom Annie Fields had given her a letter. She wore her little necklace and bracelets made of shells from the Isles of Shoals, thinking they would interest him. Mr. Browning had heard also of Mr. Thaxter's interest in his verse, and of the reading from his works in public. Browning refers to her visit in a letter written later to Roland Thaxter, but since it was so near her departure date, Celia waited until she got home to tell about her visit with him. There is no written record of it.

Celia wrote Annie, "Oh, if we could only have stayed in those heavenly southern places until it moderates," but Oscar was more than ready to return home. "He doesn't see what the Lord made any land for at all, he is so crazy to get upon that treacherous and cruel brine."

Passage for the travelers was engaged on the Malta for February second. Celia cried out bitterly, "I do not want to go! I dread the winter sea! I know it so well!" However, she knew their return was inevitable. Oscar was fretting that, with Cedric soon to be married, he would, for a while, be faced with full responsibility for both hotels at the Shoals. Celia knew, too, that her sons would need her at Kittery Point before the summer season at the Shoals claimed her also.

The necklace and bracelets worn on the visit to Browning are now in the Rare Books Collection, Houghton Library at Harvard.

16

PROBLEMS AND SEEKINGS
1881 - 1884

ON CELIA'S return from Europe in 1881, she found the Kittery house still in need of much to make it a livable home. Although invited to remain with her Boston friends, where she could resume her literary life and attend her husband's readings, she made frequent trips to Kittery. With the help of Minna Berntsen, she tried "to restore decency from the chaos of dirt and disorder which resulted from a succession of unsatisfactory housekeepers who had been unwilling to remain as servants for the two young men in their lonely situation."

Cedric Laighton was married in the spring to Julia Stowell, of Cambridge, and Celia was able to be at the Shoals to welcome them on their return from their honeymoon. With the coming of summer, she was torn between her duties on the mainland and the pleasure of reigning in her Appledore kingdom.

Now that Levi had become so much more widely known through his reading, his private life was suddenly of interest to his public. To some, their separate way of life was unconventional and therefore subject to criticism. This came to the attention of their sons by way of a letter about which John wrote his mother.

On July 3, 1881 she replied:

> . . . Send me the letter and let me see what it said. It is my most ardent wish to put an end to any kind of talk

to your father's disparagement if any such exists. I never hear of a breath or a whisper of anything of the sort and I only wish I could get hold of the person who spread such reports and keeps filling his ears with such wretched folly, such lies, such hateful nonsense. I would never neglect a chance of correcting anything disparaging to him or to any of you . . . It makes me so miserable I had rather be dead than alive. I cried all night and only wish I could get into the earth under the sod, where no one could accuse me. I want you to send me Mrs. Waldo's letter at once.

As soon as she was able in the fall, she moved into the Kittery house, and was almost overwhelmed by the physical labor involved in day-by-day living. She missed the daily servant she had always been able to depend upon at the Isles of Shoals. She found, too, that her own sons were not as self-reliant as her brothers had always been. Karl did all he could to help her with the household tasks. He lugged water from the pump to the built-in wash kettle. He kept a fire going under it. Still it is no wonder that Celia cried out after scrubbing a two weeks' wash for her young men:

. . . I am discouraged down to the very soles of my boots! So hard I strive to do the things which seem right and necessary — so hard fate strikes and strikes till I am blind with tears. How much harder does poverty make everything! I suppose we are each born to see how large a heartache we can carry and stand upright!

Her depression was lifted by visits from many of her friends. The DeNormandie family drove out from Portsmouth to see the new house, and greatly admired the beautiful farm, almost encircled by sea and creek. Julius Eichberg's pretty daughter, Annie, came to stay a while, much to the delight of the boys. Sarah Orne Jewett, the "Princess of Berwick," drove seventeen miles to see "Sandpiper," as she always called Celia. And while Celia mended and patched and worked at the endless deal of sewing, Childe Hassam arrived in October to see her and make a sketch of the house.

Roland, delayed in returning to college by an accident to his knee, invited his friend, John Storer of Cambridge, to come for a weekend of fishing and duck hunting. To Celia's horror, she saw them returning from the outing, "Stora's face streaming with blood, where both barrels of his gun had kicked back, causing a fearful irregular wound." John, realizing that help must be summoned, galloped off for the doctor, who lived two and a half miles away. The doctor returned and sewed up the wound. Since it was Saturday, however, there would be no train for twenty-four hours to return the young man home. Worry that he would be permanently disfigured added itself to Celia's other anxieties.

Levi, having secured a series of reading engagements in Boston and New Bedford, decided to share lodgings with his widowed sister, Lucy Titcomb, at 98 Charles Street, in the house of Mme. Monet. When Ronald was able to return to Cambridge, Celia remained at the farm with John and Karl, but made plans to visit Annie Fields, who was in mourning. James Fields had died after a short illness in the spring of 1881, and his loss had been keenly felt by both Celia and Levi. She had written wistfully to Annie:

. . . Brush the cobwebs out of your sweet eyes and don't shut yourself up! You should realize what happiness has been yours for twent-six years!

So different from her own troubled married life!

She wrote Annie again, trying to cheer her by describing the new farm:

Kittery Point, Nov. 15, 1881, 9 a. m.
. . . Karl's two little cats Tommy Tucker and Theodore Thomas are frisking about, the gray with a blue ribbon, the black with a scarlet one. Kate Wall's dog Punkapog, otherwise Punky lies at my feet and Silver by the open fire. It is squally dark out of doors, the sea and sky dull pewter color. I am busy putting the little parlor which leads out of this room in order — have got some carpets on the floor, hung some pictures, painted the fire-bricks and hearth red, made the brass andirons like gold, mended the sofa and am

going to re-cover the pillows — last evening I made a curtain, so pretty, for the window of two breadths of brown cotton flannel sewed together, hemmed at ends and a broad band of old gold color stitched at top and bottom nearly a foot from hem, sewing on the brass rings and now Karl has gone to straighten the brass rods we are going to arrange to hold it. And I bought an afghan of brown-green flannel for table-cover and piece of gold-green felt to stitch round for a border.

Over in Portsmouth, the other day I got such a lovely wide old armchair — it had no covering, so I got some, and brass nails and black gimp, and am going to cover it — it's a big job, but I shall accomplish it. O there's no end to the irons I have in the fire! and there's enough tailoring work on all these manly clothes to last me a year! to say nothing of stockings and under clothes to mend. But I hope to leave here the 30th of this month for your dear threshold. John means to have the pig slain the day after Thanksgiving and must be here to see about it, and the making of "sausage meat," etc. But hope to get off by Tuesday after . . . The boys do rejoice in my presence and Lony said when he was kept at home so long, he hadn't felt so infantile in his life — so much experience of Mother! So I am glad — John's birthday comes the 29th and I shall be glad to make it pleasant for him. Last year everybody left that day. . .

Nov. 12, 1881

Dearest,

I am weary of the wild and awful wintry sunrise. I love it not, its fires strike cold to my heart. I shall be glad to be in the center of human warmth, stir and interests. Yet I dread leaving these ill matched brothers to spend so many hours together. Everywhere, every moment there is needed a soothing hand to keep things straight. I am more than busy, hard at work all the time — no painting yet, only getting things nice and bright and straight as I can before I leave. I am pickling, preserving for the winter, mending and making all as snug and comfortable as I can. . .

Early Thanksgiving morning, as the sun peeped over the

ocean rim in a golden glory, Celia was getting ready to make pumpkin and mince pies. Suddenly she smelt smoke! It was pouring out of a crack in the floor, and the cellar was full of it. By the time she had awakened John and Karl and got the hired man from the barn, they found fire came also from the attic! They carried out the fire from the hearth and hacked away the bricks, disclosing a charred beam where bricks had been laid without insulation. It was a miracle that the whole house had not become a mass of flames, impossible to extinguish. But the beautiful room, which Celia had just finished painting and redecorating, was "water soaked, smoke-scented, trampled, with a gaping hole where the fire-place had been."

Their interrupted Thanksgiving over, Celia renewed her efforts to leave everything as homelike as possible for her sons. As the weather grew increasingly severe, they were almost completely cut off to the world and to Celia, it seemed, even more lonely than the Shoals. She wrote:

> . . . From the Island we looked to the land, but the view here is over miles and miles of mournful gray plain water . . . I worry especially for my little boy Karl. When they came to the Farm, his father and brothers promised to build him a little workshop of his own, where he could have his workbench and tools. But, while under the stress of other activities, this has not been accomplished. It kills me that this has been denied him. Especially as his eyesight is failing. He works patiently day after day making plans for an invention of his own, but no one but I seems to appreciate or care. Oh, if we could all have patience with each other! . . .

Well she knew that her father's temper had been inherited by her sons, added to their own father's tendency to despondency. The outlook seemed far from good.

She spent a few weeks in December with Annie Fields. She worked busily on orders for painted china and did her best to cheer Annie. They went together to hear one of Levi's readings at Mrs. Wilman's. Annie planned a Christmas dinner to which Mr. and Mrs. William Dean Howells and the T. B. Aldrich families were invited. She kindly asked John Thaxter to come also, which his mother urged him to do. This merry Christmas party was denied Celia, through the telegram from Oscar telling her of the tragedy which had befallen Minna's sisters, Annie and Ovidia Berntsen as mentioned before.

After depositing Ovidia at the insane asylum, the horror of the incident remained with Celia. She realized anxiously that Karl was to be left alone at Kittery! She left Boston again to spend Christmas with him. Instead of holiday cheer, she was greeted by an enormous bill for carpentry supplies which her "poor daft boy had contracted and which had been mounting for a long time." When she spoke to him about it "he fell into such a dreadful mood of wrath and despair" that she dared not think what might be the out- come. She decided to stay with him the rest of the winter. Having left her painting tools in Boston, she worked on making a horse blanket. She also tried to "grind out a love poem for a new illustrated journal, although in far from a romantic mood." The thermometer stood at 16 degrees below zero and the sea looked "like cotton-batting with a white column of vapor rising erect here and there, like the ghost of Hamlet, while the foghorn sounded hoots of warn- ing even in the clear cloudless day."

She wrote Annie:

> . . . Alas I dare not think of what must be the end of all this. It is a terrible night. We sit by the fire of wreck- wood and fear disasters upon the roaring sea, such a tumult of winds and water is awful to listen to. . .
>
> I am glad dear Owl is with you, I wish she would stay forever.

When Celia returned to Boston to visit the Eichbergs at 101 Pembroke Street, she dispatched part of her check from her publishers to John "to pay the girls' wages, but the gift must be kept an entire secret, because everybody talks about everything so." She goes on to beg John:

. . . not to make too much of little things and try to be
more kind to Karl and to remember that you, John, have
a balanced mind and your brother a crazy one. Poor
wretched, unfortunate fellow who has no chance in life,
and never will have one. He not only has a diseased mind
but a miserable diseased body and a complaint, so aggra-
vated and painful that it is alone enough to make him half
crazy. Be sure and exercise patience and forbearance, to
the furthest limit, it will not hurt you, John!

Her warning must have fallen on deaf ears. On January
25th, 1882 she received a telegram from John saying that
his brother was dangerous and should be put under restraint!
Celia caught the next train to Portsmouth and made her
way to the farm in a blizzard, without rubbers. She found
everything calm, with Karl tearful and penitent after the
quarrel. On January 27th she wrote Annie that she planned
"to take charge of him and help him to do some steady
work." Although he was as well as usual, the wild and unfortunate fit of passion might occur again, as she had long
feared.

Levi agreed with her that it was not yet a case for an
institution, although he was himself not able to cope with
the situation and preferred to leave it to Celia. He did find
rooms for her and Karl in the small, inexpensive and quiet
Winthrop Hotel on Bowdoin Street in Boston. Their quarters were five flights up, but with good light for her painting.
She "took the poor boy, to this sparrow's nest under the
eaves" where she could work and watch over him. Karl,
however, soon became homesick for Kittery, and was like
a fish out of water.

Levi's reading engagements were becoming very popular
and well-attended. They were a source of welcome income,
but they also took a toll of his always delicate health.

Celia continued working steadily. Although her heart
was heavy with problems, she was cheered by many visitors
who sought her out among her chimney pots. A call from
Mr. Whittier delighted her especially. Mrs. Wendell and

Mr. Paine came to see her. And everyone who came exclaimed, "What a lovely room! What a charming view!"

Roland, who had just recovered from diphtheria, was urged by his father to take a year off from his studies. From time to time there was an evening when they all attended the theatre, but not as a family unit. They saw the writer and actor, Joe Warren, and many other well-known actors of the period. Celia refused almost all invitations, devoting the daylight hours to painting and the evenings to writing, in an attempt to meet the overwhelming bills.

This pattern of life continued much the same through 1882 and 1883 — the farm in the spring and fall, the Shoals each summer. At last a good housekeeper was secured for the farm, when Annie Coleman and her little boy, Jimmy, moved into the house to remain with the family many years. With a new road from the village center, and a bridge to Cutts Island, Champernowne Farm became far more accessible.

Celia, through the years, was forever seeking some answer to the riddle of life and death. When she dropped a large anchor of ivy leaves on her mother's coffin it was a symbol of hope. She wrote Annie:

> . . . I hope all things, I believe nothing! The face of the sky is dreadful to me, I don't know when this terrible weight will wear away and I shall be able to bear the sight of the sun. . . The consolation of religion I cannot bear. I can bear my anguish better than their emptiness, though I am crushed breathless under my sorrow. It seems as if I could never fill my lungs with air again, as if I never wished to look upon the light of day.

Celia's devotion to her mother had in many ways taken the place of any set religious faith for her and the scar of grief remained with her. It forced her to face the inevitability of death and, eventually, to develop a sure stability and trust in a future life. Many of her poems had shown an awareness of God. Her earliest poems revealed her trust in a Heavenly Father, as when she held her little lantern, and waited alone for her father's returning boat, she could say in *Watching:*

> I will be patient now,
> Dear Heavenly Father, waiting here for Thee:
> I know the darkness holds Thee. Shall I be
> Afraid, when it is Thou?

And her best-known poem, *The Sandpiper*, ends:

> Comrade, where wilt thou be to-night
> When the loosed storm breaks furiously?
> My driftwood fire will burn so bright!
> To what warm shelter canst thou fly?
> I do not fear for thee, though wroth
> The tempest rushes through the sky:
> For are we not God's children both,
> Thou, little sandpiper, and I?

One of the greatest pleasures of her early married life had been listening to the sermons of the Reverend Theodore Parker and the brilliant Jewish-born Unitarian preacher, John Weiss. Then pressures and worries brought periods of doubt and of depression. In the long hours on the isolated wintry island, watching by the sickbed of her father, tending her beloved mother through the last years of helplessness, questionings and despair beset Celia. After her mother's death, she longed terribly to be as near her in the next world as she had been in this. Once, visiting the mother of her cousin Albert Laighton, who at 95 was bowed down by the loss of her four grown children, Celia had looked at the wrinkled face and bent form and begged: "Will you find my dear mother, if you can, and tell her I think of nothing but how I love her!" It gave her great comfort to send a message by someone "going through that same door out into the same road."

Perry D. Westbrook, in his book, *Acres of Flint*, gives an interesting study, "Celia Thaxter and Her Natural Religion." He felt "that because she lived so close to nature, she realized deeply the two-sidedness of the power which wrecked vessels and drowned their crews, but which could smile delightfully in a sunset or in the petals of an unfolding rose."

When Celia was forty-seven years old, a wave of interest in Spiritualism was sweeping New England, and she grasped at it. She had long sought to understand the mystery of death, and missing her mother as she did, was tempted to fall in with a group who were indulging in table tippings and Ouija-Board seances. She hoped, through means such as these, to establish some kind of communication with her mother.

In March 1882, she and her son Roland attended "a spiritual Jam-Jam for a lark and for scientific investigation" as she wrote John. She hoped she could receive a message from that mother who had died "babbling of green fields," which she had not seen for forty years. Would her mother speak through a medium, of the green pastures of the other world?

Out of her mounting interest in Spiritualism, she wrote Annie that a certain Rose Darrah had received a message from William Morris Hunt especially for Celia. It was: "Remember me to Celia, I know how lonely, how lost and hungry she is, but she is going to have very near communication with her mother, absolute tangible manifestations of her existence."

This was a very clever introduction bound to arouse Celia's intense interest. The thought that she would hear from her mother was all she needed and Madame Rose and her brother, Mr. Darrah, were urged to come to Appledore for the summer. At this time Celia was at low ebb, and had written that she wished she "could go — no matter how — I have had enough of this world!"

Now she grasped eagerly, with her usual enthusiasm, at the possibility of communicating with the next world. She prepared a little room in her cottage where she and Rose Darrah could sit together and "await experiences," which came to them as they spent long hours in the soft darkness.

Alexandan:
  "Here lie I Martin Elginbrodd
  Have mercy on my soul Lord God!
  As I would have been I Lord God
  And ye were Martin Elginbrodd!"

Isn't that a shrewd way of
putting it? Not irreverent,
surely, but an honest appeal
out of his own consciousness,
for the mercy which he would
gladly give to others,

        I hope the Shoals
paper will now go on & be
completed, while order
reigns in the "kitchen."

        With regrets for so poor
a letter I am — very truly
        & ——
                John G. Whittier

WHITTIER'S HANDWRITING: A LETTER TO CELIA

CELIA THAXTER'S COTTAGE, APPLEDORE ISLAND

INTERIOR THAXTER COTTAGE

Celia, convinced that some communication had been established, and that she had felt her mother's hands, wrote Annie Fields in strict confidence of these experiences.

Celia herself was evidently psychic, for she received many messages from various people. Weiss, who had died shortly before, called her by a pet name known only to them; Fields sent a message to his wife, and so forth.

"The scientists may call it mind reading, but we know better," she explained, and went on to tell Annie, in a letter dated June 27, 1882, that —

. . . Mr. Whittier came today. . . he was charming! I told him my tale. "Ah!" he said, "I knew something beautiful would happen to thee" . . . What a pleasure it is to talk to him. . . I am so glad, so glad. . .

In a letter to Annie dated Boston, September 26th, 1882, she described a visit to a Mrs. Philbrick, 25 Mt. Pleasant Avenue:

. . . We went upstairs to a little attic guest-chamber, all furnished in blue, she drew out a little common pine table — she had half a dozen light large slates. We sat down, two hands holding each other, two holding the slate. In a moment, raps! of all sorts each as different as human voices, all over the table. I thrilled. I was bidden to ask questions, and by the raps they were answered, who was there, then writing on the slate began vehemently, and no pencil in the room! Furiously writing and when it was ended the slate was pushed to me by no visible hands. It was from John Weiss. He said I was one of his dearest friends and helpers and that the great charity I had for him did him a world of good and so on. He touched me strongly on both arms and forehead and with an inexpressibly solemn and beautiful gesture bowed my head forward laying his whole hand upon it heavily. He said he depended on me to help him still, someone to dare to speak and help this truth that should so illuminate the world. I was almost wild with excitement.

Later Celia took Rose Darrah to the same place. Rose was frightened. Messages came from many special people, at last one from Hunt who said, "I shall never forget the Isles of Shoals, and that cold wave on which I went out! I always feel it when I come near you, every time."

Celia's enthusiasm brought her comfort for the time being, and the next year, in April, she could write from Kittery: "The pendulum will swing back into great joy from deep dark. I feel the old joy and elasticity of childhood once more!"

Partial disillusionment came after a few more experiences of Spiritualism. She was awakened to the dishonesty of some of the mediums when one of her sons concealed himself under a table and detected a hoax in one of the seances. She wrote a letter to Mr. Joshua Blake of Boston to thank him for a clipping and replying to a statement of his:

> . . . It seems a contemptible cheat doesn't it? But I had a long letter from someone else to whom I sent the same. He had held the frame of the slate on one side while "P" held the other. Three persons, above the table in the light, and writing came and answers to questions! But I don't know — I am inclined to doubt everything, and wonder if there is anything in mind reading, clairvoyance or what not.

Levi Thaxter did not share in any of his wife's Spiritualistic experiences, in spite of the fact that his friends John Weiss and William Hunt were among those from whom she seemed to receive messages. To Levi, as with Roland who was devoted to his father, science was always stronger than religion. Celia and Karl, however, were religiously curious. They read and studied together *The Bhagavad-Gita, The Light on the Path* and *The Perfect Way*. To Mrs. E. F. Waters she wrote November 16, 1886:

> . . . Karl and I are still the best Theosophists we know how to be, tho' he outstrips me every time and continually surprises me — we bless you who turned our faces in the right direction with great fervor.

Later she came under the influence of a young Hindu, Mohini Mohum Chatterji. His teachings gave her renewed peace of mind and happiness. She enjoyed the spell of his piercing eyes, and his reading of the *Song of Songs*. She wrote Mrs. Samuel Ward:

> Shoals, May 17, 1887
>
> . . . I am going to send you a photo of the young Hindu, the Brahman Mohini (Mohum Chatterji) whom we have had in Boston this winter, the most wonderful being ever dreamed of, I assure you. He is hardly to be described, but he spoke the words of angels and has been expounding the New Testament to eager listeners all winter . . . He is younger than my youngest boy, not 28. . . . All spirit, as impersonal as light, himself.

After dining with him at the home of Annie Fields, she wrote:

> . . . He is like a keen ray from the central sun, his words of fire burn not, but sere, fire that heats not, but lights the mind. . . I am become a humble and devoted follower of Christ. Now death is no longer dreadful, it has lost its terror!

Whittier wrote:

> . . . I have seen a portrait of Mohini, the young Brahman. He has a beautiful face. It seems like a spirit's. I hear that he told some of his agnostic hearers that they could have no guide and master better than Jesus Christ, and now some of them, I hear, have bought a bible!

As Celia and Karl read and studied together, the young man was moved and helped. Later she wrote:

> . . . I went to Trinity Church to hear Phillips Brooks. I was greatly struck with the fine aspect of the man, his noble port and presence, his earnestness, dignity and the purity that shines from his face, he has a magnificent head. There is something very moving in his headlong, almost boyish delivery, earnest and eager. For the matter of his sermon, it was just suited to the people to whom he spoke, no doubt the best things they could hear, but I fear it would never have moved my hard heart! After Mohini's wonderful penetrating, revealing speech, the sermon seemed like milk for babes to me, but I know it is impossible to judge in one

hearing and a man cannot carry such grandeur in his outward aspect, as does Mr. Brooks without a reason for it within. I said to myself all are here to worship God, it is no place for judgment, enter into the Spirit with which these people come together I looked about me reading the faces and I saw many things, among the rich and great who thronged the place. I also saw many with real devotion written on their faces. I was alone and it was very interesting.

Celia sometimes visited the women's prison in Boston, and read aloud to three hundred convicts there. She was delighted when Rachel Harlow put a Friend's Cap on her head. Always Mr. Whittier's simple faith had impressed her, and after his death she wrote:

> . . . I looked down at the cloak of a body he had thrown off, as a well used garment, which he had worn many years and which had, served him well, but which he no longer needed. I know he was safe with his dear ones, untrammeled, happy, that he could not forget us, and would be waiting with welcome. When our turn comes we will begin afresh to live with those we love!

In her last winters, while living in Portsmouth, she often attended the South Parish Unitarian Church where her close friend, Dr. James DeNormandie, was the pastor, but she never became a member of any church. She was able to arrive at a day by day happiness in which the "only worthwhile God-like thing is love!" This she expressed in her poem *The Heavenly Guest*, which interpreted the simple tale of Count Tolstoi, *What Men Live By*. This poem was published in St. Nicholas and it caught the simple belief by which she had always lived. The poem was never included in any of her volumes of books, until many years after her death when it was found in a portfolio which had been in the hands of her friend Sarah O. Jewett, with other of her later poems. These her brother Oscar edited and with clipping from a scrapbook in a volume entitled *The Heavenly Guest*.

17

LEVI L. THAXTER
February 1824 - May 1884

IT HAS OFTEN been asked what Celia Thaxter's husband did. How did he support a wife and three sons? What is more interesting is who were his friends and what were his interests? A summary of all one knows of him reveals a shy, scholarly man of vivid imagination, discriminating tastes, and great dramatic power. Throughout his life he read aloud in a manner to charm any listener. He was also interested in natural history in all its forms.

For the first few years of their married life the young Thaxters and the children were happy together. In their Newtonville home he took pride in introducing his intelligent young wife, his pupil, to the friends whom he enjoyed entertaining. It was hard for him to realize the fatigue of a young mother and housewife, with her many duties and small means. Though they enjoyed companionable evenings when he read aloud, he persistently put off the small, but essential household repairs for which she repeatedly asked, and which she was used to seeing her father and brothers accomplish readily. She missed him keenly when, after his shipwreck, he would not accompany her on her visits to the Isles of Shoals; but he patiently permitted her to stay if her parents asked it, for he was always devoted to his own father and mother. The senior Thaxters must have kept Levi supplied with what means he had, and he seems to have believed, if he thought of it at all, that the money would never run out.

Levi often taught his sons, the schools in Newtonville leaving much to be desired. He was a very strict teacher. Celia, in an early letter to Lizzie Hoxie, wrote:

> . . . Next winter we shall regularly set about Karly's education and a precious time we shall have of it, I expect. His papa hasn't any more patience than a teething boy, and of course will have everything his own way — I remember with a sort of agony being taught by him ages ago and faint in the prospect of seeing the children undergo something of the same torture!

When Celia was away, Levi Thaxter turned for companionship to his friends of similar age and tastes, James Russell Lowell, who was a cousin by marriage, John Weiss, and most of all William Morris Hunt were the ones to whom Levi turned in his loneliness. Hunt was his closest friend. They spent many hours together in the Newtonville house during Celia's absences at the Shoals and it was on one of these occasions that Thaxter, with difficulty, restrained Hunt from destroying the manuscript of his later-famous *Talks on Art*.

The artist often sketched from the doorway of the Thaxter house, a notable example being "The Bathers." This charcoal sketch and other drawings, together with three important portraits — one of Levi, one of young Roland, and a self-portrait — became possessions of the Thaxter family, along with Hunt's first designs for his famous frescoes in the New York State Capitol, which hung for many years in Celia's parlor at the Shoals. Annie Fields described William Morris Hunt as "one of the most dramatic characters who ever lived," and it is easy to understand why Levi was attached to him.

As a young man Levi's health was never good. Indeed it was the fresh, pure air which first drew him to visit the Isles of Shoals. Perhaps this lack of robustness is the origin of his apparently somewhat gloomy attitude, although he also possessed a keen sense of humor.

Early in the year 1869, Levi Thaxter suffered his first

serious attack of the illness from which he suffered for many years. The doctor termed it rheumatism of the chest. His ultimatum was that Levi must "flee for his life to a warmer climate."

Levi decided to undertake a journey to Florida. Since that winter he was teaching John, then thirteen, and Roland, nine, he determined to take them with him. He set out with the boys and school books to try to regain his health. In March Celia described their departure.

> . . . Did you know Karl and I are moored here for seven months? . . . Levi, Lony and John are gone down to Jacksonville, or rather to the state of Florida generally and promiscuously, with powder and shot by the ton, and arsenic and plaster ditto, and camp-kettle and frying-pan and coffee-pot and provisions and rubber blankets and a tent, and a boat, and three guns, and a darkey to be obtained upon arriving at Jacksonville, and heaven only knows what besides. They are to steam down to Enterprise and then take their boat on to the lakes at the end of the St. John's River, and then row back in their boat, shooting all the crocodiles, parakeets, mockingbirds, herons, flamingoes, white ibises and every other creature, feathered or otherwise that chances to fall in their way, until they stop in St. Augustine. . . . and in May stop for a while to examine the windfall of birds killed by the lighthouse in the spring, and then . . . . on to Nova Scotia or the coast of Labrador, still to pursue the unwary sea fowl and cure the skin thereof and bring it as a tribute to the feet of science!

In the second volume of his Journal, dated April 23, 1869, Levi describes the trip of father and sons, on their way to St. Augustine, seated in a sheltered corner of the deck of the steamer Darlington, Levi reading aloud to the boys and soon surrounded by a group of attentive passengers. When they reached port they mounted a stagecoach drawn by four horses with a trumpeter behind and started on the eighteen mile drive to the city of St. Augustine. Lony and his father enjoyed every moment, on the lookout for new wild flowers to add to their botany collection. Later after securing rooms at the inn, they went for a walk which Levi describes:

> . . . When we have refreshed ourselves with water and clean towels, we have a homely but comfortable supper with capital tea — and then emerge for a walk. Everything delights us. Narrow streets - balconies - walls - wicketed gates - gables - outside chimneys - little gardens - trees - flowers - swarthy Minorcans with foreign faces and accent, negroes, mule carts — the Plaza, the church and market, the sea wall on which we walk toward the old castle with its little corner watch turret — to the waterbattery outside where we lie down to rest awhile and enjoy the moonlight and high tide. Everything exhilerates us and so we return through the unfamiliar ways and lanes. I seem to be taking part in a comedy — only waiting for the call boy to summon me to speak my speeches in a scene where Don Diego and Inez shall figure with Lopez, Sancho, Dolores and the rest. Must I thrum a guitar and roll my eyes upward to that balcony on which Juanita with a high comb and much black lace shall come and lean down to me with answering sigh? Or, am I to stand in the shadow of that old wall breathing vengeance in a flop hat, cloak and top boots? Or to have a scene with a priest and be drawn within yon lattice gate above which I just make out the Cross and Sign Manual of the Church!
>
> John and Roland remind me that I am a Yankee father on a southern inspecting tour, and with recovered consciousness we pass up the street . . .

Levi's Journal continues, naming the flowers they saw, and birds they shot, and the old boarding house where they paid the outrageous southern price of $25 a week with meals.

He continues with his own musings, all written in beautifully expressed English, with a vividness and imagination that tells much of the man himself. He possessed great sensitivity and when Roland was taken very ill with an attack of chills and fever, Levi became depressed and alarmed with the responsibility of the situation. John was a great help and comfort to his father. He not only ran errands to the doctor, he even ventured to take his gun and go shooting by himself. The Journal continues:

> . . . John returned and presented his trophies. "There it is at last," he said, and produced a small unknown bird which may be the Tit-lark! This I skinned and cured, but Roland's condition made me feel very anxious. . . I tried to amuse him and myself too. . . I must say I suffered torments. To have a dear child sick at home with friends and sympathy at hand is bad enough, but far away among strangers, to have one sick with an unfamiliar and mysterious disease was to me terrible. I felt myself getting excited and unnerved. . .

Levi was always a most patient nurse. Celia described him to Annie when Mr. Fields was ill:

> . . . He is beautiful in sickness, gentle as a woman, with a born genius for the misses' work, and if you wanted anyone to sit with dear J to rest you, someone who would be so faithful, he would be glad to help you!

Father and sons returned north as soon as Roland was able, Levi wrote, "with much worry and some money." He found the Newtonville house "going to wrack and ruin." Celia was again at the Island. The Journal ends with a depressing description of the house, closed during their long absence.

> . . . There is a freshness nowhere during this long continued drought. Even the green along the river is meagre; but it is refreshing from contrast with the deadly dryness that has smitten this region as with a leprosy. Water lilies were tolerably plenty along the river's edge graceful as ever and sweet, their pure white petals opened wide for the glad heart of gold within to meet and embrace the loving sun. All plants are individuals to me and seem to contain a life that partakes of the human or is intimately connected with it. Nymphen I fancy to be upborne by a hand and arm of

human form, — grace of all graces — hidden beneath the
element in which they live. What is it Browning says? —
I have hunted it up in Paracelsus, my dear old yellowed copy
with brown paper binding.

> The peerless cup afloat
> Of the lake-lily is an urn, some nymph
> Swims bearing high above her head.

After this trip, there were three other expeditions, made
during later winters to Florida and Jamaica, interspersed
with part of the year spent "at home," if it could be called
such. During Celia's winter absences and all the summers
spent on Appledore with her parents, the husband and
younger sons shifted for themselves, partly through choice
and partly of necessity. For eight years Levi was more and
more alone, thrown back on himself, his thoughts and his
frustrations. William Ellery Channing well describes this
type of man:

> Poetry and contemplation was the only life for young men
> bathing in a sea of thought. They had a mania for nature
> and detested conventional ways. They talked of poetry most
> but also spiritualism, mesmerism and all dark problems.
> This emancipation from all that pertained to the serious
> business world or making a living led to fields and woods,
> where they would watch spell-bound the unfolding of a
> flower.

Levi did make a considerable contribution in the field of
ornithology. He and the boys collected specimens of all
birds found from Maine to Florida. They shot, skinned and
preserved one male and female of each, enough to fill a
huge seaman's cedar chest. This collection was given to the
Peabody Museum at Harvard.

Besides his love of nature and poetry, he had great appreciation of music. His pleasure in the opera is shown by
the following enthusiastic letter, lent me by the late Mr.
John Marquand and written to his grandmother, Mrs. Hoxie:

. . . The opera is over, and the troop departed southward

with the swallows. They were here glorifying this mundane existence for us, and suddenly they are gone. Only the blessed memory is left, and the hope of a May to come, brimful of ecstasies.

I was at the finale yesterday, to hear my beloved Stigelli. He is, you know, the German tenor, of the "Magic Flute." I liked him in that, but from liking I have developed a passionate admiration. "Der Freischutz" finished me! It gave me a new sensation and an excess of genuine youthful enthusiasm, that may be laughable to you, but which I embrace with rapture. A sexagenarian glowing with the fires of eighteen is willing to be hooted at. The opera was not very well sung, but the music was heavenly and with my beloved Stig in the tenor part, what shall I say! Even Celia with her preternatural powers of adjectives, could not set down any quite sufficient! I have heard it said that a "gin toddy went to the spot," I can only say that Herr Max has hit a spot in me, not very reachable.

The reference to Celia's descriptive power underscores his willingness and interest in assisting her along literary lines, especially in the preparation of her books for publication. He also took all necessary steps in securing copyrights, which were too often neglected in that period. Thanks to his diligence, royalties were paid to Celia, and later to her family annually, when any of her work was reprinted.

Annie Fields in the introduction to Celia's *Published Letters* says:

> The exuberant joy of her unformed maidenhood, with its power of self-direction, attracted the shy, intellectual student nature of Mr. Thaxter. He could not dream that this careless, happy creature possessed the strength and sweep of wing which belonged to her own seagull. In good hope of teaching and developing her, of adding much in which she was uninstructed to the wisdom which the influences of nature and the natural affections had bred in her, he carried his wife to a quiet inland home, where three children were soon born to them. Under the circumstances, it was not extraordinary that his ideas of education were not altogether

successfully applied; she required more strength than she could summon, more adaptability than many a grown woman could have found, to face the situation, and life became difficult and full of problems to them both. Their natures were strongly contrasted, but perhaps not too strongly to complement each other, if he had fallen in love with her as a woman, and not as a child. His retiring scholarly nature and habits drew him away from the world; her overflowing, sun-loving being, like a solar system in itself, reached out on every side, rejoicing in all created things.

Years before, Thomas Higginson, quoting in a letter to his mother, Levi's report of his wedding, added:

this I write you because you do not fully appreciate this strange and impracticable, but chivalrous and noble person, whose immediate future is hard and even sad to predict; whose past has been wayward and perhaps useless, but aspiring and stainless.

In the summer of 1879 Levi and all three sons spent the entire summer in the "Thaxter Cottage" on Appledore, to be with William Morris Hunt, who, broken in health and spirits, had decided to try to regain both in that peaceful spot. Arm in arm, the old friends walked and talked and spent pleasant hours together. On the evening when the U. S. Training Ship from Annapolis anchored in Gosport Harbor, Hunt and Thaxter sat late watching the gaiety and dancing, the pretty girls and the hundreds of midshipmen who swarmed over the island.

There were also long delightful afternoon and evening gatherings in Celia's parlor, where a chosen few congenial souls gathered for music, reading or long discussions. Levi contributed his share to these occasions by reading in his beautifully modulated voice, selections from Shakespeare or Browning.

At the tragic death of William Hunt, Levi took full charge, but the shock brought on the return of his old illness and marked the end of what had seemed the new-found happiness of the Thaxters as a family. Levi returned to Newtonville, determined to make the final, long-discussed arrangements for disposal of the property there. Henceforth his headquarters would be the Cutts Farm in Kittery Point which he had decided to buy for John.

In the spring of 1880, with the papers finally signed, he and John made plans to tear down the old house and rebuild. All through that summer his interests lay there and he readily agreed to the plan of Celia and Oscar taking their unanticipated trip to Europe in the fall.

When it became evident that the Kittery house was going to cost more money than expected to build, that the farm would need to be stocked and equipped, Levi found he needed more ready cash than was available. Remembering the success of friends' public appearances, the lecture courses of Emerson, Lowell and Fields, Hunt's talks on art, Levi Thaxter decided to attempt to overcome his shyness and try a series of readings himself. He had always admired the poetry of Robert Browning who, although gaining popularity in his own land, was considered unintelligible in the United States. Levi's keen mind seemed in perfect accord with Browning's. He seemed able to read even the most obscure passages in a way the average listener could understand and enjoy.

The first public reading he gave was in a small auditorium at No. 3 Park Street, Boston, in the Women's Club rooms. A newspaper review described the reading of *Pippa Passes* thus:

> Mr. Thaxter's reading of Browning is remarkable, his style is perfectly simple and straightforward, intelligent self-control. His voice is sweet, firm and of considerable range, his elocution clear, his pronunciation correct, and exquisitely cultivated. The source of Mr. Thaxter's peculiar power was his quick penetrating sympathy with the poet, and his poems and his perfect grasp and comprehension of their meaning. To read *Pippa Passes* in such a way as to convey its sense and comprehensibility to an audience in a hall, he performed

a real feat! No single shade was lost or blurred. Mr. Thaxter
has neither been equaled or approached as a great interpreter
of a great master!

This enthusiastic welcome and high praise encouraged
Levi to make other engagements. Several series of readings
were arranged during 1881 and 1882. He journeyed twice
a month to New Bedford where he was entertained over-
night by admirers. The still existent Thursday Morning
Club seems to have had its beginning with a meeting of a
few intimate friends to hear him. The meetings were soon
attended by the best of literary Boston. Comment is interesting on one program which included two verses of *Popularity, Italy in England, Garden Fancies, The Statue and the
Bust* and *Holber Hoh.*

> Thaxter made each line graphic, picturing the passions it
> portrayed, which were in vivid contrast to the subtle sweet-
> ness of Garden Fancies. The selections were made with dis-
> crimination and he rendered them with all the power or
> pathos, the verve and tenderness which each required, and
> his finely modulated voice gave the true dramatic effect.

Another review in speaking of the new mid-winter series
given in February 1882, says:

> . . . To be ten minutes late is like losing the entree dish at
> a banquet . . . Thaxter's natural strength makes artificial
> help unnecessary.

Only one adverse criticism has been found and it is
amusing in its Victorianism. This particular reading may
have taken place in the Hawthorne Room, directly over
Doll and Richards Gallery. It ran thus:

> April 1882
> To the Editors of the Boston Daily Advertiser:
> One critic who greatly admires and has long studied the
> poems of Browning and enjoyed Mr. T.'s interpretation, felt
> that *Pippa Passes* should not be read in its entirety to a mixed
> audience! Mr. T. is catering to a taste which he should be

the last to foster. The shrub-house scene is more indecent than books suppressed at the Public Library! Mr. T. should be forced to omit these lines by outraged public opinion! It would be impossible for a mother to take her son to such a reading! There are things intended to be done and not to be spoken of!

Thaxter's Diary of 1881 lists one series in Tremont, and goes on to mention other engagements at the homes of Mrs. Bowditch of Worcester, Miss Bedford, Mmes. Hall, Hemenway, Lockwood, Bricky and Williams. He noted that they brought in from $300 an evening, to one at Mrs. Wells' where only $15 was given or collected! These earnings seem small enough, especially when one realizes that he had lately bought the farm in Maine and built the house there.

Another critic wrote:

. . . One feels at once how sacriligious it would be to think that the desire for money was the main motive of the Thaxter readings! It is rather as if the reader were counting his treasures in the hope of sharing them with his listeners. Mr. Thaxter's quick modulation of voice from firm, fine appeal to the tenderness of eternity, is a perfect bit of nature. Each poem read, has been a faultless gem set in a few explanatory words.

During the winters of 1881 and 1882, when not at the farm, Levi lived in Boston with his sister Lucy. During the summers, however, he joined John at the newly-named Champernowne Farm. He took great interest in the progress of events — the spring cutting of ice on the pond, planting, haying, harvesting, in the herd which John was beginning to acquire. He enjoyed walking with his St. Bernards, Champernowne and Neata, and the little Skye terrier Punky, through the fields and the fine grove of oak and hickory trees near Brave Boat Harbor. He came to love the place intensely.

Celia refers in letters to two incidents which show that at

Kittery she and her husband regained some of the closeness they had lost.

Writing to Annie Fields she describes her arrival at Portsmouth from Boston, continuing:

> . . . Roland drove home, but Levi had arranged for us to be rowed five miles down the river and up Chauncey's Creek to within a mile of the house, then we walked together the rest of the way, and all was unexpectedly pleasant.

This was the same awareness of her love of a water trip which had prompted the arrangements for the long-ago row along the Charles River from Cambridge to Newtonville.

On another occasion Celia wrote to Eichberg:

> Oct. 4. 1882
>
> . . . This morning at four o'clock, Mr. Thaxter knocked at my door and asked me if I did not wish to look at the comet? I went to the window — such a supremely beautiful and wonderful sight! The East was a little red at the horizon, and through the morning twilight, steering headlong toward the sun, was this magnificent mysterious object, a round glowing orb, with a tremendous sweeping tail, taking up one third of the space of the sky, in view. Such a sight cannot occur more than once in a lifetime! . . .

She and Levi had enjoyed seeing it together.

The entire family spent a happy Thanksgiving in the new house in 1883, after which Levi returned to Boston to continue his public appearances. Before Christmas he was taken seriously ill again, with what proved to be his last illness.

Celia wrote to John:

> Winthrop House, Dec. 30, 1883
>
> . . . I go to see Papa every afternoon and would stay if Lony or Aunt Lucy would say the word, but they say there is no need — they know I am ready to come any minute. Lony said his father was getting along as well as could be expected. But he seems to suffer much, every little while. He is bright and cheerful, however, When he could be

JULIUS EICHBERG

EDWIN BOOTH AT APPLEDORE

SARAH ORNE JEWETT

LEVI LINCOLN THAXTER, AT KITTERY

GRAVE OF LEVI LINCOLN THAXTER
CONGREGATIONAL CEMETERY, KITTERY POINT

GRAVES OF LAIGHTON FAMILY

comparatively free from pain for a little, he wanted to know all the news and everything I could tell him. I hope he is going to get well soon. . .

Through the next five months Roland, who had been studying medicine, acted as nurse for his father, hardly leaving his side.

In January, Celia repeated:

. . . would gladly give up everything and stay with the invalid all the time if Lony would let me! But he won't leave his father just yet and promises to let me know if there is the least thing I can do — I go over and take him some flowers, or fruit or a book or something and sit as long as I can, till he is tired and ready to rest. Papa was delighted with the 3 wonderful crimson orchids which Frank Lee brought! . . .

Levi seemed to rally for a while, was able to sit up and walk around. Celia tried to learn the doctor's diagnosis, but wrote she could get little satisfaction. By February 13th he was forbidden to see anyone except members of the immediate family. Not even John's girl, Gertrude Stoddard, was permitted to see him, though she "brought some hyacinths and a big bunch of lilies of the valley." The flowers pleased him greatly, however. Through February and March Celia continued to write bulletins to John, and on March 9 wrote: "Papa hopes to be able to be moved to the farm."

Levi Thaxter took a turn for the worse, however. He died May 31, 1884, of the "chronic peritonitis" which finally affected the kidneys.

Following his request made years before, he was laid to rest "where the peaceful river meets the cruel sea," on a sunny bank beneath shading trees in the little Congregational Cemetery at Kittery Point. The spot is marked by an unshaped field boulder, brought from Champernowne Farm. On it were inscribed the lines written for him by Robert Browning, at the request of Roland Thaxter.

Thou whom these eyes saw never
Say friends true, who say,
My soul helped onward by my song
Though all unwittingly has helped thee too?
I gave but of the little that I knew:
How were the gift requited, while along
Life's path I pace, couldst thou make weakness strong:
Help me with knowledge for Life's old, Death's new.

R. B. to L. L. T. April 1885

On June 9, 1884, the following obituary appeared in the
Boston Advertiser. The author is unknown but it is thought
to have been written by Ignatius Grossman, the Hungarian
boy who had lived with the Thaxters in Newtonville.

LEVI THAXTER

The death of Mr. Levi Thaxter will be deeply felt by his
circle of warm and devoted friends. By the more cultivated
public of Boston and other cities, he was known and will
be remembered as the accomplished reader of Browning
from whom he drew his profoundest inspiration, and of
whom he was the most prominent interpreter in this country. Acquaintances will think of him as the courteous
gentleman whose distinguished presence made him notice-
able among all, while those who stood in closer relation
toward him must regard him as one of the most exceptional
persons whom it has been their privilege to meet. He
was a man of singular simplicity, but a born enthusiast,
a lover of beauty in all its forms; one of those true sons of
nature who feel her loveliness like a poet, and know her
secret as a naturalist. No image of him would be complete which did not include the delight he took in flowers
and the other tender growths of woods and fields. He
possessed unusual delicacy of taste and sentiment, combined
with great strength of character and a wide and ready
sympathy. He never stood mentally still, but was always
progressing and advancing. Those of the younger generation never felt themselves misunderstood or mistaken by
him; they knew that he was their friend and comrade,
that he entered into and sympathized with the feelings and

emotions which form the changing atmosphere from year to year. But the qualities which most set apart and elevated him were his absolute genuineness, his constancy to his ideal, his courage, patience and fortitude, his clear understanding of the real opportunities of existence, and his unrepining acceptance of the inevitable. In an age so largely characterized by display and pretentiousness, he was conspicuous as a hater of shams. He preferred in all cases the substance to the show. There was no brilliancy about his external fortunes or position, but he had brought his inward life to a degree of fulfillment and completion but rarely attained. His life taught a lesson, not loud, but deep, which will live always, an aiding and sustaining force, in the hearts of those he leaves behind.

18

LANE'S TURNING
1884 - 1887

IT WAS SHORTLY after her husband's death in May 1884, that Celia wrote to Annie Fields that she was back at the Shoals and working hard in her garden.

> I am out of doors all day, doing the things I love best, sleeping soundly and am better in body than I have been in years. I wish summer could go on as peacefully and that I could continue in my old clothes. I am truly dreading the coming of people to the hotel. Can it be that at last my long lane has found a turning?

From this time until her own death, ten years later, the tone of sadness and despair which had in the past so often entered into her writing is completely absent.

During the summer season she was surrounded by innumerable friends and admirers. One provided this description:

> Her downrightness was like lavender and she found life worth living, friends worth cherishing and duty worth doing! At fifty her brown hair was fast yielding to gray, but her dark blue eyes were kindly and responsive and the pose of her head was exquisits! . . . She loved the beautiful days of September, after the crowds had departed when with her brothers and the sea gulls, she could recapture the peace of the islands.

As autumn advanced she went to Kittery and visited the farm, where John, who was becoming well established, had been able to acquire more equipment and stock for his dairy. He was selling his unsalted butter in Boston. She had feared he might be lonely but his cousin, Ellery Jennison, had bought a large tract of land on Gerrish Island and the two young men rode their horses back and forth to spend the evening with one another. Roland continued his medical studies at Harvard.

For three more years Celia and Karl spent the winter months in the small Boston hotel. Karl had become interested in photography and was working on an invention of his own, and on a hand printing press. Celia, at her fine old desk, worked tirelessly at writing or painting. This was the only way she could afford a few new clothes, she said.

Through one winter she devoted most of her time to painting, to fill the orders for her porcelain cups and plates. She asked Thomas Bailey Aldrich "which design Lillian would most enjoy — a bunch of violets or a branch of peach blossoms; a Roman anemone or an autumn cluster of crimson woodbine, a dried poppy head or red rose haw, with a sad verse burned into the porcelain, or perhaps a green peacock feather?" Her friend, Helen Choate Bell, chose a delicate blue cornflower for her cup and saucer and was enthusiastic over it. All of these patterns were painted with great delicacy, born of Celia's intimate knowledge of flowers and plants. After the painting was finished each of these pieces had then to be sent or taken to the kiln in Boston for firing before they could be delivered to the buyers. Celia never attempted to do the firing herself.

In 1885 she and Karl moved into the Hotel Clifford on Cortes Street, a much more desirable situation. Before her husband's last illness Celia had begun to take painting lessons from a young artist, Ross Turner, but they had to be abandoned after seven lessons. However, she arranged for Mr. Turner to come to the Shoals in the summer and later she invited him to make a visit to Kittery Point. She wrote:

I have made ready a room, looking at the sunset, with three

windows and plenty of light and brought driftwood from
the beach and laid a fire ready to kindle in the open fireplace. I am dying to look over your artistic shoulder . . .
making heavenly sketches. I want to see you transfer the
prospect to a sheet of paper!

During the winter of 1884-1885, she resumed her lessons
with Turner at 48 Boylston Street. Her lessons and friendship with the young man were a great source of pleasure
to her and she called him "her grandson." They often attended musical programs together and she was instrumental
in having him meet some well-known people in the musical
and artistic fields who were her friends. On one occasion
she took him to the home of the violinist Ole Bull to meet
Vulf Fries and view the wondrous collection of violins, some
four hundred years old. She was delighted when she heard
of Turner's engagement to Miss Louise Phelps, and wrote
to his fiancee, March 13, 1885:

. . . May I call you Louise? I have a kind of feeling as if
I had always known you, and everything about this whole
matter seems so sweet and natural and well-established,
just what should have happened — just what could not
help happening!

I send you these little books of mine and I hope you
may find anything therein to give you pleasure. I feel
about them as if I would fain weed out of the volumes
the greater number of the poems and leave only, perhaps,
about twelve of them, which may be worthy to stand and to
live. But there they all are at your service.

You and Ross are the best poem I have read for many a
long day! I always feel as if the happiness of my friends
were my own, and I am sure there is not one in all your
lover's circle of warm friends who rejoices more sincerely
in your joy than I. How heavenly to be so happy! The
old, ever new, delicious story! don't you both feel as if
God has made it for the first time, for you alone? Do
realize fully every golden moment of this time, for nothing
so divine ever comes again in life! Every kind of good
thing may come, but not precisely this, this wondrous, holy,

unutterable joy. For the soul reaches its full height and has a fortaste of Heaven, a glimpse of the Infinite, a sense of the nearness of God . . .

Celia had been almost a child when she herself had experienced the feelings she described, but the memory of her joy had survived tribulation and heartbreak, and was, in reality, a tribute to the man who had so moved her youthful heart. Now that he was gone this memory of joy, rather than the heartaches, were most vivid to her and she could still feel the beauty of romance. She wrote to Turner on March 20, 1885:

. . . How beautiful your speech grows when you mention her! It makes me think of your pictures, something one finds in them, something clear, something strong, serene and true. You mention her golden qualities of heart and mind. . . . Ah me, were such a daughter to be mine, what joy, repose and comfort in the thought of such a one . . .

Although she did not attend their wedding ceremony, Celia continued to follow Ross Turner's career, and was worried when he moved from Boston to New York, fearing he might become lost in the larger city. Turner and his wife came to love the Shoals where a few years later a studio was built for him near Celia's own cottage.

Celia possessed empathy and identification, which made her enter into the lives of her friends, their joys and sorrows. She felt their emotions as strongly as if they were her own. Some years earlier she had written her cousin, Albert Laighton, trying to encourage him to make more of his verses by asking him to criticize one of her own poems. Sending her poem, *The Pimpernel*, in 1882, she wrote:

. . . I have copied something for you with this beastly steel pen; I never use one if I can help it — it stops my thoughts! I always use a quill which walks itself over the paper. This pimpernel — the peculiarity of the flower — it closes its petals before a storm always, you know; it grows profusely at the Shoals. I have only just finished

the poem and it will probably need much touching up —
now don't you want to criticize me? This is by way of
opening the ball, you know. I hold you to your promise to
send me something of yours straightway, so I begin. Do
you see? You dear fellow, you are in a kind of enchanted
sleep in this slumberous old city, like the Sleeping Beauty
in the wood, and I am a kind of fairy Princess to break
through the hedge and wake you up with a good shaking!
Do you know what you must do? Cherish your delicate
fancy, — yea, in spite of bank and business — you can
and you must. Don't push your divinity out in the cold,
the goddess that would fain abide with you! Put into shape
your last idea, I beseech of you, my dear cousin, and let
me have it forthwith. I give you my word not to let any
eyes save my own behold what you write. It shall be
sacred and I will tell you the truth about it according to my
light.

God bless you and yours, my dear cousin. Let me hear
from you soon and believe me always. . .

On a later occasion she wrote him, "How come on the
verses?" When he sent her some she at once replied:

. . . Your poem is truly, wholly and altogether beautiful,
and I don't see a thing to alter in it. . . . I admire it with
all my heart! How can you do such lovely things, shut
up in that sunless, airless, colorless place! You are a wonder. I send it back to you the very first opportunity. I
wish I could do anything half as good.

Later she suggested the change in one line of a certain
poem, and then advised that he send it to The Independent, who would give "five or ten dollars for it."

Before returning to the islands in the spring of 1886,
Celia wrote John a letter, encouraging him with his business and promising to do her best to persuade his uncles
to order some of the "fancy butter" which the young man
was making in his newly built stone dairy. When his
price of thirty-five cents a pound seemed too high for
the hotel menu (the Laighton brothers were currently

paying twenty-two cents), Celia suggested that John sell her some, which she would share with friends at her own table, and perhaps some of the "nabobs" would then order it personally from him. Then she wrote him a motherly sermon.

. . . Don't be unkind and unpleasant to your brother Lony, if he throws cold water on your ideas, he knows how Papa strove to save and feels you are inclined to spend too freely. When your resources are small, a half dollar here and there on unnecessary things is so hard to earn and so easy to spend! His instincts are toward saving a penny, when yours is to spend it. — Do be nice at meals; don't bring your grievances to table; if you only knew how dreadful it was for those who listen!

The next morning she wrote again, regretting her frankness and fearing she had hurt his feelings:

. . . I don't want you to think me unreasonable in speaking of your tendency to be more open-handed than Roland. Your nature is like Uncle Oscar and Lony's like Uncle Cedric. Dear boy, don't be aggrieved with your brother who is the most faithful friend you could have. I did not mean to say you were extravagant, but inclined not to be so provident, that's all!

How well she knew that pennies as well as dollars were hard to accumulate!

Her garden on Appledore was an increasing joy, but the birds disturbed her. She wrote Annie Fields:

Shoals, May 21, 1886
. . . How are you in your sweet loneliness? I think of you in that beautiful place, the place you have made so beautiful, and of your quiet and peaceful days and all your lucky doings with such pleasure! For me I am in such a busy time just now! All day long every day, beginning at 4 in the morning, out of doors, getting browner and browner, till nobody could tell me from my thievish song sparrows except by size and shape! Those beloved pirates! They

left me not one seed in the ground, but like the wise virgins, I wasn't without oil, so to speak! for I had boxes and boxes of things started and growing vigorously and I found I had so many more sweet peas than I thought that I am all right unless the wily wallowing cutworm attacks them from beneath, as the sparrows did above. Such stacks of things I have set out! Two beds full of pansies and sweet peas by the hundreds and cosmos and scabiosa and pinks and nasturtiums and myriads of scarlet phloxes and all sorts of things. The birds gobbled all my sunflowers except the few I had in boxes, Japanese and others, they made the cleanest sweep!

Never mind. Now, I strew crumbs and things for them to eat, so they'll leave me alone, and if I ever plant again I'll get a bushel of grain and scatter outside the garden for them. For I love and adore them in the face of all their thieving. How should they know, the dear things!

She described the rescue of one of her beloved birds:

. . . This morning a little after 3 I was wakened by the distressed cry of a sandpiper. I knew the dear creature had a nest in the reservoir toward which and over which one of my windows looks. I sprang up and looked out, sure enough round the brick parapet was stealing a hideous three-legged cat who got here nobody knows how and has grown wild, a terror to the birds, and we can't catch her. I saw the sandpipers distractedly flitting and piping. Everything was rosy with dawn and the sea a mirror. I threw on my dressing gown and not even stopping for stockings, slipped on my shoes, downstairs and out of the house, round the piazza, up through the green space and clustering rose and bayberry bushes, over the low fence, on to the broad low wall of the reservoir, round which I ran, at the edge of the still water, to the ledges on the other side where the tragedy was going on. I scared away the cat and the wise sandpipers stood watching on the highest part of the rock and ceased their shrieks of terror and peace descended upon the scene. The sun was yet some time below the horizon — but such a rosy world! It was heavenly, the delicate sweet air, the profound stillness, the delicious color — I quite forgot I was nearly 51, and why I didn't get my death of cold the Lord he knows, I didn't! I am a garrulous old woman. How swiftly went Mr. Whipple! How fast we fly, one after another! Who next, I wonder! Did I tell you my cousin Albert Laighton is dying of cancer, exactly as Mr. Thaxter went? Could we be but spared such lingering torture! Heaven give us swift release.

The same love of birds and her wish to spare them from senseless slaughter for the adornment of women's hats made her an active member of the Audubon Society and secretary for Appledore.

The summer of 1886 was not a successful one for either of the Laighton hotels. Celia wrote a troubled letter to Annie on June 28, 1886:

. . . I am sorry for this dry, sullen storm, no drop of rain, only black skies which keep all the people away — so much money going out to cooks, waitresses, chambermaids, fishermen, porters, bell boys, watchmen, bookkeeper, room clerk, carpenters, housekeeper, steward, captain and crew of steamer, myriads of subordinates all necessary to keep this big machine running, all being paid full wages, and nothing coming in. The storm of ten days or a week has made hundreds and hundreds of dollars difference to O. and C. You know their debt is a peculiar one, they owe no creature a cent except this one big thing, they have the greatest horror of debt. But they were able to get Star Island by the joining in their business of a cousin of ours, who became part of the firm with the agreement that he should leave it any time if he wished. So year before last he left, and they had to take it all and they owe him nearly a hundred thousand dollars, trusting to pay it little by little, year by year. But it keeps everybody so pinched and anxious, my little sister (in law) with her little ones has to be so rigidly economical and Cedric would be so glad to have it otherwise!

O, did I tell you I have a book of about fifty poems going through H. and M.'s hands, to be called the *Cruise*

of the Mystery and Other Poems. Half of them are love
songs, a new departure for me, but they have grown out of
the various experiences I have witnessed the human race
going through, from my corner here. One belonged to
Rose Lamb! But nobody knows which belongs to who, and
nobody can guess! Then I am in the midst of the 24 poems
for Wide Awake art prints, which nearly crack my small
skull, it is so difficult to circumvent their impossibility. H.
gives me two hundred and fifty dollars for them, but five
hundred would be cheap when the headaches I get from them
are counted.

John's interest in Mary Gertrude Stoddard had continued. On the night of their original meeting the special
delicacy at dinner had been mussels. John, who had beautiful teeth, bit on something hard while eating them and
broke a molar. The offending object turned out to be a
large and perfect pear-shaped pearl which he announced
his intention to keep. Several years later, his mother wrote
that she had earned a few extra dollars and he "could
now have the pearl set to give to Gertrude." This he did,
but he found the young woman reluctant to give up the
comforts and cultural activities of a city for the beauties
of a remote Champernowne Farm. At length, however,
she consented and on June 1, 1887 Celia journeyed to
Worcester, Massachusetts, for the wedding.

On June 15, Celia went to Cambridge for the wedding
of Roland and Mabel Freeman. The girl had long been
a close friend of Roland's cousin, Katharine Jennison. He
had graduated cum laude from Harvard in 1882 and was
now working at the Connecticut Agricultural Experiment
Station in New Haven. This was the first to be established
in the country! The young couple were to begin housekeeping in New Haven, Connecticut.

The Kittery estate had been held jointly by John and
Roland since its purchase, but after the death of their
father, the brothers had decided to make a division so
that each could hold land of equal value. John retained

the house and barn, the pasture and tillable land, while Roland's share included the beach, the oak grove and half of the ocean shore front. On his part, Roland built a house, to be the home of his aunt, Lucy Titcomb, for her life, but which he and his family could share with her during his summer vacations from teaching. Kittery was more accessible now, as the York Harbor and Beach Railroad ran four trains daily from Portsmouth to York Beach with a station at Kittery Point and a flag stop at Bedell's Crossing, near the northerly pasture of the farm. This and the New Road along Chauncey's Creek to Sea Point Beach, made living conditions vastly easier for the young men and their wives than at the time of the original purchase.

With both her younger sons well established in their chosen professions and homes, Celia at last, with a clear conscience, could choose where she and Karl would spend their time.

19

GOLDEN DAYS AT APPLEDORE
1880 - 1890

ALL SUMMER seasons at the Appledore hotel were much the same from year to year during the last decades of the nineteenth century. They began about the middle of June, preceded by three months of full-speed activity. Celia, whenever possible, left the mainland in March, laden with boxes of seedlings to be transplanted into her garden. She worked there daily, preparing the soil, planting and transplanting, surrounded by the furious hum of preparations for the hotel's reopening. She did not move into her own unheated cottage until the weather was warm, but stayed with her brother in the sturdy house built by their father.

As of old, she helped oversee the work of opening the hotel. This was an enormous task since everything was put away during the winter months. With spring, it all must be taken out, cleaned and put back into place. The spring cleaning was done by Norwegian girls from Smutty-nose, in addition to those employed by the family during the winter. The floating stage for the wharf was towed out from Portsmouth and put in place, the boats painted, calked and fitted out. About June fifteenth, the hotels were officially opened and the steamboat connecting with the trains from Boston began its trips.

A few families who came each season over a period of time, bought land on Appledore on which to build their own cottages. On these, gangs of workmen were often busy hammering, sawing and shouting as the structures progressed. The Warder cottage was built on the hill fronting the Thaxter cottage; Ross Turner's studio and Karl's workshop were somewhat behind Celia's. Cedric's comfortable new house was nearest the shore and Sandpiper Beach. The gardens of the sisters-in-law were separated only by a rustic fence and flowers "spilled over" from one garden to the other.

The Appledore House now consisted of three sections connected by wide, long, covered piazzas. Here was a row of large wooden rocking chairs where the guests could sit and look out over the well-kept lawn and tennis courts, the rich borders of flowers. Beyond this a boardwalk led to the pier and dock, where the steamer brought passengers, supplies and mail twice daily. All around stretched the blue sea, with the coastline from Cape Elizabeth in Maine to Cape Ann in Massachusetts, visible on a clear day. When the sun went down behind the distant hills of the mainland, the warning beacon would stream across the water from the White Island lighthouse.

Many of Celia's poems had been set to music by Eichberg, Paine and others. A universal favorite among them was *Goodbye, Sweet Day*. On Appledore then, as on Star Island now, assembled friends and guests would join in singing this beautiful song as the sun disappeared behind the New Hampshire hills.

The evening mood at the hotel was anything but quiet and sober, however. Guests always dressed for dinner, to which they were summoned by the band playing tunes from Gilbert and Sullivan. Wines were enjoyed.

Afterward guests dispersed over the rocks, through the parlors or to the billiard room. Many jokes and pranks were played by the oldtimers. On one occasion two of the artists, Childe Hassam and Appleton Brown, greatly annoyed a most temperate fellow artist, Levi's cousin,

Ellen Robbins, by sneaking into her studio and filling her Franklin stove with empty champagne bottles. She was not amused when, the next damp day, she tried to light her fire and was choked by smoke.

Sailing was a pastime especially enjoyed by the guests, who found there was always a light breeze blowing from some direction. Each morning the sun shone on a small fleet of yachts and pleasure boats anchored in the Roads of Gosport Harbor. The yachtsmen at that time dressed in the grand manner, wearing white duck trousers and striped turtle neck jerseys, with full beards or handle-bar mustaches. The wide-brimmed straw hats of their lady companions were tied on against the wind with chiffon veils. These hats were to protect soft complexions from the burning rays of the sun, for this was a day when a sun tan was unthinkable. The older ladies, who very carefully chaperoned their daughters, wore tight-fitting basques, buttoned straight down the front, and their skirts trailed the ground.

Ladies also carried fringed parasols when they ventured to wander along the shore path by day, among the wild roses and beach peas. For the many invalids who visited the island, a little carriage was provided in which they could make the mile long trip from end to end of Apple-dore. There were rustic summer houses placed at spots where the views were most beautiful and the romantic settings inspired much reading of poetry and decorous love scenes.

A small swimming pool had been created in Babb's Cove, in front of the hotel piazzas, and there the more daring young ladies swam, using water wings which had to be blown up each time they were used. Their bathing attire was elaborate. They wore long black stockings beneath a black alpaca bathing suit with baggy bloomers. Over this, buttoned on at the waist, was an ample skirt which reached to the knees. The neckline was high to

Prof. Roland Thaxter with Bobbie

Mary Gertrude Stoddard

JOHN THAXTER

MARY COWDEN CLARK IN GENOA

the throat, the short sleeves were puffed, and the whole was tastefully trimmed with white braid. Celia Thaxter, herself, never conformed to any set fashion in dress. She always wore gray, black or white in a soft material, made in a way to set off her good figure. A soft white fichu usually completed her costume. Even when she became extremely heavy — she weighed 236 pounds when she was fifty-two — her carriage was so fine that her weight was not unattractive. Far from unaware of her own good looks, she knew how to set them off to best advantage.

In the best years, more than five hundred persons were housed on mile-long Appledore Island, a total made up of guests and the large number of employees needed to keep the huge plant running smoothly. With his uncle's help, Karl had equipped the hotel with a new system of bells to and from all the rooms and the office. Oscar gleefully announced that "all a guest need do is press a knob and you have everything you want no matter how rare, strange or remote". The bootblack, "shod with silence," would steal up the stairs to gather shoes at the sleepers' doors — just as Celia returned from her early labors in her garden, laden with flowers to arrange in her parlor.

On August 22, 1882, she wrote Annie Fields:

. . . The summer scampers. It is harder for me to write than for a rich man to enter the Kingdom of Heaven. This is a hard bright Sunday morning. We have been six weeks without a drop of rain. My garden dies daily for I may not water it, the supply is so short that we fear having to send to the land for this great family of 500 or more or less. Last night 'twixt 12 and 1 midnight, I was wrestling with the hose trying to save my garden with a little drop . . . I save all bath water and carry it to my garden. . .

My Roland's injured knee is improving. I went to the Farm and got him over here. I sit at my painting table at work and he lies outside on a couch with pillows within reach of my hand. He hears all the lovely music.

On the morning of her forty-eighth birthday, June 30, 1883, she "treated herself to a lark!" She made a five o'clock visit to the bakery to see the tricks which the bakers "in spotless linen and funny caps" were accomplishing with the "snowwhite, almost aerial sensitive mass of dough." The little rolls which they turned out she had never seen equalled at home or abroad! Well she remembered the early days of the hotel when she had helped her mother to make "bushels of doughnuts and mountains of sponge cakes" day after day for the hungry guests. She sighed to herself, remembering she had "lived nearly half a century!"

In her own cottage a greatly enlarged parlor was made into "the loveliest gray-green bower with an apple blossom border". This room was a gathering place for the talented and interesting people who considered it a privilege to be allowed to enter quietly and sit for hours surrounded by the beauty created by the artists and musicians assembled there. This charming room had long sofas and easy chairs, all upholstered in olive green — comfortable furniture on which Celia's friends could sit and listen to music, conversation, story telling, or the reading of poetry. In this room every inch of wall space was covered with framed pictures, most of which had an association of some kind with the quiet woman who sat at the desk busy with her china painting. There were sketches in watercolor, oil and pastel, many of which had been painted within a few feet of where they hung. J. Appleton Brown's pastels of sunset and moonrise especially caught the spirit and feeling of the spot. There was also an oil painting by him of Celia's garden, which gave a glimpse of the sea over the tangle of flowers and vines, with a corner of the piazza. Ellen Robbins' colorful and exact watercolors made roses, poppies and yellow buttercups bloom indoors as well as out. Childe Hassam contributed his watercolor sketches of White Island Lighthouse and his more daring oils of rocks and sea.

Many friends had sent her photographs of the famous places in Europe which they wished to share with her, all these were hung around the room. Standing on the floor and easels were watercolors, oils and pastels painted by artists who hoped for a sale.

"No large social success was ever achieved upon such unwordly conditions, "Annie Fields wrote in her introduction to the *Letters of Celia Thaxter*. "She saw as much as any woman of her time of large numbers of people, and was able to give them the best kind of social enjoyment."

Aside from Annie's own gatherings in Boston during the winter, there was no similar salon anywhere else. Celia's circle had included at some time almost all those who were best known in literary and musical circles. Lowell, Emerson, John Fisk, Holmes, Hawthorne, Longfellow, Whittier, the Fields, Sarah Jewett, Sam Clemens, William Dean Howells, Thomas Bailey Aldrich were among the literary figures. Annie reported that Celia, herself, "read well, with an exceptionally beautiful voice which completely satisfied any ear."

Often Beethoven sonatas were played on the grand piano in her parlor by John Knowles Paine and William Mason. For Bach trios, they were joined by Eichberg, Ole Bull or Van Ronte on their violins. Frequently they were accompanied by Frank Jackson's fine tenor voice. These were "mornings and evenings of delight!" On one occasion a Mrs. Osgood made a great impression singing the solo from a Greek chorus. Her excellent voice drew all the people from the hotel across the lawn. They crowded around Celia's piazza and garden until every place was full. This was very unusual, because Celia was very careful that only her especial and invited friends should invade her sanctuary.

The summer residents and hotel visitors used to watch and admire her, but very few knew her personally. She spent much time and thought as friend and adviser to others in the literary world and while she enjoyed this, the strain told on her.

One of her letters to Annie tells of the involvements:

> . . . I am in the vortex of Shoals' life just now, hardly have strength to meet the demands of every day. I wish I could tell you of the lovely weather and charming people all about me. John's old friends from Southborough, Mass., Grandfather Burnett with one of Mabel's children, Jo, the image of his mother and so picturesque that he was a "fascinating object to behold." Also Ellen and Robert Bancroft from Beverly. There is a Dr. Keating here, from Philadelphia, who is, as the girls say, "just too charming for anything". French, about sixty, distinguished looking, with such a charm of manner, that all the female sex, old and young, acknowledge his fascination, so that Jo Burnett christened him "The Heartbreaker". He is very different from his friend Dr. Ford, whom I think heavy and pompous, a hopeless bore! Edwin Booth the actor was a frequent visitor.

The author, John Albee, and his friend, Edmund C. Stedman, sailed over from New Castle and talked enthusiastically with Celia about Annie Fields' latest book, about her famous husband. From York Harbor came Cora Rice and Eva Channing, and there was a Dr. Foote from Springfield, Kennie Kerly, Joanne Roche, Mrs. Angiero and many others. Charlotte Dana, sister of Richard H. Dana, used to delight the company with negro songs, accompanied by her guitar, even when she was confined to a wheel chair, pushed by her niece, Rosamond Dana Wild. Mr. Winch's favorite solo was The Wandering Wave.

The Sam Ward family, from Boston and New York, became close friends. Mr. Ward, an artist himself, took great pleasure in Celia's parlor with her beautiful and unusual arrangements of flowers. "Every rose is a study," he told her, "you ought to go about and teach the world!" The room blazed with sunflowers, small with dark centers, which were very effective. There were banks of crimson

and purple sweet peas, bowls and baskets full with light
green festal clusters of hop vine to set off their vivid hue!
There were flowers everywhere on tables, mantels and
windowsills. Tall cylinders with graceful poppies, blue
bowls heaped high with red roses, great masses of yellow
nasturtiums all made an indescribable wealth of color.

With September, one by one, the guests took flight.
Those who had cottages, the Hincklys, Andersons, Woods,
Frankles and the Wards, remained for a while after the
hotel closed. Celia's parrot Polly, hung on the piazza,
would whistle hilariously and loudly, while Celia sat in
her dismantled room where everything was stripped from
the walls for the winter. Only her desk and chair and one
picture of sunflowers were left. Yet she felt this was almost
the best part of the year, for she loved the sweet quiet,
the solitude of the last lingering golden days of Indian
Summer with the brilliant crimson bushes and seaside
goldenrod.

20

FRIENDSHIP WITH WHITTIER
1867 - 1892

THE ACQUAINTANCE of Celia Thaxter and John Greenleaf Whittier dated from the winters she lived in Newburyport. However it was not until the summer of 1866, following the death of her father, that their close and life-long friendship began. That season Whittier was a guest at Appledore House and they spent many hours together. Their correspondence shows an understanding sympathy which gave comfort and happiness to both. Through the years when life held changes and sorrows for them, Whittier increasingly cheered and encouraged Celia.

She always regarded him as New England's greatest lyric poet, "with a genius which burns clear and stands alone!" She wrote early to a friend "Mr. Whittier is the most charming man that ever was." On his part, he wrote on October 20, 1867 to Harry Fenn, preparing him to meet Celia, that she was "fearless, open, sweet, unrestrained, with a modest, refined manner in conversation".

Many letters were exchanged during their lives, and although some were destroyed, a number have been preserved. Those kept by Celia's family, a collection of only eighty-three, were given to Harvard's Houghton Library.

The first, dated New Year's Day 1867, is written on the back page of a note from his niece, Elizabeth Pickard. Whittier wrote:

> . . . I take the spare page to wish thee and thine a very

happy New Year! My sister and I often talk over the incidents of our pleasant sojourn on the Island last summer,
and the pleasure one derived from thy acquaintance. Where
is that paper for the Atlantic upon Star Island and its
inhabitants? Pray let it be forthcoming. If it is only half
as good as thy verbal account of that remarkable settlement
it will be worth reading. . . .

As Celia's great preoccupations, aside from literature,
were her mother, her eldest son and all that concerned the
sea, the flower and bird life on her island, so Whittier,
the Quaker, was chiefly concerned with his faith, his nieces
and invalid sister, and the cause of Freedom. He was
born a country boy, on a rocky New England farm, and
the memories of those early days behind the plow, or
tending the steaming cattle on snowy winter mornings,
the schoolhouse by the road, or the well-loved school-
mate — all appear in his best-known poems. The years
before he came to see much of Celia were largely devoted
to espousing the cause of abolition.

By 1867, when their close friendship began, the War
Between the States was over and Whittier, a man of sixty,
already the victim of delicate health. Celia, at thirty-two,
had been married more than fifteen years, and the enforced
separations from her husband had begun. Her father,
whom she had always regarded as a tower of strength,
was gone. Handsome Mr. Whittier, with his piercing black
eyes, his appreciation of her poetry, his love of all she
found beautiful in nature, satisfied her in many ways.

When he entered the unpopular ranks of the Abolitionists
it had not been easy to find a publisher for his poems.
In fact he waited many years to bring out his first book,
in marked contrast to Celia, who had leaped so suddenly
and so successfully into print. They both wrote vividly
of the simple familiar things which they had experienced
— he on the farm and she on her islands. In his speech
and manner he always manifested his Quaker unbringing;
he also believed strongly in the leading of the "inner light".

A bachelor, he was always surrounded by admiring feminine friends. His letters were not literary productions but mostly personal messages and descriptions of his own state of health, with some allusions to national affairs, and keen interest in the activities of his correspondents. A naturally modest man, he was always surprised at the admiration and affection showered upon him, and he ever retained, along with his keen sense of humor, enormous gratitude for friendship.

In her Personal Recollections of Whittier, Mary B. Claflin says:

> Those who have sat with him for an evening will never forget his charming vivacity and pleasant silence and repose. He never led out but always waited for someone to begin the conversation, yet once launched upon some topic that interested him he would talk for an hour with an enthusiasm and spontaneity and sprightliness that would surprise one who had only seen him in his silent moods. His feelings were so strong upon certain subjects that an hour's conversation would utterly exhaust him.

One of his early letters shows how valuable Whittier was to Celia as a critic. After the appearance of an early poem he wrote her:

Amesbury, March 29, 1867

. . . I suspect thee are in the predicament of the man who says he "woke up one morning and found himself famous." But I hope thee will still recognize thy old friends when thee meets them. Don't believe the newspapers. "Be not puffed up," says the apostle. Don't go to being blue. Don't set up for a strong-minded woman. But surely, the poem in the Atlantic is liked by everybody, and all the more that its author is not a writer by profession. It is so pleasant to know that such things can be done by a woman who looks to her own household, and makes her own fire-side circle happy, and knows how to render lighter her daily care and labors by throwing over them the charm of her free idealization. I think men are inclined to deprecate the idea of a merely literary woman. But when the charm of true womanliness is preserved, when the heart's warmth is not absorbed by the intellect and the wife and mother remain intact, and to this is added the power to move the public heart and satisfy the demands of the highest taste and culture, what can we do but admire and say God-speed!

Indeed, I don't believe in anybody's making literature the great aim of life. Greater than all books is man or woman.

Whittier wrote from Amesbury after the visit to the islands in 1867, on August 8th:

> ... It is sheer kindness of heart, my dear friend, that I owe thy pleasant letters so vividly representing life at "The Shoals." They are wonderfully hospitable letters — they give me the freedom of the island: I sit by the parlor fire in the stormy nights — I see the tossing boats in the little harbor — the islands ringed round with foam and I feel the spray as it tosses up through cleft and gorge; and I hear thee telling stories to the young folks, and half fancy myself among them, nestling close to thee with "not unpleasing horror" as the tragedy deepens. It's all very nice but it puzzlies me to know why I am favored in this way. There must be some mistake: I am getting what doesn't really belong to me.

Whittier early became and always continued to be Celia's greatest inspiration. He said: "Write thou must. It is thy Kismet." His friendship seemed to draw out Celia's best work, both in poetry and prose. She often sent him proofs of what she had written asking for his opinion. He was honest in telling her what he thought and kind in his encouragement, relaying to her what people had said to him or what he had read in reviews of her poems.

On August 24, 1867, he wrote:

> ... I know of no one who so well describes the sea and sky and the wild island scenery. Thy pictures glow with life, and color. I am only afraid I shall be tempted to appropriate them some time, they so exactly express what I feel but

cannot say. . . . As a Quaker, thee knows I cannot have
anything to do with the old heathen Nine, and so I have
made thee serve my purpose as a sort of tenth Muse. I
could not have a better.

> Dear girl, for whom all sweet flowers bloom,
> And happy birds their welcome bring
> What can my evening lend thy morn —
> Or my late autumn give thy spring?

Although Whittier wrote of the great difference in their
ages, there existed between them an accord which, had
the wheel of fate turned differently, might have led to a
satisfying and beautiful union.

Typical of their exchange is a letter written December
14, 1867. It is a vivid word picture by Whittier of Charles
Dickens as he appeared in his Boston readings.

. . . I have made "an effort" as Mrs. Chick would say, I
have heard Dickens. It was his last night in Boston. I
found myself in the packed hall sandwiched between
Richard H. Dana Sr. and Longfellow with Mrs. Fields one
side of us and Mrs. Ames the other. We waited some
half hour: a slight, brisk man tripped up the steps, sparkling with ring and chain, tight vested, wide bottomed short
frock coat, white choker, tight pantaloons enclosing, as
the Raine girl said of Judge Douglass, — "a mighty slim
staunch of legs." Somehow a slight reminder of his own
Jim Tapertit in *Barnaby Rudge*. Face marked with thought
as well as years — head bald or nearly so — a look of
keen intelligence about the strong brow and eye — the
look of a man who has seen much and is wide awake to see
more. I don't think he shows the great genius that he is
— he might pass for a shrewd Massachusetts manufacturer,
or an active N. Y. merchant. But his reading is wonderful, far beyond my expectations. Those marvelous characters of his came forth, one by one, real personages as if
their original creator had breathed new life into them.
You shut your eyes and there before you now are Peck-
sniff, and Sairy Gamp, Sam Weller, Dick Swiveller and
all the rest. But it is idle to talk about it. You must beg,

borrow or steal a ticket and hear him. Another such star shower is not to be expected in one's lifetime. After the reading I called on him with Longfellow and Mr. Fields.

It was on February 16, 1868 that Celia wrote her first long descriptive letter to Whittier. The word pictures of young moon and planet Venus, of the snow-covered piazzas of the hotel and of the parrot who imitated the sheep, the cows and the ducks and called "Celia" so pleased the poet that he suggested that she write the papers which became *Among the Isles of Shoals.*

When her mother begged her to stay, Celia lingered, but ended a letter to him:

. . . It is wrong for people to live here all winter! Well enough for women, at least better for them than for men, for they have such an incessant round of occupations in taking care of husbands and children, but it is not good for young men. These brown Viking brothers of mine are busy with boats, or capstans all day, and all evening they read, but they have been cheated out of so much! They are over 30 years old and have never voted in their lives and never wished to.

In March, 1868, she wrote again:

. . . Tonight at sunset it was dead calm and we climbed the hill and sat by the smaller cairn with all the loveliness spread out before us; a soft crimson sunset intensely vivid over the dark coast and the whole sea reflecting it, in rosy streaks near, and afar off a long red trail in the water. The tide brimmed every cove, a little icebird swam in Babb's Cove. The water came in, in such a beautiful curve that I was enchanted. First the line was marked in snow, then a few feet below it was drawn accurately in sea-weed, then below that came the living water itself, the "wan-water," the melodious water! . . .

Dear friend, you would hardly know the place! This long piazza, up and down which Youth and Romance were wont to meander through the summer evenings, is filled with snow from one end to the other and traversed occasionally by the cows and sheep; the little garden which kept me in roses so long last summer and whose golden and flame colored flowers seemed trying to outblaze the sun, is but a heap of snow and desolation. How the poppies nodded their scarlet heads between the rails; and how good you were to let me put flowers in your buttonhole!

Whittier was quick to reply:

. . . I was delighted with the graphic description of the March sea. I wish thee would write some of thy Island stories and experiences, for it is too bad to waste on me alone, the admirable bits of description in thy letter and yet I was selfish enough to be glad of it, and that it was all my own.

Whittier also visited the Thaxters in their Newtonville home. He examined the big vine climbing over the sunny side of the house, and enjoyed the pleasant sitting room, gay and beautiful with gentians, asters and ferns from the river low lands. Wherever Celia was, there must be flowers! His own picture hung in a prominent place on the wall and over the fireplace was Raphael's pensive cherub, while beside the hearth stood Celia's favorite aeolian harp. The artist, Harry Fenn, had made a charming sketch of the young woman kneeling before her driftwood fire in this same setting, a copy of which hangs in Whittier's birthplace.

In 1868, a sister poet, Lucy Larcom, told Whittier of a delightful visit with the Thaxters, which he relayed:

. . . Her very great admiration of thee must I think be henceforth shared by Mr. Thaxter, whom she speaks of with a woman's heartiest appreciation. — I wanted to run out to your place too, but I was quite unfit for visiting . . . and contented myself by looking over Henry Longfellow's poem *The Spanish Gypsy*. . . a great poem viewed as a work of art.

Whittier continued to urge her to write in prose some of the stories he had heard her tell of the fisher people she had known as a child, their way of speech and the wonderful legends of supernatural happenings on the Shoals.

Because of her husband's illness in the winter of 1868-69, Celia for a time had to give up all thought of the articles. It was not until Levi finally set forth for Florida, with John and Roland, that she found time to write at all. In February 1869 Whittier wrote her at the Shoals where she and Karl had gone:

> . . . So thee are once more on Appledore — "McGregor and his native heath!" For thy sake I am heartily glad of it. Mr. Thaxter seems to have the persistent, quiet enthusiasm of all naturalists — Wilmot, Audubon and the Quaker Bartram were ramblers in Fla., near a century ago, and are good reading still!

It was in the wintry solitude of the sea room at Appledore, while the wind roared, that Celia began work on the prose sketches, so long desired by Fields and Whittier. As a relaxation she also wrote some of her best poems — *By the Roadside* was printed in the Atlantic in August 1869, the month before the first of the Shoals articles appeared. The second installment appeared after Celia had returned from the islands to her Massachusetts home. Mr. Whittier gave his own unbounded praise and then, to encourage the author, wrote her comments of others:

> . . . It is one of the most delicious bits of writing I have ever seen — everybody praises it. Harriet P. Spofford thinks thy Shoals paper "a prose poem." Horace Greeley said, in his slow Quaker drawl, "Well, that is the best prose writing I have seen in a long time. Mrs. Thaxter's pen pictures are wonderful." Many people speak in strong terms of admiration, and hope thee will make a book, with some illustrations by Mr. Fenn. It will give delight to thousands, and I will take credit to myself for urging thee to write it.

He continues later:

> It must seem very odd to thee to exchange the wide sea room of Appledore for the leafy walled horizon of Newtonville — I suppose thee is getting used to it now. I can

imagine the pleasant sitting room, gay and beautiful with the flowers which I helped thee gather two years ago. Does your big grape vine bear well?

We are looking forward to the next Atlantic paper on the islands and hope it will appear in the Nov. number.

Hearing of Levi's second severe illness in 1870, and of his departure for Florida, Whittier wrote Celia at the Shoals:

. . . I read with much concern thy letter. Saw Weiss at the Reed Club, and he told me how thee and thine were afflicted. He said Mr. T. had been very dangerously ill. It is very sad — the breaking down of strong health, the sundering of a family — this abandonment of home — the pain of leaving old familiar places and faces — all added to thy peculiar anxieties as a mother. God comfort thee, dear friend. All thy many friends deeply and truly sympathize with thee. It is a great trial, but I think thee will meet it with thy usual courage and good nature. . .

He wrote again in March of 1870:

. . . I am glad to know thee are making thyself happy in the desolation of the wintry Shoals, by making others happy, there is no better way. Thee should have the consolation of knowing my life is made brighter and happier by thy kindness.

Summer came. In July 1870, Whittier wrote:

. . . Be thankful for sea-scented Appledore. How I thank thee for thy letter just received, bringing me the breath of wild rose and mignonette. It is as if the cool, soft sea air at the islands blew over this feverish inland. . . It is wrong for me to have so much of your time, for I know thee have many friends more deserving than myself and many cares and duties. I hope in time when I, who am not writing, am but a mummy, thee will have the consolation of knowing that my life was made brighter and happier for thy kindness — Shall we not see thee here, this fall, on thy way from the Shoals? I somehow hope it might be so.

You really will not go to Florida — thee do not mean that you are going to live there? !

Celia did stop for a little visit with Whittier. Afterwards she wrote: "I had such a happy time in Amesbury and I thank thee with all my heart. . . " To which he replied: "We felt doubly alone after thee left us. It was very good of thee to come in this way!"

His next letter, May 5, 1871 refers to her poem *Before Sunrise.*

> . . . It brings to mind the delicious evenings at Appledore — The "enchanted dusk" creeping over the sea and the cool sweet dewy fresh morning. I have no fault to find with it. I think no one interprets these gospels of nature so well as thee do. . . Mrs. Fields was right in calling it a "noble poem." I want to see all these wonderful sea pieces in a volume. I am certain of its success. . .

In 1871 when James T. Fields resigned as Editor of the Atlantic, W. D. Howells took his place and Whittier wrote to Celia:

> . . . I, too, am sorry to see Fields step out from the place he has so well occupied. He has been a true good friend to me for so many years. We shall never feel quite at home in the new house I fear. . .

Celia was encouraged to collect her best poems for publication in book form. It was ten years since she had first seen her lines printed in the Atlantic; now, with the help of her husband, she began the new venture.

Referring to the publication of her *Poems* in book form, Whittier wrote on August 24, 1871:

> . . . I was so glad to hear that the Poems are to be published. What will be the title? I am sure they will be welcomed heartily —

A fortnight later, September 9, 1871, he wrote:

> . . . How I wish I could look over thy little collection. I

could not criticize it any more than I could its author — but I would like to reassure thee, and laugh at thy misgivings. I know the book will win the hearts of friends and admirers.

As to omissions, consider thy own feelings about them. As to a name, how would *Sea Weeds and Mosses* do?. Or, as thee think so very lightly of thy work, why not call it Sea Foam by Celia T. . .

I think thee should have a set of poems — a key to the poems which follow, telling where they were sung to the music of the sea. Thee could give us a bit of beautiful description of their locality and the moods in which they were first attuned. Something of the sort seems really needed for the sake of readers who do not know the circumstances. Thee will have ample time, as the prefacing lines will not be printed until after the body of the volume. I think a good deal of Mr. Field's judgment; he has helped me in many instances.

Poems by Celia Thaxter was "entered according to Act of Congress in the year 1871 by L. L. Thaxter" and was stereotyped and printed by Hurd & Houghton, New York-Cambridge, Riverside Press. Then Levi Thaxter paid $500 for the printing and it sold for $1 a volume. Levi's investment was a wise one. The book soon went into a second edition, bound in blue with gold lettering, instead of the plain black binding of the first edition.

In a now treasured notebook, Celia has written in longhand the poems chosen for her first volume. In this book, as well as in her early correspondence, her handwriting had the conventional slight slant employed by her father and husband who had been her teachers. Later, when without a typewriter, she was sending many poems to various editors, she developed a clear and very distinctive handwriting which remained the same until her death.

Celia wrote her brother about the venture:

. . . Everything is pretty nearly ready for publication, the Lord is good, but I am scared to death when I think of the book; it is poverty stricken!

GROUP AT APPLEDORE:
R. TURNER, WM. MASON, APPLETON BROWN,
J. K. PAYNE, WM. WINCHEL

CHILDE HASSAM ON THAXTER PIAZZA

CELIA AND HER FRIENDS 1888

Young ladies visiting Appledore

Whittier encouraged her by repeating the good he heard of her collection. On May 21, 1872, he wrote:

> . . . I am delighted to know that thy poems are beginning to be appreciated as they deserve to be. I always told thee that it was thy Kismet to write and that thee could find favor with the public and Mrs. Grundy. . . Isn't it dull that thy only vulnerable point, in the estimation of critics is thy goodness! Too much piety! Solomon has a word of advice for such folks as are too good for human nature's daily food. "Be not righteous overmuch: why should thee destroy thyself?" But I think it is all nonsense — this objection of thy verses. Such nice folks as Joseph and Gertrude Cortland like them for the very thing complained of. And so do I, who am not nice.
>
> I return the letter of Mr. Albee, cordial and kind and the printed slip, which is very good although it classes thee and I with the bobolinks! Pray, who did it? . . .

Celia's reply, in part, to this letter is an interesting sidelight on her approach to faith and religion. She wrote:

> . . . All my life I have wondered at myself, of what my pen wrote of piety and moral feeling. . .

On another date Whittier wrote her:

> . . . I see in Field's "Yesterdays with Authors" that Dickens speaks highly of thy articles in the Atlantic, but declares: "I don't believe it! No, I don't! My conviction is that these Islanders must get dreadfully bored with their Islands." . . . I wish he could have seen them, as we have.

After a visit at the Isles of Shoals, Whittier wrote:

July 22, 1872

My dear friend:
    After losing the last gleam of thy white dress, we had a pleasant sail over to Portsmouth where Mr. Pitman parted as such old lover should, so affectionately as to amuse our irreverent young folks! I wish Mr. Hunt who I thought seemed a little skeptical as to the reality of the veteran

editor's sentiment, could have seen it. For as Annie Fields says "Love is not old, nor young, nor sere."

We all had a very nice visit at the Island and as usual, were sorry to leave it. I found the Atlantic Monthly here and *Tryst* (See Page 258) which confirms in type, my opinion of it in manuscript, that it is one of thy strongest poems — beautiful and terrible like the iceberg itself. . .

Again he wrote in 1872, regarding the publication of *Among the Isles of Shoals.*

. . . I am especially pleased to know that the beautiful prose papers on the Shoals are to take book form. Half a dozen of Fenn's pictures should go with them. I should be glad to render thee any service in my power.

How I thank thee for thinking of dedicating thy book to me. The dedication preferred, was I think a trifle too complimentary, however. I am sure the book will be received everywhere with satisfaction and interest and add immensely to thy reputation.

He expressed his keen interest in each of her poems as they appeared:

November 1872

. . . Thy *Discontent* is liable to the fault of being too good, too preachy, like some of my sermons! *For Thoughts* is not as good, but a great deal better, full of grace, passion and beauty.

January 22, 1873

Under the Lighthouse was called by Pres. McGill of Swarthmore College "that wonderfully beautiful poem by C. T."

November 13, 1873

Thy 2 poems are good — *Karen* sounds like a bit of Heine. *March* is admirable. I have never seen that ever-blowing month as well painted.

Whittier made constructive criticism of her work:

February 14, 1873

The long poem *Lars* — occurred to me as it now stands with the Norse names of Lars and Elsa would be under-

stood as a fancy foreign sketch. I tried to localize it by the two verses by way of introduction.
"Tell us the story of these Isles," they said.

These verses written by Whittier were later used by Celia to introduce the poem as printed in her *Collected Poems* with the change of only one word.

Among the Isles of Shoals was published with illustrations in 1873 in Boston by James R. Osgood & Co.

Referring to the new volume, Celia wrote to Mr. Fields:

. . . I shall be glad to have it done, not that I care to be in people's vestpockets, heaven save the mark, but I should be so deeply thankful to have Osgood's check in my pocket.

Whittier wrote, May 13, 1873:

. . . When thy note came, I was reading thy book. I am more than delighted with it. — I called on Mr. Anthony when in Boston. He showed me the engravings — all are good, but that of White Island is the best wood cut in America — real water and sky — A. said he had done his best to reproduce Fenn's idea. What an accomplished fellow he is! He is enraptured with thy book.

The climate of the Isles of Shoals exactly suited Whittier. Nowhere is the closeness to the ocean so strongly felt. He would wander from the piazza to the billiard room and back to Celia's parlor and sit for hours without speaking. On July 14, 1873 he thanked Celia for his visit to the Shoals:

. . . I did right in not going to the Pepperrell House: I lived fast at the Island and enjoyed every minute so much that the reaction was inevitable. A thousand thanks, dear friend, for thy kindness, "How pleasantly the days of Thalaba went by!"

. . . What a nice set of women you had at the Cottage! Mrs. Hepworth always charming. Mrs. Guild with her rare beauty and grace, Mrs. Macey reminding one of the Empress Eugenie, but far better and handsomer, Annie Fields gracious and lovely and sweet, and last, not least, the hostess herself, whose name might have the prefix of Jean Paul's: "The Only."

I found a letter waiting from Miss Sara Horner of Georgetown, originally a Professor in some college, a school in Tallahassee, Florida who says: "I look forward with the greatest pleasure to reading Mrs. Thaxter's book. Although she may be more famous she cannot be sweeter than when I saw her with her mustard-blossom wreath long ago.

On January 31, 1874 Celia wrote to Whittier in answer to another question from him:

. . . My novel? O my dear friend, it is nowhere! Twice I essayed to begin, wrote a chapter and flung it to the four winds, in wrath and scorn. Nay, good my friend, I think I'll "stick to my last." I am not to be the author of the novel, par excellence, of America, that is certain. But I do think that if I could have had some critical and sympathetic friend at hand, to whom I could have turned for advice, with whom I could have talked about it, I might have had some measure of success. . .

When in 1874 the new and larger volume of *Collected Poems* by Celia Thaxter appeared, Whittier was pleased and wrote:

June 1874
. . . Let me thank thee for thy beautiful book of poems. I have read it through — the old as well the new, and feel sure that the new poems are even better than the old ones. It is worth while to stay all winter on the island to be able to write *At Breakers Edge* alone. God has given thee a beautiful gift and thus far thee has used it well.

During her mother's last illness Celia was much cheered when in November 1876, Whittier sent her a copy of his latest volume, *Mabel Martin*, the narrative poem profusely illustrated by V. S. Anthony. On the flyleaf of the copy he sent to her he wrote a poem especially for her. The violet ink is hardly faded in spite of the fact that it was written ninety-four years ago.

A twice-told story, garnished so
Its old-time face I scarcely know,
I send thee, half ashamed to own
That one whose beard had silver grown,
Still lingers fondly where alone
The breezes of the spring-time blow,
Dreaming of morning when the day
Is closing. Pardon her essay
To sow with flowers the winter snow
JOHN G. WHITTIER

In her acknowledgment, Celia wrote:

Shoals March 1876

Dear and beautiful friend:

I am so grateful to you for your kind letter and for the exquisite book, *Mabel Martin,* how perfect it is, how could anything surpass it! I have just read it through again, the dear old ballad, and I will confess that my hard old wicked eyes, so slow to fill with tears, are wet with the tenderness of your touch; how sweet and delicate and powerful it is! My brother, reading it over last night, said, as he laid the book down, "I'll tell you one thing, this man can't be beaten!" A rudely spoken sentiment most heartily expressed, which my soul echoed with all its might.

And I can't tell you how pleased I was with the lines you wrote within, and that you did write them was such an enchanting fact! Altogether you made me most happy, and it isn't the first time, either! I have so much to thank you for, like everybody else, and the very thought of you rejoices me. Now see how I run straight into the old groove, — dear friend, you must almost be tired of love and praise, for it flows to you from all the world, forever and forever, and will follow you forever. Forgive me . . .

The years following her mother's death, Whittier was not well. No letters seem to have survived. In July, 1880, however, he wrote to say how much he longed to revisit the Island, but was unable to undertake it as he was "suffering from great weakness and pain" in his back.

. . . but I looked longingly Shoals-ward, and heartily wish I could run over and tread the happy island again — sit in thy pleasant parlor and enjoy thy gorgeous garden, and talk over old times and people. It would give me great pleasure to see Miss Jewett, also. It is long since I have seen thee and there is much to say — God bless thee! dear friend.

Whittier rejoiced over the news of Celia's projected trip to Europe, writing that he wished he could talk with her about the trip, as he knew of "no one who could more fully appreciate and enjoy such a visit." He went on to warn her "not to stay too long in Rome, to run the risk of Roman fever," and begged her "not to neglect Florence on the Arno, and Naples on its Bay!"

The next year Celia wrote from Kittery Point:

Sept. 9, 1881

My dear friend:

I am so grateful to you. How beautiful was that brief space of your stay at the Shoals! What a joy to see you again. — When you went away that morning and stood with the Morrills on the deck of the little steamer in the early sunshine, laughing to see Cedric pitching chairs overboard after his friends in such paroxysms of farewell, do you know you looked so finely, so full of life and of power, all my heart was stirred looking up at you, thinking of all you are and all you have done. — Great heaven, what eyes you have got in your head! — Now I hear you say "Hush, thee foolish woman!" But I shan't hush. I do admire the dedication of Rose Terny's book to you. She most generally does hit the nail on the head and that's a satisfaction. I'm going to write again soon as I've read her book, but I don't expect you to write to me, so don't give it a thought. You may smile at me, but you can't check or hush my admirations and enthusiasms and while the lamp holds out to burn I shall continue to rejoice in all things beautiful, admirable and glorious, yourself among the number.

Ever and ever your audacious and affectionate

C. T.

In the spring of 1882, when Celia and Karl moved into

the Winthrop Hotel in Boston, Whittier was also staying there to be near his dying brother. Being able to see him often meant much to Celia, especially at a time when she, too, was suffering from great anxiety. She wrote a poem for his seventy-fifth birthday. (See page 270)

In June 1883, Celia wrote from the cool Shoals, sympathizing with her friend for the heat of the mainland, and added:

> . . . I wish you were here. That I always do! Ten thousand yellow flowers are coming up in my garden! Will you look at them by and by? Don't give your old friends the go by, for the Pepperrell House at Kittery Point! I beg! With best love to all the household, dearest for yourself, I am ever and always your
>
> Celia Thaxter

Whittier's letter of condolence following Levi's death in 1884 did not survive, nor did any bearing on the event. On July 28, 1884, Whittier wrote from Holderness, New Hampshire, where he had gone for his asthma:

> My dear friend:
>
> It is a long time since I have seen or heard from thee. Our friends Annie Fields and Sarah Jewett are here and we wished thee could be with us also. So far I have not yet found any benefit from the mountain air — I am beginning to understand that I am an old man; and as they say of town paupers "past my usefulness!"
>
> I wonder whether thee are at Kittery, or at the Island? I would like to set my foot once more on Appledore. Has thee written much of late? I have not seen the magazine, but I was feeling rather dull a while ago, and took up an English collection of verse, and opened at thy beautiful *The Sunrise Never Failed Us Yet* (See Page 272), and the comfort of it "slid into my soul," and I thanked thee for it. Yet it is hard to realize that shadows of our lives will ever pass away, before the sun rises!
>
> Ever heartily, thy old friend
>
> John G. Whittier

Annie Fields in her Diary, tells of a hot Sunday afternoon in Celia's parlor, during one of Whittier's visits, when
the conversation turned to faith and prayer. Celia said
she "knew little about faith and had no set prayers."
Whittier told her he was sure she prayed, without knowing
it. "Pray thou must! No human being can exist without
prayer! What else do thy poems mean?"

It was on October 21, 1886 that Celia described to
Whittier her new quarters in the Hotel Clifford on Cortes
Street in Boston.

> . . . You always were so kind and encouraging to me, and I
> am proud to have done anything you can praise. I am so
> glad you did go to the Appledore this summer! It is beauti-
> ful to remember. I wish — if you come to Boston, you
> would come here and see what floods of sunshine pour all
> day into these cheerful rooms and what a bower of ferns and
> flowers I have to sit in at work all day, perfectly steeped in
> sunshine — it is heavenly. Two large high broad rooms we
> have, Karl and I, with bay window and two other windows,
> facing south, the first ray of the sun and the last one shines
> in on my beloved plants and flowers, they make me so happy!
> There is an elevator, so you would not need to climb the
> stairs and how glad, how rejoiced I should be to see you!
> It is the quietest place, an apartment house. You would not
> see a soul to bother you. It is close on the horse car track —
> but you would take a carriage probably if you came. And
> I should want to know when, because we run the elevator
> ourselves and I would come down for you — there is no one
> to run it — it is a family elevator of the most domestic
> description.
>
> My room is full of yellow — a mass of golden immortelles
> on the mantel and yellow vases, and cushions and things
> all shades of gold. And somehow it is a heavenly place!
> Mrs. Hemenway said the first day she came up here "Well,
> now I have got to Paradise! There is no mistake about it."
> . . . How did we endure that other hideous little hostelry so
> long! I wonder. But I only wanted a place to hide with Karl
> and knew no better one, and you know my life was all in

that corner under the eaves, forever at work. But it was a horrid place.

. . . With dearest love to yourself always I am, yours faithfully,

Celia Thaxter

I did not tell you that my Roland is engaged to be married. I feel so grandmotherly!

As the summer season opened in 1888, Celia wrote to remind Whittier of earlier happy days.

Shoals, June 24th, 1888

My dear friend,

How long it is since I have heard a word from you, dear friend! Not that I expect you to write, no indeed, I know how busy you are and how much writing you must do. I look at Po Hill over the way, and think of you every day of my life. I have been wondering if you and Phoebe and perhaps your cousins would not sign some of these bird pledges; the Audubon Soc. have made me local Secretary for Appledore! with power for doing its work in any place and I am after all the signatures to these pledges that I can get! If you do not find any one to sign them, might I ask you to return them to me? Keep the circular, please and if you can give me your beloved and honored name, and Phoebe's or any of the rest,, I shall be glad. Tho' no one has any uncertainty on the subject of your opinions about bird slaughter, certainly!

I am writing poems (?) by the yard to fit 26 Wide Awake art prints to be made into a Xmas book, an edition de luxe. You may believe it is no small job! I have 12 done and 14 to do. Bismillah! but some of them are posers! It takes a heap of human ingenuity to get the better of them. But I trust I shall come off victorious, tho' sometimes it does look hopeless. I have just been getting ready a new vol. to be printed in the autumn. And when I have done such a thing I always think what an idiot I am to imagine there is anything I could say worth preserving in a book, and regret my temerity.

Dear friend, would we could see you here again! The

Shoals are still moored in the old place, but life — how it changes! — Cedric's children are enchanting, two little girls, Ruth and Margaret. Ruth in her fourth year, a sweet fascinater as ever lived, and comfort to me, indeed.

I wish I could see you sometimes. They say in heaven we shall have all the people whom we love, that's my idea of heaven! But I don't believe I love a great many! like lots, but not love.

My garden is full of golden flowers in memory of you. Don't think me sentimental! truly I'm past the age — going to be 53 in a few days. But when Ruth comes to play with me, I'm just her age, not quite four! Always your loving

C. Thaxter

In a wistful and reminiscent vein she thanked him for a letter written after a long silence.

Shoals, April 11, 1889

Most dear friend:

You cannot know what a joy your dear letter is to me. I have read it again and again, every precious word of it, more glad each time, for every syllable of it. Shall I tell you — I had a kind of sorrowful feeling that you had forgotten me, or rather drifted so far away as not to care much, if any, and I love you so dearly and truly it troubled me sore. Ah, my dear friend, you speak so kindly! But who in our time has given so much strength and refreshment as you have done, not only to your friends and your country but to all the world, which has been bettered for your living in it. Never a false note have you sounded in all your sweet singing and the comfort you have been to your tried and weary fellow creatures and the inspiration for good — what a record! Forgive me — I know how you shrink from words like these. "I did not mean to," but out of the fullness of the heart the mouth speaketh.

Yes, I had a quiet, lovely winter in Portsmouth — a place for my poor Karl where he was happy, sunny windows for my beautiful blossoming plants, my brother Cedric's family, his dear little girls almost next door, and everything peaceful and comfortable. I did more writing than for years and was so well and content till about three weeks ago, I was suddenly very ill, as I have been twice before, for no reason that anybody appears able to find out except "over work," the Drs. say, in years past. . . . I never know when the bolt is going to fall and smite me, it gives me no warning. Please do not speak of it, I hate to be questioned and talked to, don't you? I know you do! So I say as little about it as possible. I do not mind the thought of death, it means only fuller life, but there is a pang in the thought of leaving my poor Karl with no one to have patience with him and comfort him. But I know the Heavenly Father provides for all. It may be I shall get quite well and strong again in this beautiful air. I hope so. But whatever befalls I am ready and know that all is for best.

We came here last Friday . . . Never did the island look so lovely in the early spring, since I was a little child playing on the rocks at White Island. O the delicious dawns and crimson sunsets, the calm blue sea, the tender sky, the chorus of the birds! It all makes me so happy! Sometimes I wonder if it is wise or well to love any one spot on this old earth as intensely as I do this! I am wrapped up in measureless content as I sit on the steps in my little garden, where the freshly turned earth is odorous of the spring. How I hope you can come to us this summer! Every year I plant the garden for your dear eyes, with yellow flowers. I never forget those lovely summers long ago when you came and loved my flowers.

I am going to send you with this a little copy of an old picture of Karl and myself when we were babes together, he one year old, I eighteen. Karl copied it. Isn't it a pathetic picture, being so prophetic of our life together . . .

Thank you so much for the beautiful poem you enclosed, it is most lovely. You ask what I have been writing — a great deal, for me. I wish I had sent you the April St. Nicholas, for in it is a version I made of Tolstoi's *Where Love is there God is also.* I had such reverence for the great author's work, I hardly dared touch it, but I did it with the greatest love. I called it *The Heavenly Guest.* Do you see St. N.? If not I will ask them to send it to you. Dear Sarah Jewett has such a sweet story begun in the April Number and my poem follows. Both Annie Fields and Sarah came to see me in Ports. that was so charming! Everybody came. I had such a pleasant winter. I love the old place, too. From my pleasant parlor windows I looked down State St. to the swift river, for the quaint house we lived in juts out a little from Penhollow St. so that we could look down State St. Oscar stayed with me a good part of the winter: that was a comfort too.

Dear friend I hope I have not wearied you with so long a letter. Please send me one little line to say if you got it and the photo. God bless you. Ever, with deep, gentle, grateful love, your   C. T.
Don't return verses, throw in waste basket. Keep the poor little photo, please.

Unfortunately, with advancing years, Whittier became fearful of posthumous publicity. He begged his dear friend "to destroy any correspondence which might fall into the hands of prying literary ghouls." This is the last of his surviving letters:

Amesbury, Nov. 23, 1890
. . . the years grow very heavy, and my sight fails so that my pen has to run without much direction. I can read very little and these long nights are rather tedious. Thanks for *My Lighthouse,* beautiful within and without, a cheering and hopeful light shines from it. As I sit alone by my lonely hearth I think of the many charming days and evenings at the enchanted island and how much I owe to thee. God bless thee for all thy kindness!

With love to thy brothers I am always affectionately thy friend

John G. Whittier

Two years later, after spending the summer at Seabrook, where he could look long and often across the waters toward the Shoals, Whittier quietly slipped away in September 1892. Annie Fields well said "Death is a low door, if it will open quickly, it brings little fear to the thoughtful mind!"

21

"MORE LIGHT"
1887 — 1894

Her parents and husband all dead, and her two younger sons married, Celia seemed at last relieved of the pressures which had for so many years filled her days. The summer of 1887 she was able fully to enjoy the daily program at the Shoals. By July 16th there was a vacancy and she wrote Ross Turner urging him to come with his wife:

> . . . Oscar says he will take care of the baby. I want you to get everything in the program that is charming — such lovely people — such music!

Appledore had become an intellectual Mecca. The assembled company became larger and more distinguished, until it seemed to epitomize the rare spirit and genius of that period and era.

Celia visited her brother, Cedric, his wife Julia and their two daughters, Ruth and Margaret, in Portsmouth for Christmas 1887.. Then she and Karl returned again to the swallows' nest under the eaves at the Hotel Clifford. Here she did much painting and wrote some poetry. One poem she sent to Thomas Bailey Aldrich, who had succeeded Howells at the Atlantic. She wrote, with uncharacteristic curtness:

Jan. 12th, 1888

Dear Mr. Aldrich,

If you don't want this poem, kindly return it in the enclosed envelope and oblige,

Yours always cordially
Celia Thaxter

The note suggests somewhat strained relations with her
old friend. The poem must have been returned, as the
Atlantic, which had previously published so many of her
poems, seems to have used none later than July 1885, when
they printed *Within and Without.*

She wrote Turner that her friend, Mr. F. J. Jameson, was
"most interested" in a plan for him to illustrate a small
book of her poems. The idea came to nothing and she
continued to make her own delicate and delightful sketches
in water color on the pages of special copies of already
published volumes.

By March 19th she and Karl were back at the Shoals
and Karl was experimenting with photographs for which
he used a new and very fine camera which his mother had
given him. Photography later became a great hobby with
him and he achieved a good measure of success. It is
through his efforts that many interesting views of the island
are preserved, and groups of summer guests on the cottage
piazza recorded. He did his own developing and printing,
and his mother saw to it that at last he had his own long-
desired workshop. Ross Turner also had a studio.

She wrote Turner on March 14, 1888:

My dear Ross,

. . . I went up to look at your quarters in the afternoon,
they are most pleasant . . . you must not forget to bring
frames and mats and have one of your pictures always for
sale in my room, on the easel, and others beside. That is
the place where they will sell best, because so many eyes
will see them . . .

Monday and Tuesday we had a terrific storm. I never saw

the waves higher, they broke over from the east and swept across the island and washed through under the piazza and joined the angry sea on the west side, rolling rocks and drift stuff all the way . . . I am working hard at my old stupid painting of books and porcelain, so that I may have a chance to work with you this summer — if I can.

There had been much new construction since the fall and Celia wrote that as she first approached the island, it looked like a little city. As always, she loved it with no one but the family and workmen about. She planted her garden and prepared for the coming of summer guests. Birds descended, as they so often did, upon the freshly-planted seeds and made havoc of the garden, so it all had to be done again. She wrote Sarah Jewett:

> . . . The birds! Poor dears, how could they know? I love them all the same, tho' they despoil my garden of its best glory. They were hungry, poor things! They knew no better!

Her trials had softened and mellowed her. As the crowds of admirers returned for the season, they were again "spellbound by her beautiful enthusiasm. She had learned to rise above their flattery as she had above the disappointments and repressions of other days," says Annie Fields in the Preface to the *Letters of Celia Thaxter*.

Worn out when the season ended, Celia wrote Mrs. Ward from the Shoals, September 17, 1888:

> . . . I have not felt like myself . . . and have so little of my old energy, that I have given up going to the continent at all.

Celia had passed her fifty-third birthday and for almost the first time in her life was not desperately needed in several places at once. Her thoughts turned back to her carefree childhood. She decided she would spend the greater part of the winter with her brother on Appledore. Karl was always happiest on the island, and she felt she could bring cheer to them both during the long days and severe storms. Fate willed it otherwise, however. She had driven herself for so long that now, with the cessation of pressure, a vital thread snapped. She suffered a sudden severe attack of illness which the doctor told her was due to over-work. The pain yielded only to injections of morphine. She wrote:

> . . . neuralgic swords playing across the region of my heart and cutting through, tearing across the spine are not very pleasant companions to deal with! It requires experience and knowledge to wrestle with them! My brother dares not risk my spending the winter on the island with him, as I had planned, for no matter how great the need no earthly power can reach the continent from the Shoals during tempests at that season. So I fear I must go to Portsmouth, for the most terrible months, which is a great disappointment to me!

Harry Marvin begged to stay out all winter to help Oscar on Appledore. There were seven cows, the pigs, hens and a large flock of sheep, which must all be cared for, besides the boats and the buildings. Marvin had learned to love the Shoals, first as messenger of the little steamer, then as deckhand, caretaker and clerk. After the death of Cedric Laighton, he was to manage the Oceanic Hotel on Star Island. For the rest of his life he was a devoted friend of the family.

Celia wrote "dearest Annie" from the Shoals, October 17, 1888:

> . . . I was very ill again — I am better now, but cannot leave the lounge where I lie most of the day. All the time my side troubles me, high up in my left side . . . my eyes look like two burned holes in a blanket. But I think I am getting over it slowly. It's curious how things arrange themselves. Surely there is a power at work under and through all things which is not man's power!

Celia and Karl moved to the mainland, taking Ella Adams to save Celia from all household cares. They were most

CELIA THAXTER 1887

Celia with her grandson Charles Eliot in 1888

CELIA IN HER GARDEN 1890

CELIA'S GRAVE ON APPLEDORE

CEDRIC LAIGHTON

fortunate to have found the two upper floors of a large
brick building on State Street, which had once been the
Armory of the Rockingham Guards. On the ground floor
there was an apothecary shop, but a separate entrance
led to the pleasant apartment above. Here were nine
rooms, which had never before been lived in and which
the landlord was glad to arrange as Celia desired. She
described her new surroundings.

> . . . This is the quaintest old place. There isn't a straight
> line in the house, and hardly a room, without seven corners
> in it. This long parlor is on the corner of the street, the
> windows are full of plants, and hanging pots, ferns and
> palms. There are three kinds of oxalis, all blooming, and
> crocus bulbs in a blaze of gold and purple.

Celia sat among them and looked down State Street to
the Piscataqua River through the bare branches of the
trees. She could see ships going out to the harbor and
the sea beyond. Across the river was the Kittery shore,
and Seavey's Island where the many-windowed Franklin
Ship House held the ways for the wooden ships being
built for the U. S. Navy.

It was a quiet, peaceful spot. She was near the De-
Normandie home, and the house where Cedric and his
family spent the winter. She was able to drive the seven
miles to visit John and Gertrude on the Kittery farm.
Roland sent word from New Haven in November that she
was a grandmother.

Having known many weeks at a time without mail
during the winters on Appledore, Celia was overjoyed that
now she could receive letters twice a day! However, she
was not physically able to write many letters herself that
winter.

She wrote S. G. Ward from Portsmouth in November
of 1888:

> . . . I have a most charming old fashioned deep window seat

in my long parlor here, full of plants, hanging pots and brackets . . .

Dear friend, I wish I could have read the article on chrysanthemums, but I don't know any language but my own, and hardly pretend to know that. I never went to school and never had any education, my lighthouse stands between me and all that — since I grew up I have been in such a whirl of work that I have never learned anything at all . . .

Celia was always modest about her own abilities.

The winter passed quietly and gradually she grew strong in her "garden window".

In the spring, Celia journeyed to New Haven to see her little blond grandson, named Charles Eliot, after his father's close friend, Dr. Charles Eliot, son of the President of Harvard University. Then began for her one of the greatest happinesses of her life, her passionate love for her grandchildren.

> *Thou little child, with tender, clinging arms,*
> *Drop thy sweet head, my darling, down and rest*
> *Upon my shoulder, rest with all thy charms,*
> *Be soothed and comforted, be loved and blessed.*
> *Against thy silken, honey-colored hair*
> *I lean a loving cheek, a mute caress;*
> *Close, close I gather thee and kiss thy fair*
> *White eyelids, sleep so softly doth depress.*
> *Dear little face, that lies in calm content*
> *Within the gracious hollow that God made*
> *In every human shoulder, where He meant*
> *Some tired head for comfort should be laid!*
> *Most like a heavy-folded rose thou art,*
> *In summer air reposing, warm and still.*
> *Dream thy sweet dream upon my quiet heart;*
> *I watch thy slumber, naught shall do thee ill.*
>
> SLUMBER SONG

As Celia's health returned she tired of the indoor pursuits of painting and writing. She delighted in working out of doors in the invigorating morning air. She loved delving in the earth, planting her seeds and transplanting all the tenderly nurtured seedlings which had been started weeks before in her sunny windows. Her garden was not always as successful as she hoped. The shallow soil and the cold winds were hard on young plants. Then came the flocks of migrating birds, hungry from their long flight north and delighted to find tender green shoots in the middle of expanses of water. Celia would patiently re-plant and laughingly scold her feathered friends. Birds seemed to sense her love of them, and often one would perch on her shoulder as she worked. She was also troubled by other devastating enemies, especially slugs. Someone told her that in France it was the custom to catch toads and sell them to gardeners to eat the slugs. Celia at once wrote to friends on the mainland to send her "toads and more toads! . . ."

To Annie she wrote:

Shoals, July 15, 1889
. . . You would have laughed to see the box of toads which came for me. Ninety toads all wired over in a box and won-dering what fate was in store for them . . . Soon as the mow-ing was done, all the million slugs charged into my poor garden and poste haste I sent for more of my little dusty pets, my friends, my saviours! and turned them loose in the fat sluggy ground and such a breakfast as they must have had! If there is one thing I adore more than another, it is a toad . . .

Just our own party here in the house now, there are others, not so interesting. The weather is so beautiful and everybody having such a good time! . . . Mr. Mason is play-ing Chopin nocturnes, preludes — such dreaming music . . . I have my hands, head and heart too full and I wish people could come by installments and not all at once, it takes the life pretty nearly out of me!

Back in Portsmouth, November 5, 1889, she begged Sarah Jewett to come to see her as soon as she was a bit rested and continued, "I am feeling so anxious about poor, poor Karl. He seems losing his hold. . . He sits and weeps for hours. . . O for some power to save him, to lift him out of it."

During the winter Celia, herself, suffered nervous prostration and wrote Mr. Ward: "I have given away all my strength all my life long and now I miss it sadly. But I trust to struggle up out of this weariness bye and bye."

And again she wrote on February 22, 1890:

> . . . I cannot answer your question about myself as I would like, for indeed I have been helpless enough all winter and am still almost too good-for-nothing to live. Still I have much to be thankful for that I do not suffer pain and am able to be about . . . Mabel and the baby are coming to stay a week with me!

Back on the Shoals, April 17, 1890, she wrote Mr. Ward:

> . . . The doctor will not let me write. I am trying to vegetate and forget that I ever had a moderate portion of intelligence . . . I must ask you — have you Tennyson's new volume, and do you not think the last poem the most beautiful? *Crossing the Bar* . . .

By May 12 on the Shoals, she could only say, "I hope I am improving in this delicious air."

All that "heavenly summer" Celia lay in her sofa corner. Gradually her health improved and many friends crowded her parlor for evenings of music and reading. Sometimes she read some of her own verses with a fullness of suggestion which no other reader could give. As always, her voice was sufficient to fill and satisfy the ears of her listeners. All who heard realized that it was her own generous, beautiful nature, unlike any other, which made her reading unique.

To those she generously invited to her parlor she always said: "If people do not enjoy what they find they must go their way; my work and the music will not cease." And this was true up to the last. She possessed the keen instincts of a child with regard to people. If they were not sympathetic to her, nothing could bring her to overcome her dislike.

"No worldly motive ever influenced her relation with human creatures," said Annie Fields.

On August 16 of that year, Celia wrote Mr. and Mrs. Samuel Ward:

> . . . I am in the vortex of the Shoals' life just now and have so little strength to meet the demands of every day life, I write but few letters, but thoughts can leap the large length of miles! My garden and my flowers have never been so lovely in spite of the dry weather. A new feature is the Shirley Poppies from white through every heavenly shade and tint of rose, to the most radiant and delicate scarlet glory — wonderful. I pile them in a pyramid on the bookcase opposite the windows in graduated shades and they are like a rosy dawn, Aurora herself.

This arrangement is the subject for one of the many Hassam illustrations in *An Island Garden*. These "Shoals" poppies remained a feature in her garden always.

In December of 1890, Celia wrote Mrs. Ward a startling bit of news:

> . . . An English syndicate is going to buy the dear Shoals. My brothers are going to sell it, they are so weary and worn with all the care. All their lives it has been their responsibility, over forty years.

The Laightons planned to build two cottages, one for Cedric and his family, and one for Oscar, Celia and Karl, on the point of land toward White Island.

> . . . I won't allow myself to think about it. Neither persons, nor places should we cling to too closely, only God. I try hard to forget it and have patience. There are many changes and deaths. We are always learning these sad lessons and being taught not to let our affections twine too closely round any mortal thing. Nothing really is except God!

The plan to sell the hotels was postponed until spring and then abandoned completely. It might have been better financially for the Laighton brothers had they sold out for a good price in 1891, but they held on for almost twenty more years. The Oceanic had a goodly number of guests, but they were of somewhat different tastes and interests than those drawn to the larger colony on Appledore, chiefly because of Celia Thaxter. She seldom visited Star Island, preferring to remember it as it was in the days of her early marriage, when she lived in the old parsonage.

In Portsmouth the next winter, Celia found that the only way she could sleep at night was by following the doctor's orders and keeping out of doors in the cold air all day, every day. When the snow was too deep along the roads for her carriage, she would drive in an open sleigh, often taking as her companion Edith, the little daughter of her lately deceased cousin, Albert Laighton, who lived on Court Street.

Celia described one such day:

> . . . exploring cart paths in the pine woods off the Gosling Road and along Great Bay, which looked heavenly, with the hills beyond sapphire blue and white with snow, The white gulls and black crows were sitting on the ice at the edge. . .

Another day she drove almost to Mt. Agamenticus on the outskirts of old York, the landmark of her childhood at the Shoals. She wrote also of another sleigh ride in the opposite direction:

> . . . I drove in a snowstorm to the beach at Wallis Sands this afternoon, and saw the wild waves lashing the coast and the murky ocean streaked with foam, between me and the islands. Tonight I hear the warning note of the foghorn, blowing constantly up the river into the town, even to our ears, as we sit sheltered from the tempest. We know it is a stormy night and many a storm will blow over those dear rocks before spring comes smiling back again. But she will come!

Celia often visited her friends, the Albee family, in New Castle. She remembered the days when she had sometimes sailed alone from Appledore, beached her boat, and donned her riding habit and gone for a brisk scamper on horseback — then sailed back to the island at sunset. The two little girls, Loulie and her sister, lovingly called her "Aunt Celia" and her poem *Footprints in the Sand* was written about them. In her old age, Loulie Albee Mathews said, "Aunt Celia was the most unforgettable person I ever knew. She had the faculty of making the one to whom she spoke, feel he was the only one in whom she was ever interested."

While Celia was not well, she carried on a very interesting correspondence with Bradford Torrey, the authority on birds. She told him of all the kinds seen on the Shoals and of their habits. She urged him to come to the Shoals the next summer. He was unable to do so and so they never met, but for the remainder of her life Celia continued to write long and enthusiastic letters to him.

Celia was becoming more and more absorbed in the new delight of her grandchildren. Roland was now a professor at Harvard and had started building a house in Norton's Woods, near Kirkland Street in Cambridge. In the autumn of 1891 Mabel and the babies came to the Shoals to stay with "Granna".

Celia wrote:

> . . . I never knew what it was to be happy, I think, until I became a grandmother! When my little three year old Eliot comes to me and says with grave intensity "Granna I adore you!" my cup of bliss is quite full! My arms and thoughts are full all the time — everything else goes, writing most of all . . .

They all stayed for two months, then Eliot stayed on with his grandmother who "worship(ed) the ground he walks on" — Celia wrote, "I never meant in my old age to become subject to the thrall of a love like this! . . . He

clings to my neck crying 'Only one Granna, only one!' "
When Eliot was ill, she nursed him and found him "perfectly bewitching. How can his grandmother do anything but fall hopelessly in love with him! There's a little girl, too, like a wild rose!"

Through the winter, Celia was busy with her window garden, which bloomed with plants. By January 17, she was starting seedlings to be taken to the Shoals two months later. It was in 1891 that she began a new method. She wrote Mrs. Ward:

> Portsmouth, January 17, 1891
> . . . I have been planting various seeds for my little garden and have my golden poppies all started in eggshells for next summer.

This method as she later explained in her book *An Island Garden,* protected the delicate roots from being blown away when placed in the ground, and eventually helped to fertilize them. Every possible method she could learn about, Celia used in making her garden a "most breathtaking riot of color".

As Celia had watched the rising summer sun while a child, she now arose at five o'clock, put on a warm dress and, taking scissors and a bucket of hot water, stepped out into her beloved garden — hers because she had worked the soil, transplanted her seedlings, weeded and tended every inch herself. She would carefully snip the Shirley poppies and at once plunge their long stems into the hot water. This method kept the blossoms fresh all day; the heads never drooped nor did the petals fall, as is the case with the untrained arranger. Then her many vases must be washed and filled. She did not plant in the manner of the formal garden, with small groups of flowers here and there and earth between where weeds could grow. Her flowers grew in a wild, beautiful disorder. Celia saved most of her seeds from year to year and planted enough so even if the pests destroyed a large number, there would still be plenty left. The piazza of her cottage was completely covered with hop-vines whose sturdy green leaves made a delightful shade and screen. Always there were yellow calendulas, in memory of the ones Mr. Whittier once allowed her to put in his buttonhole. There were bachelor buttons, favorites of Oscar Laighton, who wore one alternately with a clover blossom. And there was also the blue flax.

In her flower arrangements there were no garden club rules of balance, height or design. Celia painted a picture with her flowers and their beauty was unforgettable! To watch her handle the flowers she worshiped was also something not to be forgotten. Annie Fields tells us that "the lines of Keats — 'open afresh your rounds of starry folds, ye ardent marigolds!' " were probably oftener flitting through Celia's mind than any other since Keats wrote them.

Small wonder more and more people urged her to put her secrets between the covers of a book. She was tired and not very enthusiastic about the idea, but her dear "Pinny" offered to give all the help possible. So when she was once more settled in Portsmouth, for the winter of 1892 — 1893, she prepared her notes. She could easily journey to South Berwick to talk over her manuscript with her friend.

She wrote Sarah Orne Jewett:

. . . Thank you for your sweet letter and all your kind suggestions. I had already begun to "reef" my M. S. and perceived at once, when I read it aloud that it must be cut in ever so many places. Dear, you have given me a real helpful lift, because I have been doing this work without a particle of enthusiasm, in a most perfunctory manner, from the bits of notes I had made; my mind has been so saddened by deep shadows for many months, somehow I had no heart in it at all.

She wrote again February 5, 1893:

. . . Oh, you dear kind, wisest and helpfulest! I thought

I should remember . . . every word of your suggestions
when you spoke them, but alas! I rack my stupid and
empty brain in vain for most of them. . .

Celia gratefully planned the dedication of the book to
read:

To Mrs. Mary Hemenway, whose "largeness of heart is
even as the sand that is on the seashore," this little volume
is affectionately inscribed.

Unfortunately her benefactress did not live to read the
volume.

After the usual busy summer, Celia's tired brain found
it hard to concentrate. She wrote again on September 28,
1893 to Sarah Jewett:

. . . I am pegging away on the book and I want to ask
you lots of things. All you say is so precious, dear. I have
got a little plan of the garden, as you suggested, with places
of everything marked, — a sort of little map. I have got
the whole thing done, the writing, but there is much
copying and arranging of parts to make a proper unity.
I have been ill since the house closed, just about dead
with the stress and bother of things and people, and
feared to slip back to the hateful state of three years ago.
The doctor said, "You are going to have the whole thing
over again if you are not mighty careful," and mighty
careful I have been and I am better.

An Island Garden appeared at Easter, 1894, and her
friends were very happy with its reception and with the
exceptionally beautiful illustrations by Childe Hassam. He
painted Celia standing in her garden dressed all in white,
as was her wont, surrounded by glorious Shirley poppies,
a bit of blue sea behind. The figure is regal in its simplicity. The orginal is now part of the Mellon Collection in
the National Gallery of Art in Washington, D. C., as is
another of the illustrations, which pictures Celia and little
Eliot standing in her doorway.

The year before, 1893, Olaf Brauner had made a large bas-relief of Celia, copies of which he sold for seventy-five dollars. There was a poppy in the background — "gone to seed like the woman who is in plaster," Celia said with wry good humor. A colored photograph of her was taken in her garden, the proceeds from the sale of which went to help a little lame girl in whom Celia was interested.

The first transatlantic cables came from the Irish coast, near Bantry Bay, straight through the Isles of Shoals in 1894. Oscar Laighton was one of the first to receive an operator's license and could decode messages before they reached the Rye Beach Cable Station on the New Hampshire coast. Celia first realized the great relief this brought when, in March, Oscar and Karl had to go to Portsmouth in a severe storm. Ten minutes after their arrival a reassuring message of their safety came to her on Appledore.

Celia Thaxter had crowded more work into fifty-nine years than many persons dream of in a lifetime nearly twice as long. She was weary, but still at the beck and call of anyone in need. When she received an urgent message in June to come to Kittery, she reached Roland's summer home just in time to wrap her third grandchild, who had arrived unexpectedly early, in her own warm flannel petticoat. Little Betty opened her eyes the day after her grandmother's fifty-ninth birthday. She treasures the story, although her grandmother was to pass from the world before the baby was old enough to remember her.

A few years earlier, while gathering wild strawberries together, little Eliot had suddenly asked, "Are you very old, Granna?"

"Yes, dear," Celia said, "I am very old."

He heaved a deep sigh and said, "I am very sorry."

"But why, dear?" she asked.

"Because I don't want you deaded before I am!" The idea of losing her was even then troubling his small mind.

That summer, as if with a dim foreboding, Celia paid a

last visit to the old familiar places of a tiny world held so dear since her childhood. She called her dearest friends — Annie Fields, Childe Hassam, Ole Bull, Rose Lamb and Sarah Jewett — to walk or sail with her. She spent an afternoon on the high cliffs of Star Island and she spoke of the year spent in the Gosport parsonage, while her husband taught the islanders.

Sarah Jewett, in her Preface to *Poems*, tells poignantly:

> . . . She walked with a sure step over the rough rocks on White Island, and showed us many a trace of her childhood. . .and with a touching lovely cadence in her voice, an unforgotten cadence . . . sang some quaint old songs. . .

On Smutty-nose they sat by the Spaniards' graves and watched the sea. Most vivid of all was the afternoon on Appledore when she unerringly found her childhood playground, the stone-walled enclosures and worn doorsteps of forgotten houses. Creeping under the Sheep rock for shelter from a sudden gust of rain, she found a rare wild flower which seemed to reach up to her hand.

"This never bloomed on Appledore before," she said. "I shall come here again," and she went her unreturning way.

Celia again urged Bradford Torrey to come to the Shoals:

> July 20, 1894
> . . . When the whirl of people passes and tranquillity settles once more upon our little world . . . steal a moment . . . let us see and know you; will you not? Some of us may be slipping out of this mortal state, and we shall never know each other in this particular phase of existence, which would be a pity, I think.

Celia had not been feeling as well as usual, and on August 25, 1894, Minna Berntsen sent for Roland to come to spend Sunday on the island. He came, bringing the two older children. Celia was lying in her parlor in her sofa corner, with a few close friends who had gathered as usual.

Roland sat beside her, holding her hand as they listened to the music. Then she read a few of her poems for those who asked. Feeling a little tired, she retired early.

Minna slept in the room to be ready if needed. As the first blush of dawn lightened the sky, Celia asked that the curtains be opened so she could see the sunrise. When Minna turned from the window Celia was dead!

All were stunned by the suddenness of her passing. Oscar and Cedric were almost paralyzed by shock. Remembering their mother's death, and how strongly Celia, herself, felt — no outside help was asked. Minna Berntsen and Lucy Caswell did all that had to be done.

When the news became known throughout the island, a stillness fell over the homes, the hotel, all of Appledore.

Oscar said, "Mother came in the night and took Sister away."

On Monday morning the sad news was flashed to newspapers. Arrangements were made in the simplest possible way, characteristic of the atmosphere and the woman. Childe Hassam and Appleton Brown gathered masses of sweet-smelling bayberry and the children timidly brought flowers and more flowers! Dr. DeNormandie conducted the simple service. Celia lay in her parlor made radiant with flowers. Then, carried by those closest to her, she was borne out around the house and up the path to the spot where her mother and father had been laid. There was no appearance of a grave, for all was covered with green leaves, and the flowers she loved were brought by the children to cover her completely. As the words of the last prayer were spoken, a little bird was seen to flutter skyward.

The family and intimate friends returned to her parlor, and Mr. Mason played for two hours the music which had meant so much to Celia Thaxter when she, also, had been sorrowful. As Annie Fields said: "It was a Poet's burial!"

Celia's farewell message to her sons, brothers, and host

of friends whose lives had been touched and inspired by hers, can be found in the letter she had written her cousin, Albert Laighton, when she learned he was dying of cancer:

. . . It is so long since death was robbed of any terror or distress so that I cannot look upon it in the way people generally do at all. It is a purely natural process, and no more than casting off your worn out coat for a fresh one, no more, no more! I know it! It is only leaving your dear ones here for a little space; it means having your little Arthur in your arms, the mother you loved clasping you, the brothers, sisters, friends, all welcoming you — I know it. And after a little while these dear ones whom you cling to here will join you, nor will you lose sight of them meanwhile. To me it is a happy, comforting, delightful thought that I shall put off this dress of my body which grows old and tired, presently, and have all my dear ones, there and here, at once! What can be more beautiful to think of? Do not be cast down, there is every reason for joy — be of good cheer — let the tired body go, it is nothing. No harm can come to that dear, pure noble soul which is you and the only you; happiness is waiting for it, of that I am sure. May the coming joy bring you peace beforehand; may the thought of the comfort in store help you every hour . . .

The memory of Celia Thaxter still surrounds the Islands she loved and has been passed down to succeeding generations, by those of whom she spoke when she said:

"What a joy friendship is! I grow warm thinking of what friends God has given me in this little life of mine. I should glow warm at the thought, if all the glaciers of the Alps were heaped over me."

EPILOGUE

After reading the book many persons have asked that I bring the story up to date by answering such questions as What became of Karl? What is there on the Isles of Shoals now? So in a few words I will try to round out the picture.

After his mother's death Karl was a lonely, rather pathetic figure. He boarded with friends in Portsmouth and continued his interest in photography. He was much helped by his strong religious faith. He was especially kind to children and would take large groups on an all-day picnic to the Isles of Shoals or to the farm at Kittery. He was so generous in completely outfitting some shabby little girl like the one in the photograph with new dress and shoes, that his brothers feared he would overspend the small income left him by his mother. He drifted from Portsmouth to Newton and then to Worcester, Mass., where he died alone in 1912.

Two years later came the end of the Appledore Hotel, which had passed out of the hands of the last of the Laightons some years before. After a poor season with the new management, a mysterious fire broke out in the boiler room and all the buildings connected with the hotel and Celia Thaxter's cottage were burned to the ground September 4, 1914. The few remaining cottages left standing on the southwestern end of Appledore were for a few years used for the summer Extension Headquarters for marine research and study of the University of New Hampshire. This project which gave promise of a revival at Appledore had to be abandoned when in 1942 the Island was closed to the public and a Coast Patrol group of U. S. Army was stationed there. Since the end of the war the hand of vandalism has completely demolished the interiors of the sturdily built cottages. Mother Nature has run riot over the whole Island, intertwining blackberry vines with poison ivy in a way to make the old paths impassable. The few nostalgic persons who succeed in landing, share with the wild roses and the sea gulls the memory of a gone but not forgotten era!

Quite differently across Gosport Harbor the very active Star Island Association continues each summer to occupy the Oceanic Hotel built by Mr. Poor. Now many new buildings and improvements have been added to Old Gosport.

From mid June until Labor Day the Island is crowded with happy Shoalers enjoying fellowship, religious and scientific study and most of all the Island charm! A good steamboat runs twice daily from Portsmouth and trippers are allowed to picnic and given a tour of the Island by an historical guide. Included in the tour is a visit to the Henry G. Vaughn Memorial Cottage, one room of which is devoted to a Thaxter-Laighton Museum. Here have been placed many mementoes of the family. These include many beautiful pieces of china painted by Celia and a vast collection of material of all sorts most interesting to examine.

A vast collection of photographs, books and other mementoes of the day when Appledore flourished in all its glory, have been saved and almost tearfully brought for preservation in the little museum. Here persons giving any souvenir of the Golden Days at the Thaxter Cottage and the Island garden, will know these treasures will be lovingly catalogued and preserved. One may spend a morning reading old clippings and looking at photographs. Celia's little writing desk, which once belonged to her son Karl, stands under a sketch of the young girl by her driftwood fire. Also the round tiptop table and the same Windsor chair which can be seen in the photograph of Celia's parlor. These furnish the room, which has a beautiful view of the early lighthouse home.

When the museum room was opened, three of Celia's grandchildren, Rosamond, daughter of her son John, and Roland's son Edmund, and daughter Betty, now Mrs. Eliot Hubbard, and her husband, Dr. Eliot Hubbard, journeyed from Cambridge for the dedication. Mrs. Hubbard has the proud distinction of having had the only great grandchildren, two sons, Eliot and Jack Hubbard, and a daughter, now an artist in her own right, Celia Thaxter Hubbard.

STAR ISLAND CHAPEL—VAUGHN COTTAGE—
THAXTER MEMORIAL ROOM

POOR'S FIRST HOTEL

THAXTER HOUSE AT KITTERY POINT

At the dedication ceremony the youngest of the first Celia's great, great grandchildren, Nathaniel Hubbard, recited "Sandpiper" at the age of seven! Cedric Laighton's daughter, Celia's own niece, Mrs. Barbara Durant, gave a few of her memories, and Rosamond told of her book, the story of her grandmother.

Katharine Thaxter, the other granddaughter, was not present at the time, but visited often since, as has the other great grandson Jack, and his family of four.

The memory of dear Uncle Oscar Laighton still lingers where the last twenty of his ninety-nine summers were passed. On Star Island his blue eyes, ruddy complexion and beautiful white beard were a welcome to all visitors. He lived for a time on Londoner's Island and made daily trips in his sturdy motorboat "Twilight," where he told his passengers about "dear Sister" and her poetry. He also wrote his memoirs in his delightful book "Ninety Years on the Isles of Shoals." Two months before his 100th birthday, still quoting poetry, he closed his eyes, holding this author's hand.

There will be no more Laightons or Thaxters, in the direct line, but eight young Hubbards seem to feel a love for the Isles of their heritage. Also there are many descendants of Cedric Laighton's daughter Margaret who married Edward Forbes, and Barbara, Mrs. William Durant.

The Islands of Smutty-nose and Malaga, purchased by Thomas Laighton in 1837, have never passed from the family. They still belong in part to Rosamond Thaxter. For 200 years descendants of Thomas have felt pride in ownership, as he did, and are drawn back in memory and in reality to the Enchanted Isles!

The door of my little cabin is always open and a welcome extended to all who wish to enjoy the peace, the calm and beauty of the Islands and to think back over the years to the lives of their forebears.

ROSAMOND THAXTER

July 1967

THE FOLLOWING LETTERS HAVE
RECENTLY COME TO LIGHT

This letter written to young Roland by his mother as from his little dog has lately come to light. Saved in an old desk.

Appledore
March 6th, 1869

My dear little Master,

I miss you very much. I was very seasick coming over in the boat and didn't know what was going to be done to me. I watched my chance and scrabbled up out of the cabin thinking I could feel better if I could get out, but bow-wow-wow! O-o-o-o! It was dreadful up on deck, I couldn't keep my feet, though I had four to stand on, the wind blew and horrible cold water dashed over me. I managed to crawl to your Uncle Cedric and got as close as I could to him, but it wouldn't do. The water was too dreadful and I scuttled down again and was a miserable dog till I got on shore. When we got to the house they gave me a good bone, but I didn't have much appetite. I scratched at the pump till they gave me some water of which I drank a great deal and went and lay down behind the stove.

I have a pretty good time but I miss you and John very much. I am round a good deal in the day time and bark at the cows and horse. They have a most improper way of coming up and my sense of the impropriety of it is so great that I nearly bark myself into fits on the doorstep, but they don't move a jot for all my noise. It wouldn't be allowed for a moment in Newtonville! A man from Star Island came here the other day and I dutifully rushed at him and fixed my tooth in the heel of his boot. His name was John Cook and he made such a noise that your mother came out and called me in. Another one named Jud came day before yesterday and I flew at him and bit his trousers through and through, whereupon he and your two uncles set up such a roar of laughter that they had to sit down and rest themselves. I couldn't see anything to laugh at, for my part. I had the pleasure of shaking the life out of a rat the other day and heard his back bone snap with satisfaction, and everybody patted me and said I was a good dog, which made me feel very proud, so that I winked and blinked more foolishly than usual, with my hair all over my eyes. In the evenings, while your mother is reading aloud, one or other of your uncles always holds me on his lap and altogether I'm very much petted indeed. They leave me here in the parlor for the night and when they go away, I'm always lying very innocently behind the stove, but the minute they go, up I hop on the sofa and then I pass a pleasant night till Jenny comes and puts me out of doors at half past five o'clock in the morning. There I run around and snarl and bark and cough a little and then come and scratch at the door till they let me in, and I go and lie down behind the stove where it's nice and warm.

I want to see you very much. How I'll bark when you come! I send you a lock of my hair. I've been washed over but I go round among the coal and in the mud and dust after rats, and it's of no manner of use, washing me! I never *did* see any use in it! Bow, wow, wow! I am your affectionate little dog.

Sil.

Celia's parents had been married for 25 years and this was almost the only time they had been separated.

Appledore, Isles of Shoals
Sat. Oct 4, 1856

My cherished and beloved wife,

A week has elapsed since you left our peaceful home and to me that week, brief though it be, appears a little eternity. You cannot imagine, my dear wife, how necessary your presence is to the happiness and comfort of my life. Your absence and Oscar's at the same time is the tearing away of the best part of our home — he is the music and you the sunshine of our solitary life. But the time wears away, and then, to meet you again, safe, contented, and happy, what a glorious moment it will be for us all.

Give yourself no uneasiness about our well doing. We are getting along famously as can be possible to do, without you. Though I must confess I regard everything as unsettled with us until I again hear the merry music of your sweet voice in our own home.

God forever bless you, my own dear wife, that you may enjoy yourself and return early to your devoted friend and ever loving husband, is the prayer of

Thomas B. Laighton

This letter was recently found in the Yale Collection:

7 Coloseum Terrace,
Albany St. Regent's Park, W.
Jan. 28th '81

My dear Mr. Browning:

I am in fear lest Mr. Moncure Conway should have written to you asking you to call on me if you were at liberty on Sat. or Sunday from five to six. I am going to Annie Thackeray Ritchie at five on Saturday.

My husband is your willing bondsman, your devoted lover, your apostle, preaching your gospel to crowds in America — for his sake I wish much to see you, but I never should have dreamed of taking such a method of bringing it about and was filled with dismay after Mr. C. had left me saying he should ask you to come and see me. I wrote to Mrs. Ritchie asking her to tell you, but afterward Mr. Lowes Dickenson gave me your address, which I could not wholly remember so I venture to write to you myself. I must plead as excuse my short time in London — I have but three days.

You were interested in Wm. Hunt. It was with us he passed his last summer — it was my fate to find him, when all the rest sought him in vain — to find him "freed by that throbbing impulse we call death, floating on the still pool under the sky."

I hope it may be my fortune to see you!

Yours very truly

Celia Thaxter

POEMS

LAND-LOCKED

Black lie the hills; swiftly doth daylight flee;
  And, catching gleams of sunset's dying smile,
  Through the dusk land for many a changing mile
The river runneth softly to the sea.

O happy river, could I follow thee!
  O yearning heart, that never can be still!
  O wistful eyes, that watch the steadfast hill,
Longing for level line of solemn sea!

Have patience; here are flowers and songs of birds,
  Beauty and fragrance, wealth of sound and sight,
  All summer's glory thine from morn till night,
And life too full of joy for uttered words.

Neither am I ungrateful; but I dream
  Deliciously how twilight falls to-night
  Over the glimmering water, how the light
Dies blissfully away, until I seem

To feel the wind, sea-scented, on my cheek,
  To catch the sound of dusky flapping sail
  And dip of oars, and voices on the gale
Afar off, calling low, — my name they speak!

O Earth! thy summer song of joy may soar
  Ringing to heaven in triumph. I but crave
  The sad, caressing murmur of the wave
That breaks in tender music on the shore.

OFF SHORE

Rock, little boat, beneath the quiet sky;
Only the stars behold us where we lie, —
Only the stars and yonder brightening moon.

On the wide sea to-night alone are we;
The sweet, bright summer day dies silently,
Its glowing sunset will have faded soon.

Rock softly, little boat, the while I mark
The far off gliding sails, distinct and dark,
Across the west pass steadily and slow.

But on the eastern waters sad, they change
And vanish, dream-like, gray, and cold, and strange,
And no one knoweth whither they may go.

We care not, we, drifting with wind and tide,
While glad waves darken upon either side,
Save where the moon sends silver sparkles down.

And yonder slender stream of changing light,
Now white, now crimson, tremulously bright,
Where dark the lighthouse stands, with fiery crown.

Thick falls the dew, soundless on sea and shore:
It shines on little boat and idle oar,
Wherever moonbeams touch with tranquil glow.

The waves are full of whispers wild and sweet;
They call to me, — incessantly they beat
Along the boat from stern to curvèd prow.

Comes the careering wind, blows back my hair,
All damp with dew, to kiss me unaware,
Murmuring "Thee I love," and passes on.

Sweet sounds on rocky shores the distant rote;
Oh could we float forever, little boat,
Under the blissful sky drifting alone!

THE WRECK OF THE POCAHONTAS

I lit the lamps in the lighthouse tower,
   For the sun dropped down and the day was dead.
They shone like a glorious clustered flower, —
   Ten golden and five red.

Looking across, where the line of coast
   Stretched darkly, shrinking away from the sea,
The lights sprang out at its edge, — almost
   They seemed to answer me!

O warning lights! burn bright and clear
   Hither the storm comes, Leagues away
It moans and thunders low and drear, —
   Burn till the break of day!

Good-night! I called to the gulls that sailed
   Slow past me through the evening sky;
And my comrades, answering shrilly, hailed
   Me back with boding cry.

A mournful breeze began to blow;
   Weird music it drew through the iron bars;
The sullen billows boiled below,
   And dimly peered the stars;

The sails that flecked the ocean floor
   From east to west leaned low and fled;
They knew what came in the distant roar
   That filled the air with dread!

Flung by a fitful gust, there beat
   Against the window a dash of rain:
Steady as tramp of marching feet
   Strode on the hurricane.

It smote the waves for a moment still,
  Level and deadly white for fear;
The bare rock shuddered, — an awful thrill
  Shook even my tower of cheer.

Like all the demons loosed at last,
  Whistling and shrieking, wild and wide,
The mad wind raged, while strong and fast
  Rolled in the rising tide.

And soon in ponderous showers, the spray,
  Struck from the granite, reared and sprung
And clutched at tower and cottage gray,
  Where overwhelmed they clung

Half drowning to the naked rock;
  But still burned on the faithful light,
Nor faltered at the tempest's shock,
  Through all the fearful night.

Was it in vain? That knew not we.
  We seemed, in that confusion vast
Of rushing wind and roaring sea,
  One point whereon was cast

The whole Atlantic's weight of brine.
  Heaven help the ship should drift our way!
No matter how the light might shine
  Far on into the day.

When morning dawned, above the din
  Of gale and breaker boomed a gun!
Another! We who sat within
  Answered with cries each one.

Into each other's eyes with fear
  We looked through helpless tears, as still,

One after one, near and more near,
    The signals pealed, until

The thick storm seemed to break apart
    To show us, staggering to her grave,
The fated brig. We had no heart
    To look, for naught could save.

One glimpse of black hull heaving slow,
    Then closed the mists o'er canvas torn
And tangled ropes swept to and fro
    From masts that raked forlorn.

Weeks after, yet ringed round with spray
    Our island lay, and none might land;
Though blue the waters of the bay
    Stretched calm on either hand.

And when at last from the distant shore
    A little boat stole out, to reach
Our loneliness, and bring once more
    Fresh human thought and speech,

We told our tale, and the boatmen cried:
    " 'Twas the Pocahontas, — all were lost!
For miles along the coast the tide
    Her shattered timbers tossed."

Then I looked the whole horizon round, —
    So beautiful the ocean spread
About us, o'er those sailors drowned!
    "Father in heaven," I said, —

A child's grief struggling in my breast, —
    "Do purposeless thy children meet
Such bitter death? How was it best
    These hearts should cease to beat?

"O wherefore? Are we naught to Thee?
    Like senseless weeds that rise and fall
Upon thine awful sea, are we
    No more then, after all?"

And I shut the beauty from my sight,
    For I thought of the dead that lay below;
From the bright air faded the warmth and light,
    There came a chill like snow.

Then I heard the far-off rote resound,
    Where the breakers slow and slumberous rolled,
And a subtile sense of Thought profound
    Touched me with power untold.

And like a voice eternal spake
    That wondrous rhythm, and, "Peace, be still!"
It murmured, "bow thy head and take
    Life's rapture and life's ill,

"And wait. At last all shall be clear."
    The long, low, mellow music rose
And fell, and soothed my dreaming ear
    With infinite repose.

Sighing I climbed the lighthouse stair,
    Half forgetting my grief and pain;
And while the day died, sweet and fair,
    I lit the lamps again.

THE SANDPIPER

Across the narrow beach we flit,
　One little sandpiper and I,
And fast I gather, bit by bit,
　The scattered driftwood bleached and dry.
The wild waves reach their hands for it,
　The wild wind raves, the tide runs high,
As up and down the beach we flit, —
　One little sandpiper and I.

Above our heads the sullen clouds
　Scud black and swift across the sky;
Like silent ghosts in misty shrouds
　Stand out the white lighthouses high.
Almost as far as eye can reach
　I see the close-reefed vessels fly,
As fast we flit along the beach, —
　One little sandpiper and I.

I watch him as he skims along,
　Uttering his sweet and mournful cry.
He starts not at my fitful song,
　Or flash of fluttering drapery.
He has no thought of any wrong;
　He scans me with a fearless eye.
Stanch friends are we, well tried and strong,
　The little sandpiper and I.

Comrade, where wilt thou be to-night
　When the loosed storm breaks furiously?
My driftwood fire will burn so bright!
　To what warm shelter canst thou fly?
I do not fear for thee, though wroth
　The tempest rushes through the sky:
For are we not God's children both,
　Thou, little sandpiper, and I?

TWILIGHT

September's slender crescent grows again
  Distinct in yonder peaceful evening red,
  Clearer the stars are sparkling overhead,
And all the sky is pure, without a stain.

Cool blows the evening wind from out the West
  And bows the flowers, the last sweet flowers that bloom, —
  Pale asters, many a heavy-waving plume
Of goldenrod that bends as if opprest.

  The summer's songs are hushed. Up the lone shore
  The weary waves wash sadly, and a grief
  Sounds in the wind, like farewells fond and brief.
The cricket's chirp but makes the silence more.

Life's autumn comes; the leaves begin to fall;
  The moods of spring and summer pass away;
  The glory and the rapture, day by day,
Depart, and soon the quiet grave folds all.

O thoughtful sky, how many eyes in vain
  Are lifted to your beauty, full of tears!
  How many hearts go back through all the years,
Heavy with loss, eager with questioning pain,

To read the dim Hereafter, to obtain
  One glimpse beyond the earthly curtain, where
  Their dearest dwell, where they may be or e'er
September's slender crescent shines again!

THE SPANIARDS' GRAVES
At The Isles of Shoals

O sailors, did sweet eyes look after you
  The day you sailed away from sunny Spain?
Bright eyes that followed fading ship and crew,
  Melting in tender rain?

Did no one dream of that drear night to be,
  Wild with the wind, fierce with the stinging snow,
When on yon granite point that frets the sea,
  The ship met her death-blow?

Fifty long years ago these sailors died:
  (None know how many sleep beneath the waves:)
Fourteen gray headstones, rising side by side,
  Point out their nameless graves, —

Lonely, unknown, deserted, but for me,
  And the wild birds that flit with mournful cry,
And sadder winds, and voices of the sea
  That moans perpetually.

Wives, mothers, maidens, wistfully, in vain
  Questioned the distance for the yearning sail,
That, leaning landward, should have stretched again
  White arms wide on the gale,

To bring back their beloved. Year by year,
  Weary they watched, till youth and beauty passed,
And lustrous eyes grew dim and age drew near,
  And hope was dead at last.

Still summer broods o'er that delicious land,
  Rich, fragrant, warm with skies of golden glow:
Live any yet of that forsaken band
  Who loved so long ago?

O Spanish women, over the far seas,
    Could I but show you where your dead repose!
Could I send tidings on this northern breeze
    That strong and steady blows!

Dear dark-eyed sisters, you remember yet
    These you have lost, but you can never know
One stands at their bleak graves whose eyes are wet
    With thinking of your woe!

WATCHING

In childhood's season fair,
On many a balmy, moonless summer night,
While wheeled the lighthouse arms of dark and bright
  Far through the humid air;

How patient have I been,
Sitting alone, a happy little maid,
Waiting to see, careless and unafraid,
  My father's boat come in;

Close to the water's edge
Holding a tiny spark, that he might steer
(So dangerous the landing, far and near)
  Safe past the ragged ledge.

I had no fears, — not one;
The wild, wide waste of water leagues around
Washed ceaselessly; there was no human sound,
  And I was all alone.

But Nature was so kind!
Like a dear friend I loved the loneliness;
My heart rose glad, as at some sweet caress,
  When passed the wandering wind.

Yet it was joy to hear,
From out the darkness, sounds grow clear at last,
Of rattling rowlock, and of creaking mast,
  And voices drawing near!

"Is't thou, dear father? Say!"
What well-known shout resounded in reply,
As loomed the tall sail, smitten suddenly
  With the great lighthouse ray!

I will be patient now,
Dear Heavenly Father, waiting here for Thee:
I know the darkness holds Thee. Shall I be
    Afraid, when it is Thou?

On thy eternal shore,
In pauses, when life's tide is at its prime,
I hear the everlasting rote of Time
    Beating for evermore.

Shall I not then rejoice?
Oh, never lost or sad should child of thine
Sit waiting, fearing lest there come no sign,
    No whisper of thy voice!

ROSAMOND THAXTER

Shoals. 27th March
1876

Dear Sadie Cabot :

Ever since I came
home I have been thinking of you &
longing to write to you, but I have
been so busy about all sorts of
things! It seems a thousand years
since that lovely time in Boston, &
like a dream at that. We have had
all the fury of the winter spent upon
this disastrous month of March. Upon

CELIA THAXTER'S MATURE HANDWRITING

COURAGE

Because I hold it sinful to despond,
   And will not let the bitterness of life
Blind me with burning tears, but look beyond
   Its tumult and its strife;

Because I lift my head above the mist,
   Where the sun shines and the broad breezes blow,
By every ray and every raindrop kissed
   That God's love doth bestow;

Think you I find no bitterness at all?
   No burden to be borne, like Christian's pack?
Think you there are no ready tears to fall
   Because I keep them back?

Why should I hug life's ills with cold reserve,
   To curse myself and all who love me? Nay!
A thousand times more good than I deserve
   God gives me every day.

And in each one of these rebellious tears,
   Kept bravely back, He makes a rainbow shine;
Grateful I take his slightest gift, no fears
   Nor any doubts are mine.

Dark skies must clear, and when the clouds are past,
   One golden day redeems a weary year;
Patient I listen, sure that sweet at last
   Will sound his voice of cheer.

Then vex me not with childing. Let me be.
   I must be glad and grateful to the end.
I grudge you not your cold and darkness, — me
   The powers of light befriend.

A TRYST

From out the desolation of the North
    An iceberg took its way,
From its detaining comrades breaking forth,
    And traveling night and day.

At whose command? Who bade it sail the deep
    With that resistless force?
Who made the dread appointment it must keep?
    Who traced its awful course?

To the warm airs that stir in the sweet South,
    A good ship spreads her sails;
Stately she passed beyond the harbor's mouth,
    Chased by the favoring gales;

And on her ample decks a happy crowd
    Bade the fair land good-by;
Clear shone the day, with not a single cloud
    In all the peaceful sky.

Brave men, sweet women, little children bright,
    For all these she made room,
And with her freight of beauty and delight
    She went to meet her doom.

Storms buffeted the iceberg, spray was swept
    Across its loftiest height;
Guided alike by storm and calm, it kept
    Its fatal path aright.

Then warmer waves gnawed at its crumbling base,
    As if in piteous plea;
The ardent sun sent slow tears down its face,
    Soft flowing to the sea.

Dawn kissed it with her tender rose tints, Eve
  Bathed it in violet,
The wistful color o'er it seemed to grieve
  With a divine regret.

Whether Day clad its clefts in rainbows dim
  And shadowy as a dream,
Or Night through lonely spaces saw it swim
  White in the moonlight's gleam,

Ever Death rode upon its solemn heights,
  Ever his watch he kept;
Cold at its heart through changing days and nights
  Its changeless purpose slept.

And where afar a smiling coast it passed,
  Straightway the air grew chill;
Dwellers thereon perceived a bitter blast,
  A vague report of ill.

Like some imperial creature, moving slow,
  Meanwhile, with matchless grace,
The stately ship, unconscious of her foe,
  Drew near the trysting place.

For still the prosperous breezes followed her,
  And half the voyage was o'er;
In many a breast glad thoughts began to stir
  Of lands that lay before.

And human hearts with longing love were dumb,
  That soon should cease to beat,
Thrilled with the hope of meetings soon to come,
  And lost in memories sweet.

Was not the weltering waste of water wide
  Enough for both to sail?

What drew the two together o'er the tide,
  Fair ship and iceberg pale?

There came a night with neither moon nor star,
  Clouds draped the sky in black;
With fluttering canvas reefed at every spar,
  And weird fire in her track,

The ship swept on; a wild wind gathering fast
  Drove her at utmost speed.
Bravely she bent before the fitful blast
  That shook her like a reed.

O helmsman, turn thy wheel! Will no surmise
  Cleave through the midnight drear?
No warning of the horrible surprise
  Reach thine unconscious ear?

She rushed upon her ruin. Not a flash
  Broke up the waiting dark;
Dully through wind and sea one awful crash
  Sounded, with none to mark.

Scarcely her crew had time to clutch despair,
  So swift the work was done:
Ere their pale lips could frame a speechless prayer,
  They perished, every one!

IN KITTERY CHURCHYARD
"Mary, wife of Charles Chauncy, died April 23, 1758,
in the 24th year of her age."

Crushing the scarlet strawberries in the grass,
I kneel to read the slanting stone. Alas!
How sharp a sorrow speaks! A hundred years
And more have vanished, with their smiles and tears,
Since here was laid, upon an April day,
Sweet Mary Chauncy in the grave away, —
A hundred years since here her lover stood
Beside her grave in such despairing mood,
And yet from out the vanished past I hear
His cry of anguish sounding deep and clear,
And all my heart with pity melts, as though
To-day's bright sun were looking on his woe.
"Of such a wife, O righteous Heaven! bereft,
What joy for me, what joy on earth is left?
Still from my inmost soul the groans arise,
Still flow the sorrows ceaseless from mine eyes."
Alas, poor tortured soul! I look away
From the dark stone, — how brilliant shines the day!
A low wall, over which the roses shed
Their perfumed petals, shuts the quiet dead
Apart a little, and the tiny square
Stands in the broad and laughing field so fair,
And gay green vines climb o'er the rough stone wall,
And all about the wild birds flit and call.
And but a stone's throw southward, the blue sea
Rolls sparkling in and sings incessantly.
Lovely as any dream the peaceful place,
And scarcely changed since on her gentle face
For the last time on that sad April day

He gazed, and felt, for him all beauty lay
Buried with her forever. Dull to him
Looked the bright world through eyes with tears so dim!
"I soon shall follow the same dreary way
That leads and opens to the coasts of day."
His only hope! But when slow time had dealt
Firmly with him and kindly, and he felt
The storm and stress of strong and piercing pain
Yielding at last, and he grew calm again,
Doubtless he found another mate before
He followed Mary to the happy shore!
But none the less his grief appeals to me
Who sit and listen to the singing sea
This matchless summer day, beside the stone
He made to echo with his bitter moan,
And in my eyes I feel the foolish tears
For buried sorrow, dead a hundred years!

WHEREFORE

Black sea, black sky! A ponderous steamship driving
  Between them, laboring westward on her way,
And in her path a trap of Death's contriving
  Waiting remorseless for its easy prey.

Hundreds of souls within her frame lie dreaming,
  Hoping and fearing, longing for the light:
With human life and thought and feeling teeming.
  She struggles onward through the starless night.

Upon her furnace fires fresh fuel flinging,
  The swarthy firemen grumble at the dust
Mixed with the coal — when suddenly upspringing,
  Swift through the smoke-stack like a signal thrust,

Flares a red flame, a dread illumination!
  A cry, — a tumult! Slowly to her helm
The vessel yields, 'mid shouts of acclamation,
  And joy and terror all her crew o'erwhelm;

For looming from the blackness drear before them
  Discovered is the iceberg — hardly seen,
Its ghastly precipices hanging o'er them,
  Its reddened peaks, with dreadful chasms between,

Ere darkness swallows it again! and veering
  Out of its track the brave ship onward steers,
Just grazing ruin. Trembling still, and fearing,
  Her grateful people melt in prayers and tears.

Is it a mockery, their profound thanksgiving?
  Another ship goes shuddering to her doom
Unwarned, that very night, with hopes as living
  With freight as precious, lost amid the gloom,

With not a ray to show the apparition
   Waiting to slay her, none to cry "Beware!"
Rushing straight onward headlong to perdition,
   And for her crew no time vouchsafed for prayer.

Could they have stormed Heaven's gate with anguished
      praying,
   It would not have availed a feather's weight
Against their doom. Yet were they disobeying
   No law of God, to beckon such a fate.

And do not tell me the Almighty Master
   Would work a miracle to save the one,
And yield the other up to dire disaster,
   By merely human justice thus outdone!

Vainly we weep and wrestle with our sorrow —
   We cannot see his roads, they lie so broad:
But his eternal day knows no to-morrow,
   And life and death are all the same with God.

ALL'S WELL

What doest thou here, young wife, by the water-side,
    Gathering crimson dulse?
Know'st thou not that the cloud in the west glooms wide,
    And the wind has a hurrying pulse?

Peaceful the eastern waters before thee spread,
    And the cliffs rise high behind,
While thou gatherest sea-weeds, green and brown and red,
    To the coming trouble blind.

She lifts her eyes to the top of the granite crags,
    And the color ebbs from her cheek,
Swift vapors skurry the black squall's tattered flags,
    And she hears the gray gull shriek.

And like a blow is the thought of the little boat
    By this on its homeward way,
A tiny skiff, like a cockle-shell afloat
    In the tempest-threatened bay;

With husband and brother who sailed away to the town
    When fair shone the morning sun,
To tarry but till the tide in the stream turned down,
    Then seaward again to run.

Homeward she flies; the land-breeze strikes her cold;
    A terror is in the sky;
Her little babe with his tumbled hair of gold
    In his mother's arms doth lie.

She catches him up with a breathless, questioning cry:
    "O mother, speak! Are they near?"
"Dear, almost home. At the western window high
    Thy father watches in fear."

She climbs the stair: "O father, must they be lost?"
  He answers never a word;
Through the glass he watches the line the squall has crossed
  As if no sound he heard.

And the Day of Doom seems come in the angry sky,
  And a low roar fills the air;
In an awful stillness the dead-black waters lie,
  And the rocks gleam ghastly and bare.

Is it a snow-white gull's wing fluttering there?
  In the midst of that hush of dread?
Ah, no, 'tis the narrow strip of canvas they dare
  In the face of the storm to spread.

A moment more and all the furies are loose,
  The coast line is blotted out,
The skiff is gone, the rain-cloud pours its sluice,
  And she hears her father shout,

"Down with your sail!" as if through the tumult wild,
  And the distance, his voice might reach;
And, stunned, she clasps still closer her rosy child,
  Bereft of the power of speech.

But her heart cries low, as writhing it lies on the rack,
  "Sweet, art thou fatherless?"
And swift to her mother she carries the little one back,
  Where she waits in her sore distress.

Then into the heart of the storm she rushes forth;
  Like leaden bullets the rain
Beats hard in her face, and the hurricane from the north
  Would drive her back again.

It splits the shingles off the roof like a wedge,
  It lashes her clothes and her hair,

But slowly she fights her way to the western ledge,
  With the strength of her despair.

Through the flying spray, through the rain-cloud's
    shattered stream,
  What shapes in the distance grope,
Like figures that haunt the shore of a dreadful dream?
  She is wild with a desperate hope.

Have pity, merciful Heaven! Can it be?
  Is it no vision that mocks?
From billow to billow the headlong plunging sea
  Has tossed them high on the rocks;

And the hollow skiff like a child's toy lies on the ledge
  This side of the roaring foam,
And up from the valley of death, from the grave's drear edge,
  Like ghosts of men they come!

Oh sweetly, sweetly shines the sinking sun,
  And the storm is swept away;
Piled high in the east are the cloud-heaps purple and dun,
  And peacefully dies the day.

But a sweeter peace falls soft on the grateful souls
  In the lonely isle that dwell,
And the whisper and rush of every wave that rolls
  Seem murmuring, "All is well."

MODJESKA

Deft hands called Chopin's music from the keys.
   Silent she sat, her slender figure's poise
Flower-like and fine and full of lofty ease;
   She heard her Poland's most consummate voice
From power to pathos falter, sink and change;
   The music of her land, the wondrous high,
Utmost expression of its genius strange, —
   Incarnate sadness breathed in melody.
Silent and thrilled she sat, her lovely face
   Flushing and paling like a delicate rose
   Shaken by summer winds from its repose
Softly this way and that with tender grace,
   Now touched by sun, now into shadow turned, —
   While bright with kindred fire her deep eyes burned!

SLUMBER SONG

Thou little child, with tender, clinging arms,
   Drop thy sweet head, my darling, down and rest
Upon my shoulder, rest with all thy charms;
   Be soothed and comforted, be loved and blessed.

Against thy silken, honey-colored hair
   I lean a loving cheek, a mute caress;
Close, close I gather thee and kiss thy fair
   White eyelids, sleep so softly doth oppress.

Dear little face, that lies in calm content
   Within the gracious hollow that God made
In every human shoulder, where He meant
   Some tired head for comfort should be laid!

Most like a heavy-folded rose thou art,
   In summer air reposing, warm and still.
Dream thy sweet dreams upon my quiet heart;
   I watch thy slumber; naught shall do thee ill.

TO J. G. W.
ON HIS SEVENTY-FIFTH BIRTHDAY

What is there left, I wonder,
  To give thee on this glad day?
Vainly I muse and ponder;
  What is there left to say?

There is winter abroad, and snow,
  And winds that are chill and drear
Over the sad earth blow,
  Like the sighs of the dying year.

But the land thou lovest is warm
  At heart with the love of thee,
And breaks into bloom and charm
  And fragrance, that thou mayest see.

Violet, laurel, and rose,
  They are laid before thy feet,
And the red rose deeper glows
  At a fate so proud and sweet.

Gifts and greeting and blessing,
  Honor and praise, are thine;
There's naught left worth expressing
  By any word or sign!

So, like the rest, I offer
  The gift all gifts above
That heaven or earth can proffer, —
  Deep, gentle, grateful love.

GOOD-BY, SWEET DAY
FOR MUSIC

Good-by, sweet day, good-by!
I have so loved thee, but I cannot hold thee.
Departing like a dream, the shadows fold thee;
Slowly thy perfect beauty fades away:
Good-by, sweet day!

Good-by, sweet day, good-by!
Dear were thy golden hours of tranquil splendor,
Sadly thou yieldest to the evening tender
Who wert so fair from thy first morning ray;
Good-by, sweet day!

Good-by, sweet day, good-by!
Thy glow and charm, thy smiles and tones and glances,
Vanish at last, and solemn night advances;
Ah, couldst thou yet a little longer stay!
Good-by, sweet day!

Good-by, sweet day, good-by!
All thy rich gifts my grateful heart remembers,
The while I watch thy sunset's smouldering embers
Die in the west beneath the twilight gray.
Good-by, sweet day!

"THE SUNRISE NEVER FAILED US YET"

Upon the sadness of the sea
The sunset broods regretfully;
From the far lonely spaces, slow
Withdraws the wistful afterglow.

So out of life the splendor dies;
So darken all the happy skies;
So gathers twilight, cold and stern;
But overhead the planets burn;

And up the east another day
Shall chase the bitter dark away;
What though our eyes with tears be wet?
The sunrise never failed us yet.
The blush of dawn may yet restore
Our light and hope and joy once more.
Sad soul, take comfort, nor forget
That sunrise never failed us yet!

IMPATIENCE
E. L.

Only to follow you, dearest, only to find you!
  Only to feel for one instant the touch of your hand;
Only to tell you once of the love you left behind you, —
  To say the world without you is like a desert of sand;

That the flowers have lost their perfume, the rose its
    splendor,
  And the charm of nature is lost in a dull eclipse;
That joy went out with the glance of your eyes so tender,
  And beauty passed with the lovely smile on your lips.

I did not dream it was you who kindled the morning
  And folded the evening purple in peace so sweet;
But you took the whole world's rapture without a warning,
  And left me naught save the print of your patient feet.

I count the days and the hours that hold us asunder:
  I long for Death's friendly hand which shall rend in twain,
With the glorious lightning flash and the golden thunder,
  These clouds of the earth, and give me my own again!

MY GARDEN

It blossomed by the summer sea,
  A tiny space of tangled bloom
  Wherein so many flowers found room,
A miracle it seemed to be!

Up from the ground, alert and bright,
  The pansies laughed in gold and jet,
  Purple and pied, and mignonette
Breathed like a spirit of delight.

Flaming the rich nasturtiums ran
  Along the fence, and marigolds
  "Opened afresh their starry folds"
In beauty as the day began;

While ranks of scarlet poppies gay
  Waved when the soft south-wind did blow,
  Superb in sunshine, to and fro,
Like soldiers proud in brave array.

And tall blue larkspur waved its spikes
  Against the sea's deep violet,
  That every breeze makes deeper yet
With splendid azure where it strikes;

And rosy-pale sweet-peas climbed up,
  And phloxes spread their colors fine,
  Pink, white, and purple, red as wine,
And fire burned in the eschscholtzia's cup.

More dear to me than words can tell
  Was every cup and spray and leaf;
  Too perfect for a life so brief
Seemed every star and bud and bell.

And many a maiden, fairer yet,
　　Came smiling to my garden gay,
　　Whose graceful head I decked alway
With pansy and with mignonette.

Such slender shapes of girlhood young
　　Haunted that little blooming space,
　　Each with a more delightful face
Than any flower that ever sprung!

O shadowy shapes of youthful bloom!
　　How fair the sweet procession glides
　　Down memory's swift and silent tides,
Till lost in doubtful mists of gloom!

Year after year new flowers unfold,
　　Year after year fresh maidens fair,
　　Scenting their perfume on the air,
Follow and find their red and gold.

And while for them the poppies' blaze
　　I gather, brightening into mine
　　The eyes of vanished beauty shine,
That gladdened long-lost summer days.

Where are they all who wide have ranged?
　　Where are the flowers of other years?
　　What ear the wistful question hears?
Ah, some are dead and all are changed.

And still the constant earth renews
　　Her treasured splendor; still unfold
　　Petals of purple and of gold
Beneath the sunshine and the dews.

But for her human children dear
　　Whom she has folded to her breast,
　　No beauty wakes them from their rest,
Nor change they with the changing year.

APPEAL

The childish voice rose to my ear
   Sweet toned and eager, praying me,
"I am so little, Granna dear,
   Please lift me up, so I can see."

I looked down at the pleading face,
   Felt the small hand's entreating touch,
And stooping caught in swift embrace
   The baby boy I loved so much.

And held him high that he might gaze
   At the great pageant of the sky,
The glory of the sunset's blaze,
   The glittering moon that curved on high.

With speechless love I clasped him close
   And read their beauty in his eyes,
And on his fair cheek kissed the rose,
   Sweeter than blooms of Paradise.

And in my heart his eager prayer
   Found echo, and the self-same cry
Rose from my heart through heaven's air,
   "O gracious Father, lift me high!

"So little and so low am I,
   Among earth's mists I call to Thee,
Show me the glory of Thy sky!
   Oh lift me up that I may see!"

FAITH
(My Lighthouse)

Fain would I hold my lamp of life aloft
  Like yonder tower built high above the reef;
Steadfast, though tempests rave or winds blow soft,
  Clear, though the sky dissolve in tears of grief.

For darkness passes, storms shall not abide:
  A little patience and the fog is past.
After the sorrow of the ebbing tide
  The singing flood returns in joy at last.

The night is long and pain weighs heavily,
  But God will hold his world above despair.
Look to the East, where up the lucid sky
  The morning climbs! The day shall yet be fair!

NOTES

Page 6: Thomas B. Laighton's candidacy is usually reported as having been for the post of Governor. According to the latest careful research by Mr. Lyman Rutledge, there is no substantiation for this legend.

Page 14: Richard Henry Dana visited the Isles in August 1842 and describes his impressions at the age of 28. He writes "the rocks of Star Island are very grand, rugged and broken. Some large crevices and ravines seem to have been formed by the wasting of many centuries, or some great convulsion of Nature. They are the grandest rocks I ever saw — none can equal them unless it be those of Nahant and a part of the shore of San Juan Capistrano in California."

Page 16: Haley also erected salt-works and manufactured excellent salt for curing fish, he stretched a ropewalk over uneven ground 270 feet, he set up windmills to grind wheat and corn grown on Smutty-nose Island, and planted an orchard. Most helpful of all, he built a sea-wall connecting his island with Malaga and thus forming a safe harbor. The funds to construct this wall he acquired when he discovered four bars of solid silver under a large flat stone on the Island, left there by one of the many pirates who often buried their treasure on or around the Isles of Shoals.

Page 18: During the period of time not spent on the mainland, Thomas Laighton devoted himself to his fishing business. In April, 1844 the diary states he paid his brother Joseph $400 and bought out his half of the five whale boats with their oars and sails and tackle. Then he acquired the four wherries and the four punts complete with oars and paddles. There was also the large Seine Boats with cordage, grapples, anchors, box for seine and drip nets, in fact everything connected with the fishing business owned by J. W. Laighton and Co. and Jonathan Marshall Esq. of Salisbury, Mass. — which consisted of moorings, kelloks, splitting tables, gaffs, bait mills, butts, hogsheads, crocks, barrels, kegs, baskets, scales, weights, measures, hand barrows, fish flaker and flake stuff, buoys and net buoys, fishing lines, leads, hooks and reels. This made up the equipment used for the catching of fish off Hog and Smutty-nose Islands.

Page 47: The Mansion House still stands. It was owned by

the late John P. Marquand, a great-nephew of Mrs. Curzon. It was the setting for his novel, Wickford Point.

Page 59: Mrs. Field's diary gave an interesting description, May 27, 1872, of the ballad *All's Well* which told of Levi's shipwreck:

. . . Celia Thaxter came in on the wings of a glorious spring morning. She brought one short poem with her, also an unfinished ballad. Before beginning to read the last she told me in a natural way enough but with very great fervor of the squall which the ballad records in which her brother and husband came as near to Death as they ever can till they are actually carried to the other shore. She said Mr. Thaxter has never wished to get into a boat since. Her whole description, as she spoke of watching the wind lift the boat out of their vision and set it down on the rocks at her side high and dry, was one of the most breathless and impressive of relations of which human spirit is capable. I could hardly judge of the ballad after her story — but I thought it very fine, inasmuch as it really lost nothing, but rather gained after the previous telling, the epithets being all quite natural as well as forcible.

Page 62: People who do their boating with the roar of a motor in their ears, should shut it off and listen for this sound familiar to those who sail!

Page 72: This quilt is a treasured possession of the author.

Page 79: The little family graveyard on Appledore contains a white marble shaft to Thomas B. Laighton, b. 1804 d. 1866, stones to him and his wife, father and mother, also to their three children, with stone for each:

    Celia b. June 29, 1835 d. August 26, 1894
    Cedric b. September 4, 1840 d. June 1899
    Oscar b. June 30, 1839 d. April 1939

The path leading to it is now so overgrown with raspberry and blackberry vines, and poison ivy, that it is impossible to reach the spot.

Page 91: This was one of the largest eagles carved by the far famed Charles Bellamy and had spread wings.

Page 98: All during the summer of 1873 excursion boats came from Newburyport, Rye, Hampton, and even Boston, loaded with persons morbidly eager to visit the scene of the tragedy. Money-minded local people painted rocks and bits of wood with fake bloodstains and sold them to the credulous souvenir hunters!

Page 107:
Terms at Appledore House — 1880:
Transient   .$3.75 per day
by week   3.00   "   "
4 weeks   2.50   "   "
Children under twelve, not occupying separate room, 1/2 price
Double room occupied by one person $4.00 or $5.00, according to size and location
Servant and child $2.75 per day
extra dinner   1.00

Page 112: Musician Julius Eichberg, a violinist who lived in Boston, came to Appledore in the summer. The whole family were great friends of Thaxter.

Page 118: Banting, or Bantingism, was a method of reducing through avoidance of foods containing much farinacious, saccharine, or oily matter, so named from the London undertaker and writer who originated it.

Page 122: Appleton Brown's oil painting of the Thaxter garden now hangs in the author's home and another copy is in the possession of the Clark family in Portland.

Page 134: On this territory in 1663 Champernowne chose a site for the home where he lived with his wife and her sons. Between the old house and the seashore was planted a magnificent English elm tree, whose noble trunk and wide spreading branches are the wonder and admiration of all who now visit the Thaxter homestead.

Page 156: This Hassam sketch is now owned by Calvin Hosmer, Jr. and hangs a few miles from where it was painted.

Page 160: The pet names of the three friends were: Celia Thaxter — "Sandpiper," Sarah Jewett — "Owl," Annie Fields — "Little Flower." They often used these in very personal letters.

Page 168: In the long poem entitled "The Fire in the Crystal," William Rose Benet describes an imaginary and absolutely unfounded romantic friendship between Celia Thaxter and William M. Hunt. Hunt was Levi Thaxter's close friend. It was the good Quaker John G. Whittier who gave Celia her greatest inspiration through sincere friendship and admiration.

Page 176: Quoted from Letters of T. W. Higginson now in Craige House, Cambridge.

Page 181: The bronze plaque on the grave of Levi Thaxter has been lately added to the original field-stone, the lettering on which had become unreadable.

Page 182: Ignatius Grossman went to college on his own and then to live in New York City. There he met the beautiful and talented daughter of the actor Edwin Booth who was a frequent summer visitor at Appledore and close friend of the Thaxter family.

Page 195: Wines were freely sold in spite of the fact that Appledore Island is in Maine which was a dry State!

Page 214: When Greely the explorer returned from an Arctic expedition when for some time all thought that there would be no rescue, Greely took pains to seek Celia Thaxter out and tell her that in those grim days of despair he had read aloud to his men from her book of poems. Many of which had an appeal to the rough sailors and they had especially found comfort and hope in her poem "Tryst."

Page 215:

    "Tell us a story of these isles," they said,
        The daughters of the West, whose eyes had seen
    For the first time the circling sea, instead
        Of the brown prairies' waves of grassy green;
    "Tell us of wreck and peril, storm and cold,
        Wild as the wildest." Under summer stars,
    With the slow moonrise at our back, I told
        The story of the young Norwegian, Lars. . .

Page 215: The Pepperrell Hotel was the first of four hotels which later flourished in Kittery Point; Champernowne, Parkfield and Pocahontas being the others.

Page 225: "More light" were Goethe's last words.

Page 231: The box containing the toads became unwired on the steamer and the small creatures caused consternation as they hopped among the feet of the lady passengers — "An Island Garden"

Page 242: Celia Thaxter once said, "When I go I hope it will be quickly, also I hope Minna will be with me when I die."

INDEX

Adams, Ella, 228

Aldrich, Thomas Bailey, 152; publisher of *Atlantic Monthly,* 225-226

Among the Isles of Shoals, 66; 89; 102; 207; publication of, 215

An Island Garden, 236; publication of, 238

Appledore, town of, 3; 23

Appledore Hotel, contract for, 21; end of, x (see Appledore House)

Appledore House, construction of, 23-25; opening of, 25; enlargement of, 73; 86; 101-102; 195

Appledore Island, 20 (see Hog Island); move to, 22; life on, 194-201; last summer on, 240

Appledore, The, steamer, 114

Atlantic Monthly, The, 61; 72

Babb's Cove, 25

Baker, Mr., 22

Bateman, Clara, steamtug, 87; 119

Becker, Captain Fabius, 35

Berntsen, Annie, 99; 109

Berntsen, Minna, 123; 155; 241

Berntsen, Ovidia, 99; 109; 123

Boon Island, 104

Brauner, Olaf, 239

Brave Boat Harbor, at Kittery Point, Me., 134

Brock, Rev. John, 3

Brooks, Phillips, 167

Brown, Appleton, 120; 129; 195; 241

Browning, 154; 181

Bull, 240

Cambridge Riding School, 125

Caswell, Lucy, 241

Champernowne Farm, 162; 179 (see Cutts Farm)

Champernowne, Capt. Francis, 134

Charles River, 52

Chatterji, Mohini Mohum, 166; 167

Chauncey Creek, 135

Christiansen, Anethe, murder of, 93-95

Christiansen, Ivan, tragedy at Smutty-nose, 93-96

Christiansen, Karen, companion to Eliza Laighton, 89; murder of, 93-95

Claflin, Mary B., 204

Clarke, Mrs. Cowden, 150

Clarke, James Gordon, 153

Clifford, Hotel, in Boston, 185; 220

Coleman, Annie, housekeeper, 162

Collected Poems by Celia Thaxter, publication of, 216

Conservatory of Music, Boston, 89

Cruise of the Mystery and Other Poems, 191-192

Curzon, Margie, 18; 47

Cutts Farm, Kittery Point, Me., purchase of, 134; 177 (see Champernowne Farm)

Cutts Island, 135

Dana, Richard H., 14; 17

Darby, Lucy, 140

Darrah, Rose, 164

DeNormandie, family, 156

DeNormandie, Dr. James, pastor of So. Parish Unitarian Church, Portsmouth, 168; funeral service for Celia Thaxter, 241

Dickens, Charles, 81; 206

Dodge, Mary Mapes, editor of *Young Folks,* 83

Driftweed, book of poems, 130

Duck Island, 50; 63; wreck on, 98

Eichberg, Annie, 156

Emerson, Ellen, 83

Emerson, Ralph Waldo, 83

Out On The Shoals

Twenty Years of Photography on the Isles of Shoals

by Peter E. Randall

This extended photographic essay will delight lovers of coastal New England. Since 1973, Peter Randall has been photographing the magnificent Isles of Shoals, located about six miles off the coast of New Hampshire. The result of many trips to the islands in all seasons is a book of spectacular color photographs covering the Shoals from sunrise to sunset, from wildflowers to Celia Thaxter's garden, and from unique bird colonies to the surprising colors of the intertidal zone. Picturesque buildings on Star Island, the rugged beauty of Appledore, crashing waves on White Island and its famed light, and abandoned stone walls of Smuttynose all are captured by Randall and his camera in an unforgettable portrait of one of New England's most exceptional natural places.
64 pages, paperbound, ISBN 0-914339-52-4$ 16.50

The Poems of Celia Thaxter

Introduction by Jane E. Vallier

Celia Laighton Thaxter, the most widely published woman writing poetry in America in the last half of the nineteenth century, lived a life of mythic dimensions. Born in Portsmouth, New Hampshire, in 1835, Celia developed into a woman who came to embody all that American women of her time could hope to achieve without the support of wealth, position, or even good fortune.

She grew up on the Isles of Shoals, off the coast from Portsmouth, New Hampshire, spending an idyllic childhood playing with her two brothers along the rocky shore watching the birds and many moods of the ocean. Married at age 16, she moved to the mainland and turned to poetry to express the loss of her beloved islands. With one emotionally disturbed child and a well educated husband who nevertheless failed to provide proper financial support for the family, Celia Thaxter was forced to fend for herself as an adult mother, writing poetry and prose to earn money.

Eventually she returned to spend summers on Appledore Island

where her family operated a resort hotel. Here she entertained her friends, some of America's best known writers, poets, musicians, and artists. She died on Appledore in 1894 and two years later her close friend Sarah Orne Jewett edited this, the most complete volume of Thaxter's poetry. The publisher has added other poems and a few short stories to make this comprehensive new edition of the works of Celia Thaxter.
340 pages, paper, ISBN 0-914339-57-5 . . . . $20

Poet On Demand

The Life, Letters, and Works of Celia Thaxter

by Jane E. Vallier

During the last quarter of the nineteenth century Celia Thaxter was the most popular of America's woman poets, surpassing in importance many others whose names are better known today. Yet Celia's fame began to wane even before her death in 1894. Perhaps, as Jane Vallier suggests in this study of Thaxter's life, adverse financial circumstances forced the poet to try her hand as a folklorist, juvenile author, freelance journalist, dramatic actress, naturalist, and illustrator, as well.

In this, the first extensive literary biography of Celia Thaxter, author Vallier explains the meaning and symbolism of Thaxter's poetry and describes how Celia's unhappy marriage and her life on the Isles of Shoals colored her poetry and prose. Included in this reprint of the original 1982 edition is a new introduction with additional photographs, fifty-three of Thaxter's poems plus a reprint of "A Memorable Murder," the story of the killing of two women on Smuttynose Island in 1873 and first published in *Atlantic Monthly*.
285 pages, paperbound, ISBN 0-914339-47-8 . . . . . . $14.95

Among The Isles of Shoals

by Celia Thaxter

A reprint of Celia Thaxter's classic 1873 human and natural history of the Isles of Shoals, a group of nine islands off the coast of Portsmouth, New Hampshire. In addition to a description of the scenic and natural beauty of the islands, this extended essay also includes stories, both poignant and humorous, about the hardy folk who inhabited the islands, making a meager living from the sea. Indexed with additional photographs and maps.
188 pages, paperbound, ISBN 0-914339-49-4 . . . . . . $12.50